Roll 'em! Action!

Roll 'em! Action!

How to Produce a Motion Picture on a Shoestring Budget

by
HARRY M. JOYNER, JR.

McFarland & Company, Inc., Publishers
Jefferson, North Carolina, and London

All photos and illustrations provided by the author except where noted

British Library Cataloguing-in-Publication data are available

Library of Congress Cataloguing-in-Publication Data

Joyner, Harry M., 1936–
Roll 'em! Action! : how to produce a motion picture on a shoestring budget / by Harry M. Joyner.
p. cm.
Includes bibliographical references and index. ∞
ISBN 0-89950-860-X (lib. bdg. : 50# alk. paper)
1. Motion pictures—Production and direction. I. Title.
PN1995.9.P7J69 1994
791.43'0232—dc20 92-56656
CIP

©1994 Harry M. Joyner. All rights reserved

Manufactured in the United States of America

McFarland & Company, Inc., Publishers
Box 611, Jefferson, North Carolina 28640

Table of Contents

Acknowledgments vii
Introduction ix

1. A Learning Experience Making *Body Shop* 1

2. A Learning Experience Making *Marley's Revenge* 12

3. Financial Considerations 28

4. You Have to Decide... 35
   Shooting Ratio 35
   Film/Tape Size/Format 35
   Labs 36
   Opticals 36
   Optical Houses 37
   Videotape and Film Stocks 37
   Full Coat 38
   Single System vs. Double System 38
   Work Prints and Time Coded Dupes 39
   Edge Number (Coding) and SMPTE Time Code 39
   Director or DP? 40
   A Caterer! 41
   Sound Effects—and Foley 41
   Mechanical FX 42
   Editing and Conforming 43
   Optical or Magnetic Sound Track 44

5. Techniques for Making Screen Titles 46

6. Advice for the Director 52

7. Visual Effects 59
   Traveling Mattes and Miniatures 59
   The Schufftan Shot 64
   Rotoscoping 66
   The Camera as Printer 68
   Glass Shots 68
   Hanging Miniatures 70

8. Communication 77
   Good Instructions 77
   Writing a Useable Script 77
   Script Form 84

9. Location, Personnel, Financing and More 90

10. Equipment Choices 104
    VHS, Beta, and 8mm Video 104
    Super VHS and High-Band 8 104
    Industrial Cameras and Recorders 104
    The Top of the Line 105

11. Less Common Equipment Options 106
    What About Super/16! 106
    Techniscope 108
    Anamorphic 109
    Three-Perf 110
    The Dolly 111

12. Strange Equipment 114
    Why Not Standard 35? 114
    70mm—On a Cheap Movie!? 115
    Super/8!—For Feature Filming? 116
    Since We're on the Subject of Videotape... 118
    Other Uses for Video 118

13. Cheaper Lighting Possibilities 121

14. Music 130

15. It's a Wrap! 132

Appendix A: Official Checklists 133
   GENERAL 133
   Tool Box 133

Table of Contents

    CAMERA AND SUPPORT SYSTEM *134*
        Camera *134*
        Sound *134*
        Lighting *134*
        Grip Equipment *135*

Appendix B: Forms 137
    SUMMARY PRODUCTION COSTS *138*
    PRODUCTION COST STATEMENT *139*
    MOTION PICTURE COST ESTIMATE SHEET *146*
    TRANSPORTATION/LUNCH SHEET *153*
    CALL SHEET *155*
    SCRIPT BREAKDOWN *156*
    CAMERA AND ACCESSORY LIST *157*
    LENS LIST *158*
    LOCATION REQUIREMENTS *159*
    DAILY PRODUCTION REPORT *161*
    MODEL RELEASE *162*
    LOCATION SURVEY *163*
        Interior and Exterior *164*
        Local Supply *165*
        Food Catered to Location *166*
        Electrical *166*
    COPYRIGHT FORM *167*

Glossary 171

Index 179

Acknowledgments

This work is by no means mine alone. Were it not for technicians, producers, service agencies, product providers, and a list that reads like the perpetually continuing credits at the end of a film, the issues that brought to mind the need for this book would not exist.

There are those whose contribution to this work is direct and, therefore, deserves a direct "thank you."

The photographs herein, each of which is worth more than ten thousand words, were made over a 32-year period by Chris Allen, John Autry, John Clifford, Jet Eller, Marie Heptig, Martin Hill, and Hugh Peralta. They all were gracious to do some digging in their personal archives to provide me with them.

A notable amount of research and technical information was contributed by Chris Allen, Martin Hill, John Autry, Dave Floyd, Mark Overton, Bob Carroll, Tony Elwood, Chris Wilson, and Charles Reynolds.

Thanks to Ralph Carpenter and Tony Elwood for their illustrations.

I realize how painful it is to be coerced into reading copy on a subject that is not one's cup of tea. Since I am more literate than literary, Harry Cosgrove, Will Espin, Ruth Pentes, and Palmer Senn were pressed into doing so. Correcting my mistakes was their only reward.

In the case of normally budgeted pictures those who get a screen credit typically get a pretty fat check to go with it. The pictures I've worked often purchased the total dedication of the talent and crew with nothing more than a screen credit and an opportunity to do another picture—one on which they would earn nothing more than a screen credit and an opportunity to do another picture, hoping and believing that success eventually would arrive. They really deserve more than simple acknowledgment but the list is too great to offer more. They do have, nonetheless, my gratitude together with my wishes and prayers that they achieve their goals.

Introduction

Every paragraph in this book—whether interesting or dull—has a small message in it, a little instruction of some kind. You'll have to sort out what it is and how it applies to you, but it's there and you'll find it if you look for it.

Each experience noted here is a lesson and there's no reason that you can't learn from it without repeating the experience yourself. Even so, you'll always learn more from your own mistakes than from being instructed or by accidentally getting it right.

Here's what you're going to get. First, you'll read about *Anitra,* a successful, incredibly low budget picture, which was a nightmare while it was being done, but looking at it retrospectively, it was...still a nightmare. Its fitting ending was tribulation as was its distribution. Produced in the early 1970's, an era before the VCR, it was shot on 35mm film solely for theatrical release.

Then, glossing over a couple of others, you'll learn about a tightly budgeted film produced twenty years later, *Marley's Revenge, the Monster Movie.* Its production was ravaged with mistakes which the producer has been kind enough to allow me to mention so you won't have to repeat them. Had the film been a failure none of these comments would have been worthwhile. *Marley's* was produced exclusively for videotape release and was shot on 16mm film.

One of the two stories points out a great number of errors you can either make or avoid. The other confirms the lesson the first one teaches. Both stories are short and worth reading, providing money-saving information, tips, and how-to's.

You'll note as you read along that we had access to a lot of equipment that you probably won't have, if your movie is a super cheapie. But be reminded that our goal was to produce a worthwhile film while spending as little as necessary. Neither trying to break a minimum budget record nor writing a book about how cheaply it could be achieved was, by any means, our motive.

Here you will find some specific principles regarding what will save you money and some of the ways you can apply them.

Keeping notes, whether in your head or on paper, is a mark of experience. That note taking is called memory, if you are young and vital, but those of us whose memory is shot must resort to physical note taking—even if the notes are written on brown paper bags.

A good definition of education is the compilation of all the notes from on-the-job training and book learning along with the recollection of tales told by the hangar pilots who are now too decrepit to fly. Fly, in this case, may be applied to the range of enterprises falling at any point between neurosurgery and post hole digging.

You doubtlessly have heard the old adage about the second lieutenant who, in the heat of battle, whined, "It wasn't like this at the Point." What he was saying, in effect, was that knowing "the three R's" alone is insufficient. Without him, all his subordinates in the trenches had no dictum to follow, no purposeful course of action, in spite of their experience. In other words, no matter how much you know about music you can't play the piano until your fingers learn to wiggle the right way.

You're getting notes from me, not because I am wise, experienced, or especially intelligent, but because I took the time to prepare them for you. What makes them valuable is that most of my experience resides with uncommonly cheap movies. If you knew me, you'd not be surprised at all to learn that the original manuscript was written on a paper bag. (In fact it was not, but it did begin on a paper napkin during lunch.)

Despite this little forewarning, you will get no advice here regarding procurement or distribution of funds because cheaper or more efficient production is the thrust of this writing.

There is some paperwork laid out for you that you probably could find elsewhere, but now you won't have to. As long as you were in school, the librarian and all your teachers kept telling you, "Don't write in the books." My nephew and partner, Will Espin, takes exception to that idea and brought it to my attention. He suggests writing in the book. Use a yellow marker to highlight points and issues you want to refer to later. Make notes in the margins, and circle things you want to bring to your own attention.

In doing so you'll be committing the thoughts to *your* own mind. The ideas will be a part of *you.* If you do this, not only will the book be yours but the thoughts will become yours, too.

I second his notion. Just don't do it in a library book—you might get me in trouble!

SCENE 1, TAKE 1
(A Note About the Author)

By age 12, Harry Joyner had saved 2,000 pennies in a cigar box, and he used them to buy his first movie camera. It was a used 8mm which, of course, was the only size within the grasp of someone that age. As one would imagine, a child with a movie camera would not stand still for pictures of the family standing still. Action was the thing.

So he, together with his friend Martin Hill (same age), spent many an hour setting up fight scenes, effects shots, single frame animation, or anything else they could implement with a Keystone 8.

Harry stuck to photography in the Air Force, and his tour turned into a civilian profession which lasted all through the 1960's, 1970's, and the early 1980's. By then, Martin had established himself as a dealer in motion picture equipment.

Harry had become a commercial photographer and a documentary film maker. A technician more than a businessman, he unwittingly developed an expertise in using gadgetry instead of first class equipment while his competitors were investing in good equipment and getting the clientele who had the bucks.

One of the proper offerings of a commercial photographer—so he thought—was to shoot movie film for a customer who needed it. Harry considered himself prepared for film production on the basis that he had a Bolex camera and had enough requests for occasional short pieces of film to pay for it. His clientele got the result they wanted while he took a back seat financially. His family was not deprived, he simply was a poor businessman. He had, for that reason, tired of picture taking, but was still intrigued with film making, especially with the prospect of making a feature. A local documentary film producer had concocted techniques to do the documentary and travelogue film with pizazz, but precious little equipment. His films had the pretty picture, the deep and mellow voice, and the bouncy music, but they were enhanced by the illusion of lip-sync sound from beginning to end; unlike the competition's product, in these films everything that made a sound was heard. It wasn't really lip-sync sound, but you'd never have guessed it.

This was the era of the Kodachrome Esso travelogue narrated by a deep, resonant voice—music in the background and stems of dogwood buds blowing in the wind, in the foreground—the days when news film had no sound track, and the only accessory you really needed for your camera was a tripod.

These were the days when doing a Hollywood sound track required the use of a Hollywood sound truck, packed to the hilt with equipment.

This producer's novel technique required no more equipment than would fit in a desk drawer and the cost followed accordingly. It simply made his product better than whatever came in second place.

When Harry was offered a job with the company, he readily accepted it and learned much from the experience. Mostly he learned to be innovative. He later went on to produce documentaries on his own. But he still hadn't done a feature.

In time, theatricals were done in the Charlotte, N.C., area. Harry had the good fortune to perform in the various capacities of producer, associate producer, technical adviser, screen writer, director of photography, editor, assistant director, miniature and model builder, special effects director, mechanical effects supervisor and chief "cinemaphotographer"—a credit he chuckled at until he saw the same credit in *Gone with the Wind*.

While a number of his experiences were associated with Hollywood films, most were drawn from very low budget regional or local ones which gave him the background upon which this book was written.

1
A Learning Experience Making *Body Shop*

In spite of what the hardworking movie stars say on TV talk shows, every painful moment of movie making is more joy, for those of us who love it, than winning a jackpot in Las Vegas. Investing in one is surely a greater gamble.

Almost everybody—including you—has been affected in some small way by the late, sort of great Pat Patterson. Pat was the unchallenged "king of the cheapies."

The phone rang.

"This is J.G. Patterson," he said with authority, and stated that he planned to make a movie in Charlotte. "I understand you have a Mitchell."

(The Mitchell camera, originally built in the 1920's by George Mitchell, is still the industry standard, yielding to Panavision only recently—and even they use the Mitchell type movement. Expensive stuff, and most impressive!)

"Well, yeah," came an answer, "Got about seventeen of 'em."

"I'm serious," he said. "Someone told me you had one."

"I do, seventeen of them."

"You have seventeen 35mm Mitchell cameras?" he asked incredulously.

"Well, not exactly."

He moaned, believing he'd gotten the upper hand. He was, of course, being victimized by the playing of a silly little game.

One of them is 70mm," came the retort. "Only sixteen of them are 35's." (The 70mm was basically useless, but the comment was impressive to Pat.) He gasped in response, sensing the comment was a serious one.

"We need to get together!" Without determining my capability, he went over all the qualifying steps. "What would you charge to shoot a picture for me on a ten day schedule?"

At that moment he was subconsciously making a statement that would surface again some 17 years later from another producer. "Plan ahead? Who needs it?"

He also assumed that possessing a camera was the primary criterion for the prospect of making a movie. I didn't know any more than he did so I answered his question.

"Well, to tell you the truth, the equipment isn't my own. It belongs to an associate of mine. We'll have to discuss it."

"Keep in mind," Pat added, "that the picture is a low budget one and that I'm a little short."

"No sweat, I'll talk to him today and get back to you," I closed, nonchalantly hiding my Promethean exhilaration. Taking down his phone number I hung up and called Martin.

Martin lived out in the country in a little house worth about the same as one of the well-used Mitchells which he had gotten on a government surplus deal. It was a time when his family ate sandwiches made of radishes from his garden for financial reasons. He was in the formative stages of what was to become a lucrative film equipment business. Fortunately he always managed to keep his phone bill paid and answered when I called.

We discussed the thing for a while. Knowing we were confined to a $20,000 budget, and desperately wanting the screen credit as a stepping stone, we worked out a deal we felt Pat couldn't refuse.

"Let's charge him only $1,000 just to get the assignment," suggested Martin. "We'll pay Chris $200 as camera assistant and split the remaining $800." (Chris Allen had just gotten out of the Air Force and was looking for work. He got the work when what he really needed was the money. Didn't we all!)

I went for it. Chris went for it. So did J.G. We met him the next day at Anderson's Restaurant and made our proposal. Mr. Patterson readily accepted. "They call me Pat for short," he said. He was barely 5 feet 6 inches and had cast himself as the leading man. "Suckered again," says I to myself, "he *is* a little short."

Scene 2, Take 1

We later met him at the place he had selected as his studio. It seemed reasonable enough to me that since no feature had ever been filmed in Charlotte, there would be no sound stages available. But that wasn't why he chose a vacant space for rent between the Paper Doll lounge and the Wilmont Launderette. He got a deal on it, that's why.

We had our brief meeting in the foyer, then stepped into the studio area. It was roomy enough for a reasonable set, I reckoned, even though the 12-foot ceiling was a bit low for movie making. At worst, it would be adequate. At that point, I never dreamed adequate would be as good as it got for the next six weeks—except for the presence on the set of several young lovelies.

He presented each of us with the script of *Anitra* and painted verbal images of grandeur, a talent which he used liberally for as long as I knew him.

Pat wrote the screenplay himself, and also produced it, directed it, and starred in it. He designed and produced the special effects and the advertising poster, known as the one-sheet. (I told you before that this guy was king of the cheapies. You ain't seen nothing yet.)

"You'll get publicity you never dreamed of," he promised. He hadn't lied. In a short time both Martin and I got substantial publicity. And we never dreamed that when we got it we'd never be identified. We were gingerly referred to as the director of photography whose vision was such and such, or the cameraman whose skill did this or that, or the technicians whose expertise afforded the picture one thing or another. Anyway, you get the picture. In the long run, we were ecstatic to be anonymous.

Having a business to run, I stayed away for most of the first several days while casting was taking place. When I returned, I discovered what his criteria for casting talent were. For males it was, "The part pays $25. Will you work for that price?" For females it was, "You have a nice figure. The part pays $25. Will you work for that price?" Obviously the answer was yes, because they did. Actually a couple of parts paid a little more. It was the expectation of prestige they were really working for. We shot the picture with a cast of around 30 people, all of whom sounded just like Gomer Pyle, except Jeannine Abernathy (or "Little Jenny" whose Chicago accent was equally unremarkable.

You'd have to see the script to *Anitra* to believe it. It was a good, basic story modeled somewhat after *Bride of Frankenstein*. While it was obviously well thought out, it was not at all well written.

While 130 pages are typical, *Anitra* was comprised of a total of only 35, including dialogue. Even then, some of the pages were almost blank except for the heading. That made the script infinitely easier to write and certainly left the director with plenty of latitude. Additional notes in pencil or pen are typical for any script.

Having read these pages doesn't leave you with much information so here's the plot in a nutshell: The picture begins at the closing of the funeral of Anitra, a "perfect" woman and the wife of Dr. Don Brandon. Being distraught over her loss, he decides to create another "perfect" woman by killing young women and taking the best parts of their anatomy, later combining and reanimating them in his lab. Greg, his mute hunchback assistant, willingly helps him in hopes that someday the doctor will correct his physical defect. Several reanimation experiments fail, but ultimately the mad doctor succeeds in reviving the assembled body parts as the new Anitra. After he educates her empty brain, she drifts away in search of the "perfect" man, leaving the doctor to lose his mind.

SCENE 3, TAKE 1

We worked well together in spite of knowing little about what we were doing and nothing about what anybody else was doing.

Pat had worked on features before—some horror films—and he had been assistant to the producer. His talent was procurement, cheap when necessary and free when possible. He usually got what was needed without charge.

Whatever he was exposed to on those other pictures definitely rubbed off on him. And it took. What he didn't know about movies technically, he made up for in foresight. His abilities of observation were acute, and he retained all of what he took in, even those things he didn't understand. The one thing that I did agree with was his attitude about cost effectiveness.

"The less it costs to begin with," he would say, "the faster you'll get your money back." He was right.

I took exception, however, when he rejected the suggestion of redoing a shot which could be made better on the grounds that "If it looks any better, then the 'marks' will realize how bad the rest is" and "If we make it better it will have to cost more and I'd rather take the cheaper route." He was unquestionably wrong, but then I didn't know how to argue with his logic!

By the end of the first week most of the casting had been completed, the primary set was well under way, and I had compiled a list of supplies and support equipment that I would require.

Fortunately, Martin furnished most of the camera equipment; that is, a second unit camera, tripods, and four SunGuns. I had stands for the SunGuns. The list of supplies for local purchase was totally denied on the premise that if we can't get it for free we probably don't need it.

Four SunGuns do not a movie make, so, in order to support our own self-image as filmmakers, the crew (me) gave in and built the rest of the lights used on the picture using materials like aluminum flashing and a collection of electrical stuff.

The homemade lights were not intended to be professional movie lights. Their only goal was to highlight certain elements on the set, without increasing the ambient light level. They did, in fact, together with the SunGuns, offer enough light of the desired quality and quantity to shoot 5247 film which was rated at ASA 100. (It was ASA then, it's ISO now.)

The set was lit with either two or three SunGuns and sometimes one or two naked photofloods. While the lighting was not classy, it was certainly effective.

Every single interior shot in *Anitra* was shot at f5.6. Fortunately, Pat allowed us to buy 200w light bulbs and photofloods with petty cash. As time passed and the need for an item presented itself, he would give in and buy it. By the time we were supposed to be finished shooting, we had begun to shoot.

Anyone having left Hollywood and walking on our set would have assumed himself to have left Earth and walked onto Planet Dork.

Martin, who was the director of photography, was also the dolly pusher and sound recordist. Chris, who was the second unit cameraman, was focus puller and camera assistant. Joe Lamb, who'd just worked on his first feature in Atlanta, was production manager and served in any capacity from microphone holder to Roman candle shooter. Worth Keeter, special consultant who turned 16 during the shoot, served in precisely the same capacity as Joe. (After escaping from *Anitra*, Worth further developed his career and, in the ensuing years, directed over 27 feature films before going to Hollywood and continuing.)

From the very first day work began, the lack of planning and organization was conspicuous. Pat refused to recognize that fact as a problem and continued right along in his dream world as we all slowly pulled his dream together.

Pat had ordered ends (short, leftover rolls) from a "second hand" film supply company in Hollywood. It was these ends which we were loading into the magazines. He would look at the script and elect to shoot scene number so-and-so on the basis that the scene would take about 20 seconds plus slate. The magazine probably had enough film to thread the camera and shoot 30 seconds. We had four magazines, and each time we had three or four shots, Chris had to reload all four of them—with film whose length was determined only by intuition.

Note that I said shots, not takes. We usually got the shot on the first take. Of course, we rehearsed each bit several times before we filmed it, but if the actor didn't fall down or throw up, the take was accepted as printable.

We began by using the longest rolls first. As time went on, the rolls became shorter and shorter until finally, we ran out of film a number of times before we could clap the slate. Since we were using rolls so short, the *cameraman* (usually me) called action as soon as the camera was up to speed. If we hadn't run out of film by the end of the take, we would, tail slate the shot. If indeed, the magazine supply spindle stopped turning, we would know we had run out of film, and using a fresh load, would pick up the same shot on a different angle at that point.

It was unfortunate that Pat could not stand back and look on to direct himself. Each time the "mad scientist" heard the word "action," he withdrew from his smock pocket a pack of cigarettes and ponderously lit up as if in deep thought. It was a distinct attempt to be theatrical. While his lighting of the cigarette offered little to the pacing of the action, the smoke he generated added substantial dimension to the surgical scenes. His habit was profound, a mark of his nervousness, and it doubtlessly contributed to the cause of his early death.

SCENE 4, TAKE 1

The greatest frustration was the lack of organization. Early calls followed by endless hours of inactivity led to a serious lack of productivity. This is highly detrimental to any project. No doubt it would have been especially so to this one had the talent and crew been paid by the hour. In any case, the delays persisted for the two-month duration of the ten-day shoot. It was this fact that promoted an early onset of perpetual and hilarious wisecracks, puns, and one-liners on the set. We all became punchy, much as one does when he's stayed up too late. Perhaps five to ten times a day the entire staff would break up in side-splitting laughter.

The set was designed not unlike that of the *Frankenstein* lab, and many shots were established from a high point of view to emphasize that fact.

While Dr. Frankenstein used natural forces to provide his electricity, the *Anitra* set had electrical and electronic equipment that was representative of the 1940's and 1950's yet set in a 1970's environment. Pat had gotten the obsolete equipment from a surplus dealer who, no doubt, was delighted to get rid of it at any price and Pat was ecstatic to have picked it up for a pittance. Because of consummate disregard for the script, set, and prop design, the electronics equipment from a modern-day jet bomber would have served him equally well. The chrome steel surgical instruments were procured much the same way, this time by Martin, and arrived—literally—by the barrelful.

Once the sinister looking set was finished and lit, few changes were ever needed. We had flying walls and movable props which gave us ample space to reposition—or to dolly on the only two occasions we did so. The ceiling was only 12 feet high which ordinarily is not enough to light a set properly. On the other hand, we didn't have enough lights to put up there, so we managed to make the world's best use of our few SunGuns and homemade lighting units. Each of the lights was on a conventional light stand and there was ample floor space to move them around as needed.

We shot for about three days before we saw our first rushes. I had previously converted my den at home to a screening room and we used it five times a week to screen the dailies.

4 A Learning Experience Making *Body Shop*

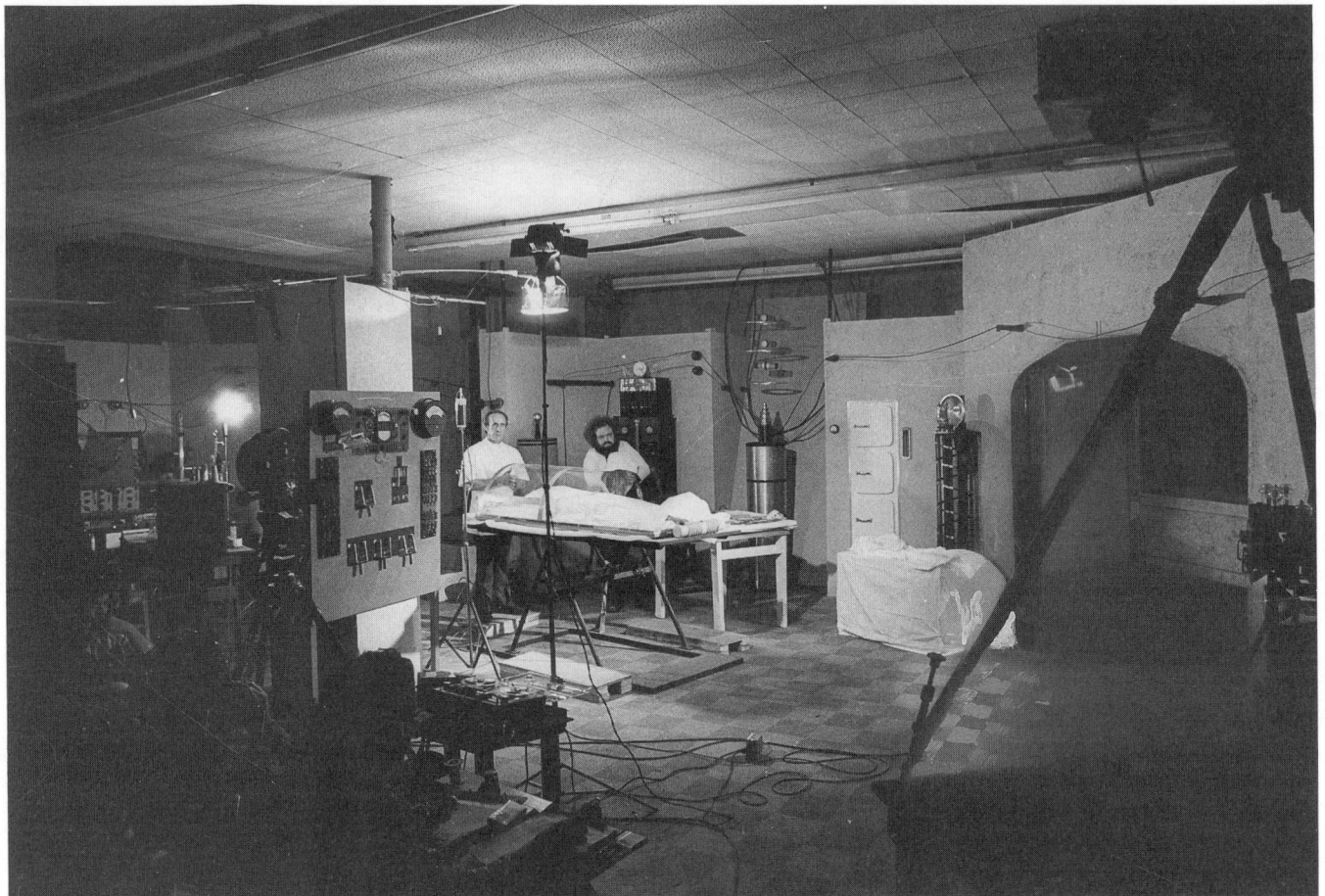

The leading man and "mad scientist" was 5 feet 6 inches and doing his part standing on apple boxes—reading his lines to his leading lady of almost 6 feet, Genny Driggers. (Photo by Hugh Peralta.)

Not sensing that my head was getting a little large for my hat, I was most pleased with the fruits of my labors. So was Pat until an occasional shot went in upside down! I didn't know why they were upside down at the time but I found it to be no cause for worry since I knew it was fixable. Pat worried. Although he said nothing, everybody in the room could feel his ulcer acting up each time an inverted scene went by.

As it turned out, some of the ends had been rewound before photography while others had not. The lab had inverted the former ones so the edge numbers would print through. (Simply turning the film around—flopping it—would also have put the numbers on the correct side but then the picture would have been backward. Confusing?)

In any case, we simply pulled those shots, replaced them right side up and the problem ceased to be. Others didn't. More than once, as Chris began to thread a camera, he discovered that the emulsion was a different color from other rolls. It turned out to be black and white film and therefore unusable. Fortunately, every time, he was alert enough to catch the error and prevent it from causing us a serious problem.

Scene 5, Take 1

We had to shoot a few exteriors. December is relatively warm in the North Carolina Piedmont so the shooting of exteriors did not present a serious inconvenience. One sequence was a picnic under a huge oak tree at Martin's, followed by a trek in the woods nearby.

Additional footage was shot of Pat and Big Genny smooching in the moonlight and riding in a rowboat on the pond of my nephew, Will. We always had to choose our angles wisely in order to mask the fact that Genny was half a foot taller than her leading man. We were not always successful, but we got some pleasant "postcard" footage.

The first exterior scene we shot was the burial of Anitra, the "perfect woman," who had presumably died in an automobile accident. It was among the shots made at Martin's home and was a bit disconcerting to his ten-year-old son who arrived home from school that day to discover a funeral taking place in his backyard. On the sound track, we can hear a school bus pull to a stop as the country preacher is reading the twenty-third Psalm, "though ah wauk, thoo th' valley o' the shadder adeath, ah'll fare no ayvul..."

A Learning Experience Making *Body Shop*

As the graveside ceremony ended, we cut to a tight shot of Anitra's husband, the "mad scientist," picking out one of the roses from those lying on the casket.

Keeping alive the memory of the dead Anitra was represented in the film by keeping the cut rose alive. Accordingly, having a rose that would not change from day to day was imperative, so Pat sent Reggie Belk to buy an artificial one. He came back with a half dozen which looked good, each of which had a wire stem about three feet long. Pat chose one and told Reggie to put it in a ceramic pot with some dirt to make it look alive.

Throughout the shoot, we would cut to the mad doctor's pampering and feeding the rose to reinforce the idea that the doctor, in some weird way, was keeping the essence of Anitra alive.

For the last day's shoot before Christmas eve, we had a 9:00 A.M. call. No one on the payroll was late, but Pat did not show up on time. We waited and drank coffee. We drank coffee and waited. Pat spent the entire morning in his "office." Let me describe his office.

It was a typical office desk pushed against the wall. Two sheets of 4×12 foot plywood leaned against the same wall forcing him also to lean forward over the desk. That was it! The telephone had no bell, only a light, which wouldn't spoil a sound take in case it rang—or flashed—while we were shooting, since the office was right on the set.

Noon came so the crew went to lunch. We came back and drank more coffee while Pat continued to wear out his inner sanctum. At 2:45 P.M. Pat came out and gave the first order of the day. "Load up the vehicles. We're going to shoot on location today."

We loaded up. By then, it was 3:15 and Pat stood there pondering a few moments with his chin in his hand and asked, "Does anybody know where we can find a large, grassy expanse with trees in the background?"

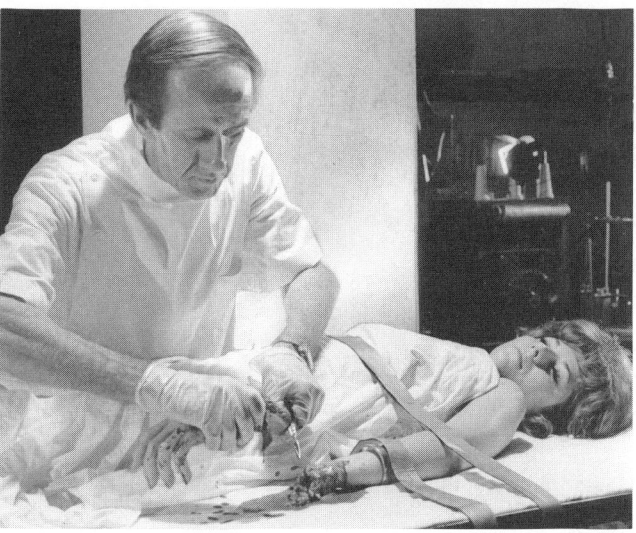

Every performance deserves a hand. Here Pat is getting one from Little Genny.

As it turned out, nobody did. So, knowing that it would be dark by 4:30, we launched our caravan of cars and a single, beat-up step van and set out on the quest of a grassy expanse with trees in the background.

Before dark, we got two minutes of really nice lovey-dovey, pitter-patter-through-the-woods footage, took the equipment back to the studio and went home for Christmas, 1971.

Christmas came and went. January came. Unlike December in the Carolinas, January can be cold, and it was. The script required Greg, the hunchback, to rob a grave. It was a night-for-night shot so (again in Martin's backyard) we dug a shallow grave—with great effort, I might add. It was double cold, the ground was frozen and our two SunGuns were casting out their light in chips. We dug that grave *one foot deep*. (When the director of photography and the cameraman are doubling as grips, that's how deep you dig a grave in frozen soil.)

Shooting up at Pat from ground level with a wide angle

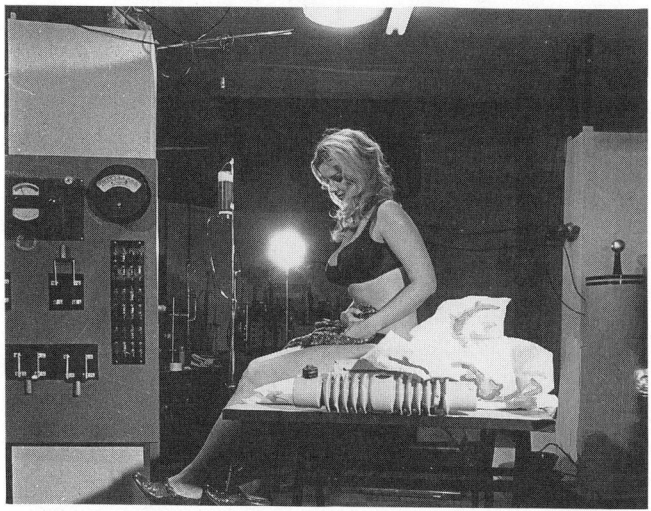

The very much alive Anitra, Genny Driggers. The staff called her Big Genny because she was so well-endowed. (Photo by Hugh Peralta.)

"Who died?" Marty, Martin's ten-year-old son, might have asked, walking from the school bus to his backyard.

6 A Learning Experience Making *Body Shop*

When there is no need for location recording, shooting with lighter equipment is in order.

lens established the hole as grave-deep. Roy Mehaffey, truly an extraordinary actor and our only professional one, lay down in that shallow hole and, on cue, climbed out pushing a body ahead of himself as if he were standing. He executed that bit with the expertise of a seasoned magician performing a grand illusion.

It's a shame that Roy (Greg) had no lines. He was the only professional actor regularly on the set, but his character was a mute. He could steal a scene simply by the use of a facial expression, a grunt or a raised eyebrow.

We continued shooting the lab shots in the studio. The only continuing technical problem we had was that each time the director said "action," somebody would drop a dime in a clothes dryer next door. The problem became so serious that eventually we sent Worth over there to record a couple of minutes of "dryer" so we could insert it where we needed to maintain background noise continuity.

Anitra was the assembly of a human jigsaw puzzle. Like the Frankenstein monster, it was necessary to use some type of gimmick to bring her freshly united parts to life. While the idea was not exactly unique, Pat elected to use electricity—actually, to simulate it. By putting probes here and insulators there, attaching them to this device or that, the mad doctor cranked up all his electrical eyewash and closed the circuit.

On cue, several people lit Roman candles aimed at the Plexiglas crucible in which the dead body parts kit (but much alive Genny Driggers) lay. One Roman candle fired a single shot and stopped. Another sizzled briefly and died. A third did nothing. It was not a good take.

In an effort to discover the problem I took one of the fireworks into the bathroom and lit it. It worked flaw-

Most of the romantic footage had a "postcard" look.

lessly. Unfortunately, once lit they have to run their course so I fired six perfect shots into the toilet.

Knowing now that the Roman candles were o.k., we set up to do a second take. It was a perfect repeat of the first. "Bang, fssssst, poof, and nothing."

I took another into the bathroom and lit it. Six perfect rounds into the john again. We were running low on Roman candles now. We set up the shot again. This time every available person stood in the safest place possible and held a Roman candle, carefully poised and aimed at Genny's crucible. We needed a minimum of three and we figured we were covered by having a half dozen or more. On Pat's signal, everyone lit his Roman candle. They all worked perfectly, six times each. We had plenty of light, plenty of fireballs and plenty of opportunity to burn down the Wilmont Launderette.

Probably all the fireballs hit the crucible. But being half-cylindrical, it deflected them. They went over the set, under the set, into the set, and into the tile ceiling. It looked like the Fourth of July.

Pat, who was standing perhaps three feet from the

Filming in the woods went quickly and easily—we just had to watch our angles.

crucible, probably never touched the floor more than twice between the first shot and the last. His first move, once he came down, was to check the ceiling for fire. There was none. The take was worth the problem. It was indeed impressive, but the fun was not over. The mad doctor's goal with the new 1971 model Anitra was to have what was his idea of the perfect woman, that is, six feet of empty minded pulchritude.

When the life-giving electrical display subsided, the doctor and Greg removed the crucible cover where the new Anitra lay, wrapped in gauze. From the camera's point of view, she looked like a L.A. Rams' fullback found in an ancient Egyptian pyramid.

"I've done it, Greg! I've done it," said the mad doctor, checking her heartbeat with his stethoscope. "She's alive!"

They tilted the surgical table up, putting her in a standing position. With a pair of scissors, he removed the bandages from her eyes and Anitra looked about the room, seeing right through the doctor with her void expression.

The scene was intended to be laden with emotion. The doctor would pluck the rose which symbolically held the original Anitra's essence of life. Destroying it would transfer that theoretical substance to the new, perfect woman. The "Wedding March" played in the background as the doctor kissed his unresponsive bride. The scene ended with a close up of Greg as a tear of glycerin ran down his cheek. His emotion appeared to be directed less toward sentiment than toward the prospect, "Why didn't he bake me one while the oven was hot?"

The scene, of course, works in the finished film, but the first take was a doozy! Because Pat believed it to be a scene of complicated moves, he elected to use two cameras to film it. Martin manned the Mitchell while Chris operated the Arri. I directed.

The scene began. Pat delicately cut the bandages and put down the scissors. "Give me the rose," said the doctor. Greg complied. Pat gently grabbed the stem and pulled, expecting the wire stem to simply slide out of the dirt. It didn't. He pulled a little harder. It didn't budge. He yanked vigorously and the artificial flower yielded, casting peat and dirt all over his smock and Genny's mummy-like wrappings. And there stood the mad doctor—about to be married—holding a pot in one hand and a rose with a three-foot, spring-coiled wire stem in the other. The expression on his face was exactly what you would expect.

"Cut!" he said sheepishly and beginning to break up, "Did you get that?" "I ran out of film just as you put down the scissors," answered Martin. "Sorry."

"I got it," said Chris. Unfortunately, he hadn't. His roll was double exposed.

Not all the goofs were somebody else's.

Needing an acid vat to dispose of unused body parts I donated some information I had once heard. Dye some sawdust green and float it on top of water. When you're ready to use it, dump in an appropriate amount of Alka-Seltzer, Bromo-Seltzer, or dry ice for bubbles. The suggestion was approved.

That evening I dyed some sawdust green with food color and dried it out in the oven to hold fast the color. The next day we put the sawdust into the "acid" vat— where it promptly sank to the bottom.

Scene 6, Take 1

Typically we did not work on Sundays. But one Sunday morning, Pat called and asked if I would ride up to Asheville with him. I agreed and it was during that short trip that I got to know him much better.

He had been a vaudeville-type magician. He had also done some live, late night horror shows on TV. Each time he was about to "make it really big," the act he had done became generally obsolete. But making movies was what he wanted to do. And if you're making money doing what you want to do, that's as good as it gets.

Pat was not a cheapskate. He simply had limited himself by thinking small, a symptom of working in television in its infancy when budgets for shows were ludicrously low; sometimes as low as $18 for a one-hour show, including props and talent.

Often he was that talent and furnished props for the shows which always played live on Friday nights. If he had nothing going on in the meantime that could mean a week with earnings of less than $20. He never escaped the fear of falling back into that trap.

Pat had procured a number of locations for us to use. The finding of Overlook was both a stroke of luck and a stroke of genius. Its use was inspired by the whimsical suggestion of a passer-by. Nothing about it had been written into the script. Previously none of us was even aware of its existence.

Overlook Castle in Asheville (not to be confused with Biltmore House) was constructed as the 1800's yielded to the new century. Since childhood the original owner had wanted a castle. In 1903 he laid the last stone and died that very day, leaving perhaps a single day's work to complete the edifice which to this day is unfinished.

It wasn't until the 1920's that a tile bathroom was installed far away in the back hall of the castle. Then bathrooms were seldom put indoors. The building had electrical service installed by Thomas A. Edison himself, a friend of the original owner. While separate power was directed to the chandeliers only, a single 15 amp circuit was distributed through the entire 30 or 40 rooms for main service.

After blowing the only fuse for that circuit the third time in rapid succession, we continued by shooting with the available light which, incidentally, resulted in some rather pleasing photography as well as strong production value. A sensible amount of furniture for a typical house

8 A Learning Experience Making *Body Shop*

A dead Anitra (and live Genny)—attacked by 36 Roman candles and protected by only a thin wall of Plexiglas.

left the living room in the mansion looking like a football field with an occasional sofa.

The castle had a turret in which a spiral staircase led to a vault not unlike a dungeon. The castle was so big that while we were in the basement we discovered a room that the owners were not aware of.

When we visited Overlook, it was owned and occupied by a Jerry Steinberg, his wife and their young daughter. Contracting the use of the castle was executed quickly, simply and efficiently. "Hey, lady. How would you and your daughter like to be in the movies for free?" They were kind enough to do it, certainly not because it was free but to accommodate Pat. In the movie, the viewer will see the Steinbergs walking up the winding driveway to the entrance of Overlook as Dr. Don Brandon drives past them in his Lincoln Continental, Greg hanging out the window ogling them.

By writing similar contracts, Pat got authorization to shoot the exterior of the Drawbridge Restaurant, the interior of the Paper Doll Lounge, the Open Kitchen, the Photo-Lab, Martin's property and my house.

By inserting Overlook footage into footage shot elsewhere, the classic appearance enhanced the picture immeasurably.

The exteriors we shot at the Drawbridge represented the entrance for a restaurant and bar sequence we shot in the Paper Doll. A dining scene we shot in the Open Kitchen offered dialogue that established the plot, that is, since Dr. Don Brandon wanted the perfect woman he'd have to create her himself. The comment was made tongue-in-cheek by Paul Woodhouse, who was played by Mike De Strom, but the doctor would take it seriously and decide to take the best parts from various women whom he would kill and put together as the perfect woman. Later, he would murder Paul Woodhouse who made the suggestion because "he knew too much."

Somehow the sound tape to that sequence was misplaced and, rather than loop it or reshoot it, Pat scrapped the shot literally murdering the character who spoke the dialogue. Not having that short sequence leaves the viewer in a bit of a quandary but offers him the opportunity to figure out what's going on without benefit of dramatic institution. (In postproduction Pat did do a narration over another scene which helped to clear up the mystery somewhat.)

Pat also worked out an arrangement with Bill Hicks who wrote and sang the musical compositions which were used in the picture: "Sugar and Spice" (the theme), "The Lovin' Tree," and "A Heart Dies Every Minute." The songs added both appeal and production value and were

Chris Allen and the author set up a shot at Overlook. (Photo by Martin Hill.)

good enough that I'm surprised that none of the three compositions ever went anywhere in the music market.

The script called for one of the mad doctor's victims to be drowned in the ocean after a brief love scene on the beach. On the warmest January day we could pick, we loaded up everybody and everything we would need and took a 200 mile trip to the Charleston, South Carolina, beach.

It was a comfortable temperature, pretty and sunny, except within eyesight of the surf. Everywhere we went within 200 yards of the ocean, it was so foggy that you could barely see the surf from 50 paces.

We had no choice but to shoot everything we could in the fog or return another day. We opted for the former. A minimum amount of script rewrite left us with a need to shoot only three shots at the beach. The first was the doctor and his victim running hand in hand toward the surf, the second was his return from the surf carrying the girl's lifeless body, and the last was a seagull or two for cutaways.

The first shot went well and quickly. When we tried the second, the camera became sluggish and jammed. After several tries we got the shot. The humidity in the fog was so high that the camera was shorting out and the film emulsion was sticking in the gate. We got a couple of shots of the gulls, loaded up the vehicles (including several boxes of sand) and headed home.

The next day we laid a blanket on the studio floor, put some sand around the periphery, lit it to look like the beach and finished the sequence by shooting from a high angle. It worked.

Shooting at my house and The Photo-Lab took little negotiating since both belonged to me. Besides, it gave Pat, my daughter then 12, an opportunity to be in her first and last X-rated movie (as an extra, I hasten to add).

That's right. *Anitra* got rated X because of the blood. This picture gave new meaning to the words "bare bones."

SCENE 7, TAKE 1

Anitra was made at a time when the quality of a horror movie was measured by the number of buckets of blood that were spilled. I was amazed at what startling effects could be achieved by the use of two dollars worth of beef and chicken fat together with a quart of white Karo syrup and red food color.

Taking into account that the doctor's goal was to seduce a woman into his lair, deprive her of the body parts he required, and dump what was left of her into the nearest acid vat, a notable amount of gore would naturally ensue.

On the long shots, we used pieces of mannequins dressed in beef and chicken fat. On the close ups, we used real human body parts. Fresh ones are quite easy to come by and nothing looks quite so effective as the real thing. "Repulsive!" you might think. Not at all. Everyone knows you have plenty of body parts. The trick is to do long shots and medium shots of artificial body parts, and then use those which are still alive and firmly attached to the proprietor in the close up shots.

It was about the fourth week that we did a great deal of the hand amputation photography along with legs, feet, arms, and eyeballs. We had such a good thing going that to do these episodes of gore, we used the longest roll of film we had—twice! That's right. We shot that roll and, somehow in the confusion, loaded it up and shot it again. It was the one we had used to shoot Anitra's wedding scene.

Imagine this. All the shots on the camera were of gory activity. When it was threaded up in the camera again, tails first, the subsequent shots of similar business were superimposed over the first. Looking at the result, we had action proceeding normally and right side up. Double

"Hey lady. How would you and your daughter like to be in the movies for free?" (Photo by Martin Hill.)

10 A Learning Experience Making *Body Shop*

The combination of light from the window and that of the chandeliers made very pleasing photography.

exposed over it, we had action which was upside down and running backwards! It was the most ridiculous stuff you ever saw.

"So much for that roll," you'd think. No, sir! We used that sucker! No sense throwing away two days' work. After delivering some eloquent dialogue through prison bars, the doctor is revealed to be in a padded cell. (This makes little since since he can beat his brains out on the iron bars if he chooses.) We used the double exposed roll in the sequence to depict his demented thoughts. With the appropriate music, it worked perfectly.

Editing was a snap. Pat had shot so tight a ratio that the outtakes could be carried away in two cigar boxes. Editing was simple because the editor was deprived of editorial latitude; he could cut it only the way it had been designed. Period.

The original audio recording was good and the sound track was transferred from a single roll full coat together with a quarter inch music track recorded from a synthesizer.

While at the lab, Pat decided to change the film's name to *Body Shop*. Ten prints were struck from the original negative and were put into distribution by Bob McClure

The castle was obviously spacious, a fact easily seen when watching the film or video.

who was both a distributor and the single backer of the film.

The rating system in those years was relatively new and laws were being passed right and left on the basis of the not-exactly-legal system. The picture, having gotten an "X" rating, became a white elephant and was hardly worth the effort of distribution. Once Bob had recovered his investment, he ceased distribution.

In the mid 1980's a poor looking videotape—one obviously made from a print—was released under the title *Body Shop*. At the same time, a very good looking tape made from the original negative went on the market under the title, *Dr. Gore*. The latter release opened with a special introduction by the master of gore, Herschel Gordon Lewis, under whose guidance Pat had learned production technique.

Body Shop became a cult classic—an achievement

The demented mad doctor was "put away."

which is never a goal—and it is demonstrative of films of its sort. It is unquestionably a fine example of a really cheap, worthwhile picture. Twenty years later, it is remarkably still generating revenues through sales and rentals.

The $20,000 budget on *Body Shop* was exceeded by $3,000. This is still one whale of a triumph, especially in light of the fact that its technical accomplishment, poor though it may be, exceeds that of many pictures costing 10 to 20 times as much.

A Learning Experience Making *Body Shop* 11

REVIEW

'Body Shop' gets a tuneup with blood, guts, satire

By EVIE STAUNTON
Gazette Staff Reporter

The photography is superb. The scenery is beautiful and in glorious color. The music is melodic and heartwarming.

That — in a nutshell, describes "The Body Shop," an 85-minute motion picture shown in its world premiere in Gastonia Friday.

Written, produced and directed by Pat Patterson, a native Gastonian, it is the first full-length motion picture to be made in its entirety in North Carolina. The 85-minute horror-love story was produced by Metrolina Motion Pictures Corp., of Charltote and starred Patterson in the male lead.

Starring with Patterson is Jennie Drigger, a lovely blonde Charlotte model. As Anita, Miss Drigger, portrays the perfect woman, created in the laboratory of the mad doctor. While it is Miss Drigger's first motion picture role, her acting and dialogue is natural and relaxed. As the naive girl, created from portions of other girls' bodies, she brings the house down with a throw-away line when she asks a truck driver "Are you going to haul my ashes?" Clad in a brief bikini, she has followed another truck driver from the castle where she lives with the scientist. The second driver stops to give her a lift. "You're a man," she says, and adds "Will you love me? Women are made to be loved."

Patterson's technique of sawing off the legs, arms and torso of his victims is so realistic that stumps of hands and arms can be seen quivering on the operating table.

But the picture is more than blood and gore. It is a passionate love story of a grief-crazed man who falls in love with his own creation and ends up in a mental cell when she disappears.

The music, composed and sung by Bill Hicks, also of Gastonia provides a background for the love scenes. The audience is s y m p a t h e t i c with the mad scientist when Hicks, a youthful Burl Ives type, sings "The Heart Dies a Little Every Minute."

Other tender scenes show the doctor and his new mate strolling through an Asheville park. He pauses to carve a message into a large oak tree, while Hicks' music of "The Loving Tree" is played. H i c k s later sings the song in a Charlotte night club.

Comic relief breaks the tension of bloody horror scenes when a hunchback, the doctor's faithful servant, leaps into the air as a mutilated body rises from the operating table. The girl, whose torso has just been cut off, rises from the table after a restraining strap breaks.

If realism and bloody gore is your cup of tea, "The Body Shop" will add the spice. Another ironic twist in the production is a nursery rhyme song that is hummed throughout the picture.

Patterson's dialogue is somewhat stilted, but his pantomine and glassy eyed looks of the h y p n o t i s t is so frightening, y o u ' l l find yourself looking away from the screen. The doctor's old flame played by Nita Shaw, seen in the closing reel, delivers a convincing line when she visits the mental hospital with a new boyfriend and tells the doctor he's through. Miss Shaw is Patterson's wife in real life.

A review in the Saturday, June 3, 1971, *Gastonia Gazette*..

The final incarnation of *Anitra*.

2
A Learning Experience Making *Marley's Revenge*

Whatever it is that makes people think I know more than I do worked on Jet Eller. We met at a time when I was doing special effects for several films and he, being fascinated by it, became my fan.

I had seen a film he had done a couple of years earlier called *I Walk with the Dead*. It was shot in black & white Super/8 and had a running time of about 20 minutes. I was startled to discover the sound had been added in post production since I remembered his lip sync being flawless.

It was an excellent piece of work for someone who'd never worked on a film before. It was hardly a prize winner because prizes are won by folks with more experience. I was impressed, though, that he was using a sound-installation technique that I had learned 25 years earlier at a time when it never officially existed.

Jet, 20 years my junior, and I became a mutual admiration society.

Jet told me he planned to do an updated, improved version of *I Walk* in 16mm for videotape release.

I questioned both his motives and his methods. His motive was that he was determined to produce a feature film and that was that. Regarding his methods, he had bought a camera and recorder and, beyond that, was open for suggestions.

"Let me know if I can help," I recklessly offered.

"Will you shoot it for me?" he recklessly asked.

"Sure," I recklessly answered. "When do we start?"

"Tomorrow night," he answered gleefully.

It was at that moment that I realized that "sure" was as shortsighted an answer as "When do we start?" was an impulsive question. To offer a major position on a film crew for a shoot beginning tomorrow ought to have been a clear indication that there had been little, if any, preproduction planning. Enter shades of Pat Patterson. I failed to pick up on the "clear indication."

Like *Body Shop*'s preproduction, this one had involved little more than buying some film, and sure enough, we started "tomorrow night."

Sharing the foolhardiness with Jet pleases me because he made as many mistakes as I, or vice versa. Either way, the budget had to finance *everybody's* errors.

Marley's Revenge, the Monster Movie (the new title) was written in about 15 percent daytime interiors, ten percent daytime exteriors, and the rest in the woods *at night*. You'd imagine the interiors and daytime exteriors would be a snap, and they were. But those long, drawn out weekends in the woods!

Before offering me the assignment of shooting he had already shown me a storyboard of the effects shots, mostly those of the monster. The monster represented a reanimation of dead things from the forest floor—and the underworld—which Marley had created using his voodoo powers. Boy, was he ugly.

He was built of styrofoam, broomsticks, two-by-fours, and cotton string. The quality of his appearance, his "ugly," was inspiring. The majesty of his 14-foot altitude was a credit to his designer and builder, Ralph Carpenter (not to be confused with John).

Ralph, who also had done the striking storyboards, is not ordinarily a special effects man but was in charge of processing Kodachrome at a photo finishing plant. He, like the rest of us, also played a part in the picture.

In the truest sense of the word, it was not principal photography which had begun. The object was to shoot an exciting ten minute segment, edit it, and present it to a potential backer.

I disagreed with Jet on that course because I had once taken the approach and found it fruitless, but he was hell bent on doing it. He had planned it and he had organized it—or so he thought—and he had it ready to do, so I wasn't going to stand in his way.

The schedule for the first evening's business was to shoot a demon, one that Ralph had built, walking and stalking through the woods. Also scheduled was a zombie rising from his grave, and for the character, Howard (played by the same Ralph Carpenter), to be snake bitten.

That was a pretty ambitious schedule for the first evening but we pulled it off successfully. (Ultimately, the demons were scrapped in editing because they looked like what they were, effects).

The crew that appeared there that evening were Jet's friends whom he had chosen only on the basis that they

I told you he was ugly! (Illustration by Ralph Carpenter.)

were friends. It would have been great to have chosen his friends who were actors as actors, his friends who were technicians as technicians, and so on, but he didn't. He chose them on the basis that they too wanted to make a movie and were willing to follow his lead. They followed well.

Donnie Evans, being a member of a band, had access to a half dozen 500w stage lights which he brought. Jet had brought some 300w quartz parking lot lamps which he had gotten on special at a hardware store. I furnished ten 12-foot indoor light stands and a handful of ColorTran units.

The stage lights were put on Hi-Riser stands (which Jet had procured at no charge other than the promise to sand and repaint them). These lights were used to create three quarters rear moonlight streaming through the trees. Several 600w ColorTrans and some of the 300w quartz were put at about 30 yards away, modified with a one half blue gel. They faced the camera using a tree here and there to flag the lamp. These illuminated the background fog which was laid in by using a rented fog machine. The rest of the lights simply illuminated the talent, some with one half or full blue gels and some with none at all, to simulate people in the woods. Looked great!

The very first shot we did was of nondescript silhouettes coming through the woods with flashlights beaming through the fog. It was shot (as was everything) on the film stock 7292. I rated it at 320 as Kodak suggests. Looking through the finder worried me though, because the image was so dim I couldn't bring myself to believe I was getting sufficient exposure. After the first take, I opened up a stop on everything else I shot that night.

Getting a perfect exposure is the one thing that must be expected of any cinematographer. No matter how good or bad he is, he ought to be good enough to read a meter correctly. Although Jet liked it, I was embarrassed with that first shot and the subsequent ones which I was pressed into shooting wide open. Those shots were a stop underexposed. Sometimes one stop under can be corrected, but not when you intend for a correct exposure to render a dark image in the first place. That was one on me. I should have had the guts to demand from the outset that we would *not* shoot until after we had tests. By not doing so, my photography embarrassed me.

Experience over the next few sessions would tell us that nighttime shots with very heavy fog could be filmed at ASA 250, but all shots in the woods without fog had to be shot at ASA 200, about one third stop difference.

While some nighttime photography can be successfully done at ASA 320, the exposure will be close enough to the edge of correctness that you will bite your nails. The foliage in the woods simply drank up light as did the darkness when there was no fog between the trees to keep the light dancing around to create ambience.

For the duration of the picture, we stuck with a straight ASA 200 on night shots. Even then, I cheated by opening up a quarter to a half stop except on extreme close ups. In fact, when we changed exterior night locations we read the key light once and eyeballed everything else for the rest of the evening. The ensuing work print was more consistently even and more accurate than ever before.

Since everyone on the project worked elsewhere for a living, we were restricted to shooting on Friday nights, Saturdays, and Saturday nights. At one time or another, each of us took a turn at screwing up the schedule because of prior commitments or family emergencies. Having begun on such short notice, prior obligations caused me to be the first absentee by missing half of the second session and all of the third.

Upon arrival at the second session, I was both stunned and pleased to discover the lights had been shifted to a different location, but set up precisely as I would have had it done. Donnie, together with Chris Berkebile and Lee Roberts, obviously had retained what I had explained about lighting. Having seen what they had done and knowing that Jet could handle the photography, I felt somewhat reassured having to abandon the crew that third night.

My confidence was rewarded. While I was able to see some difference between my style and theirs, they proved they could get along without me. It took me 35 years of diverse, self-inflicted education to learn the subtleties of lighting the way I do it. Then two printers and a pork skin salesman from Mint Hill figure it out in the woods on a single Friday night! That was sufficient evidence that I was dispensable and ought to have been there. Thereafter I was.

By the end of the fifth session, the show piece that Jet had intended to make was in the can. We had seen the dailies and were pleased. He was excited that we were on a roll and didn't want to stop. I had mixed emotions regarding that issue because of some of the problems that existed.

14 A Learning Experience Making *Marley's Revenge*

The monster was dubbed "Big Daddy" after "Big Mamma" in *Alien*.

Having recently settled a modest insurance claim, Jet knew he'd have enough money to continue for a while. The greatest drawback was that the script at this point was only a synopsis. He and Donnie Broom, a costar and cowriter, jumped headfirst into the script writing process and, staying only hours ahead of each weekend shoot, continued writing the script. That was the crux of my reservations. Not only because writing in that fashion was a problem but that it was yet another indicator of a lack of organization.

Continuing wasn't a good idea, but we did anyway. Each Friday or Saturday everyone would show up on the location having absolutely no idea of what to expect, save that we were going to shoot in the woods. The inexperienced talent (all of our talent) would have to learn their few lines on the spot, pick up on their blocking, and do their most serious rehearsing as the camera went with them on the walk-through's. More often than not, only Jet knew what was going on. No one else understood enough even to make a suggestion.

Knowing Jet's choice of locale, the grips would have already established the lighting by the time I arrived, leaving me with only a little tweaking to do. I then would take a reading which was invariably f/4. That would appease me knowing that I could get an adequate exposure at f/3.5. Typically f/5.6 would be my preferred f/stop but if f/3.5 was all we had, it was all we had! So I would set the lens on f/3.5 and use that stop all evening being excruciatingly careful with my focus.

From a technical standpoint, start up wasn't so bad because all we had to do was light a slightly different area for a moonlight situation. In the woods, you can pan 45 degrees or shift six feet and appear to be in a completely different location. By doing that, you can pan incrementally 360 degrees over the course of a few sequences and do two days' work without treading on new ground. That, unquestionably, is a time saver.

Not being professionals almost everybody had foolish cause to slow down the project. Probably the first occasion was the grip/electrician team had forgotten to bring the electric cables. Not some of it—all of it. We waited calmly in the dark until they drove 20 miles round trip to fetch it. They were the first to forget something vital but, unfortunately, not the last.

The season of the year or the geographical location can have great impact upon your script and production expenses, requirements, operational speed, and techniques. We began to shoot late in October. After several weekends, it was becoming too cold to shoot. Besides, the leaves had begun to fall, dispelling any possibility of matching photography. Stopping at that point offered a number of advantages. We had the opportunity to regroup our thinking and plan for the springtime shooting sessions. Many lessons had been learned by the experience. Our problems required research and analysis.

The respite gave Jet the rest of the winter to finish the script, but he didn't. It gave Ralph time to finish building the monster, but he didn't. And it gave me time to convince Jet that organization would lead to finishing the film more efficiently, but I didn't. I found all three to be most disconcerting.

A number of people—outsiders—by now had become aware of what was going on and had begun to develop an interest in the project. Jet needed more money to continue and these people wanted to invest. Hallelujah!

Because of their trust in Jet, each invested with nothing more than a handshake as security. (Not a good idea for either party but an overwhelming vote of confidence.)

Harry Cosgrove later produced a plan where the cash investors and the sweat-equity investors—the crew who were not being paid in money—would be compensated upon the sale of the film or the rights to it. It was a good and fair plan and everybody later signed a loosely written contract to that effect.

When the time came to reckon who had done what and how much of it, the precise paperwork Trena Davis had done finally paid off. Her record keeping had not been done according to accepted standards, but she had a record of every financial transaction—who had been on the set on which days, for how long. She even had a model release for everybody who showed up, even if he didn't get photographed.

We had already concluded that the picture was destined to be a good one but we all agreed that it lacked production values; that is, it needed some additional pizazz. My recommendation, since we were dealing with an island, was to blow up the boat that got the characters to the island.

We had chosen to use a cabin cruiser which belonged to a friend, so we made a number of photographs of it from every necessary angle. From the photographs we drew up a loose set of plans. Several sheets of Luan, some hot glue, styrofoam, and bailing wire were all the materials needed to build an eight-foot model of the boat—a one quarter scale model.

Harry Cosgrove, while not a pyrotechnist, knew where he could buy some black powder so we proclaimed him to be expert and had him do the deed.

We decided that since the boat was eight feet long we would need an explosion that would render a mushroom cloud from eight to 12 feet above the boat. Also a welder, Harry made several mortars of varying depths and widths with which to experiment. After several tries at a safe distance and taking notes, he chose to use this mortar with that amount of Pyrodex and so much napalm. He rested assured that when the time case he could effect a predescribed explosion on demand.

The time came. We elected to shoot on a Wednesday evening so no crowd would be around. We used the two-acre pond on Martin's property. Our model was carefully rigged with electric lights and with string to position it in the water precisely where we wanted it.

Harry's mortar could be found nowhere. A rusty three-inch iron pipe welded to a six-inch square of iron plate, it evidently had been picked up and taken away by someone believing it to be scrap. Not one to waste the evening, Harry elected to substitute and calculate.

He rigged his Pyrodex in a plastic bag together with the electric squib and put it in a small cardboard box in the floor of the boat. On top of that, he put a predetermined amount of napalm in another plastic bag and put that on top of the Pyrodex. He extended 100 feet of electric wire from the boat and announced he was ready.

Meanwhile, referring to my American Cinematographer Manual, I had verified the appropriate camera speed for an exploding model and had set up a Bolex, a Cine Special, and two Kodak model K cameras on tripods and was ready to shoot as soon as it was dark.

The purpose for the four cameras was twofold. I wanted to use a medium shot and a long shot in case making an editorial cut was in order, and I wanted to have a back up camera for each of the two shots since we would have only one opportunity. (In retrospect, I wish I had elected to put another pair at a different angle just to have a greater variety of choice.)

Lights were set up to simulate back-light by moonlight and the fog machine was put into position to screen out trees which otherwise might have been seen beyond the boat, giving away the fact that it was a miniature.

Finally, when dark fell we were ready. The lights were lit, the fog was blown into position, the cameras were started and Harry was given his cue.

He depressed the 110 volt button and blew the boat to Pittsburgh. The shot looked great going up, and sometime later, coming down.

The winter months came and gave us a little time to get ahead. It also gave me time to make life masks of several actors which I was assigned to do.

The heads of Jet, Trena, Donnie and Gary Vaughn were to be used in various special effects. Gary's head was bitten off by the monster, Donnie's was to expand when he was bitten in his (normally) inflated midsection, and Trena's (representing an hallucination) rapidly decomposed by melting. Jet's was to be used as a machete decapitation, but after three remakes to get it just right, it wasn't used at all. Neither was Donnie's. It looked good, worked well, but serving only as a close up it required a prior medium shot to support it. We had none and since there was a skin texture difference between Donnie's skin and that of the duplicate we were unable to use it. I enjoyed making them anyway and Jim Lawrence did a whale of a job painting them to look natural.

Jet had spent the winter writing and rewriting and, we

16 A Learning Experience Making *Marley's Revenge*

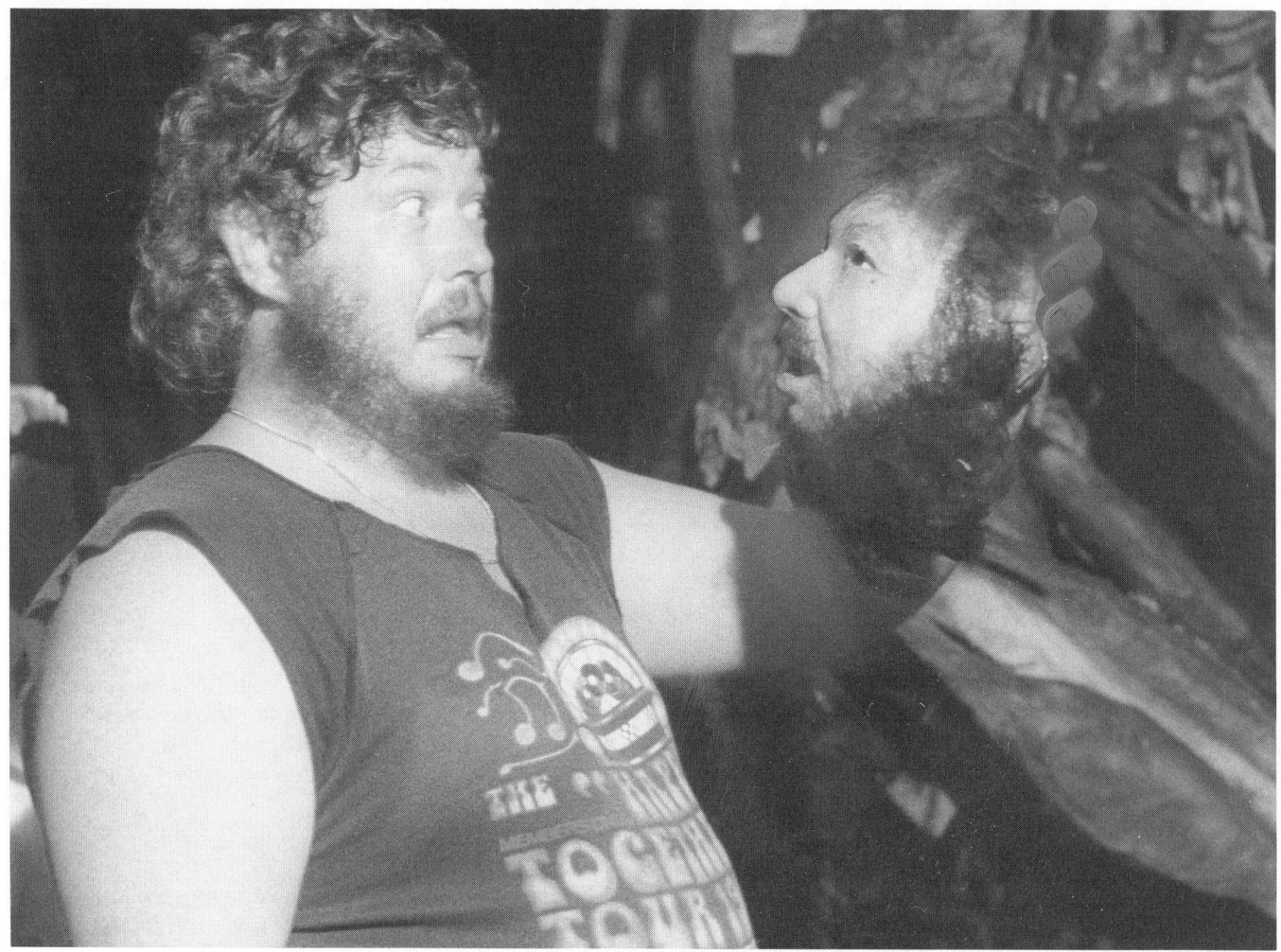

Speaking of heads, Donnie Evans, on the other hand, is holding his own. (Photo by Marie Heptig.)

thought, organizing and reorganizing. We all could see the wheels turning in his head but we never were quite able to read his thoughts. As it turned out, we had erred. Jet's turning wheels were steered toward his writing which was nearly finished but he had paid no attention to reorganization. This being his first real project he had deluded himself into believing that producing and directing were synonymous. He knows now that they are not.

Before the weather got warm, we had the opportunity to shoot our interiors. Not having a sound stage, we used Jet's house as the house of the two leading characters. It was compact for a shooting area, but since we had only two characters to deal with and only two rooms to be represented, the shoot went well and was more or less efficiently executed.

No tragedies took place during the shoot, but each time there was a requirement for something as simple as a 40w bulb or a hammer and nail, there was none available. Ever! What about a hand mirror or an extension cord? A piece of string, a coat hanger, some Scotch tape or a paper clip? It was as if he knew today what things I would ask for tomorrow and would purge his apartment of them tonight simply to deprive me of their use! I doubt if there is anyone else in this country who has a house but not a hammer and nail.

To make a long story short, the "more-or-lesses" didn't interfere much because we managed to get by without them or we sat around for 15 minutes while somebody went to the hardware store. Since Trena always had a pot of coffee ready, the wait was a respite anyway.

The filming of the apartment now behind us, we had two interiors left to shoot. Next came the bar. Needing the look of a truly red-neck bar, Jet had contracted with the owner of Mr. Ed's to let us shoot in his place of business. It was an extraordinarily good choice and gave new meaning to the word "dive."

Since such places stay open most of the night, and because we could work only on weekends, we were confined to shoot on Saturday mornings. Early—at 5:00 a.m., an hour which I assumed had been universally discontinued shortly after I got out of the service.

In exchange for a screen credit and small part in the picture, Ed was gracious enough to stay late to let us in to set up. Jet had, of course, agreed to pay any expenses which might accrue because we were shooting there. For two months in the late winter and early spring we would show up at Mr. Ed's Bar, not at all wide-eyed or bushy-tailed, to set up for that morning's shoot which was always to be at 8:30, but never was.

Invariably, there would be an obstacle. On the first occasion we discovered we had too few electrical cables. The second Saturday we had enough cables, but we blew a circuit and still had to shoot around the problem of not having enough light. The third week we blew yet another circuit and had to get an electrician out of bed at 5:45.

The following week, while installing a light fixture to the ceiling, one of the grips stepped on a beer cooler door and bent it, giving Jet an opportunity to replace it.

Not wanting to break tradition, the next Saturday morning we managed somehow to screw up the compressor. I'm not sure what compressor it was or what we were compressing, but it was $300 worth and Jet agreed to pay $150 next week and the balance a week later.

He did, in cash. And Mr. Ed forgot it because in a bar everybody pays cash. And being the businessman that Jet is, he almost never got a receipt for anything during the entire first half of shooting the picture. But Trena did! It is good that Ed is as kind and trusting a soul as Jet is, because on the simple word of a mutual friend who witnessed Jet's paying, Ed agreed that the bill had been settled.

A word to the wise whatever your business: The IRS may choose not to accept only a check as proof of payment. If you don't have a bill or a receipt to go with your canceled check, they can infer that you simply cashed a check rather than making a deductible purchase and charge you income tax on the amount.

The film shot on the seventh and final session was irretrievably scratched by the lab. The unfortunate accident could have happened at any lab so they readily admitted the fault and said they were sorry. We readily agreed that we too were sorry and asked them to pay for a reshoot. They readily said "No," but replaced the roll and credited Jet for the processing. We reshot it the following Saturday wrapping up the bar sequence.

Customarily, labs do not pay for reshoots since that's what negative insurance is for. They do, however, replace the film stock and do not charge for the processing.

The first exterior daylight sequence we shot was a somewhat intricate sequence of Donnie and Alvin Johnson leaving their house to begin the trip.

We set up two five-light FAY lamps to bring up the shadows and powered them by a 70 amp generator that had been bought for such use but had not been tested. As it turned out, the generator's circuits were divided in such a way that no five-light unit could be powered by a single circuit. Since rewiring the lamps on the spot would not have been practical, we spent the next hour and a half making reflectors which we ought to have had to begin with.

The unfortunate surprise caused us to take eight hours to do what should have been done in two.

Topping off an otherwise great day, our dailies (which we got weekly) revealed that all our footage from that session was fogged. Not knowing right away just where the light leak had occurred we switched from using Jet's CP-16 to my Auricon Pro-600 Special. It had an identical lens, the same movement, and equal film capacity, and we knew it was dependable in the sunlight. (The magazine proved to be the culprit on Jet's camera. The problem was corrected and we continued using Jet's camera.)

By now, Mark Overton had come to work with us. Finally we had a second crew member who had some practical experience! Mark worked in lighting on a number of features and many commercials. Being a workaholic, he fit in quite well with the rest of the crew.

During a daylight auto-tracking sequence the following Saturday, John Clifford, our video and second unit cameraman, was substituting as sound man for Dick Walters. To our great chagrin he discovered he was using a roll of tape which had previously been recorded! Placing the blame was less important than finding a way to preclude a recurrence. Fortunately, most of the audio we lost represented the picture that was scratched by the lab. Shades of *Body Shop* enter again. The lesson we ought to have learned was to account for all the property concerned with a shoot. But somehow we didn't.

Because we had no individual to account for props, whoever was to use a prop was usually responsible for bringing it. That wasn't a rule, simply an expectation. As often as not, someone would appear for the shoot having forgotten a vital prop causing a course change in mid flight—potentially a very destructive problem.

None of us were experienced with car mounts for cameras, but we needed a number of shots through each side window and through the windshield. I had built a mounting device not unlike a curb service tray but it had proved too shaky.

Fortune was with us that day. Hugh Esco, a grip from Atlanta and a friend of Mark's, had come up to visit. He had no sooner arrived than we put him to work. Having had considerable experience with car mounts, he tightened our mount with bungies and bailing wire, and using the camcorder, we tested its performance proving it flawless, absolutely rock steady.

Our first shot was through the passenger's window. We used Martin's Arri BL which provided perfect shots. We stopped several miles away from the starting point to changed the mount to the other side. We remounted the camera and began the take. Twenty seconds later, the magazine jammed. We were losing the sun and were far enough away from the starting point that it would have been fruitless to dash back, load the Auricon magazine,

18 A Learning Experience Making *Marley's Revenge*

Note (directly under the camera) the sliding camera mount screw for shifting the camera from front to back to find the nodal point. The tripod mounting plate is at the top of the jig, left on the photo.

thread the camera and pick up where we left off. So we took a chance.

Knowing that the shots we were about to shoot could be divided into several short ones and that we were going to have to loop the sound, we mounted my Cine Special which has a long spring wind. It provided us with excellent results, and much to our surprise, the sound was in sync!

Even though it was winter there were insert shots that could be made. My son, Kurt, and his wife make frequent trips to Wilmington, North Carolina, to visit. I gave him a Bolex and one hundred feet of film and explained that I needed a shot of the surf with the horizon dividing the frame in half with the surf and sand in the foreground, a tilt down and a pan right. I added that later I would matte in an island on the horizon, since nowhere on the east coast of the United States exists an island like the one we wanted.

They brought back a shot whose beauty far exceeded my need or expectations. It was as I requested but stippled with shells all about the glossy, wet sand and framed by foliage bobbing in the breeze.

Using the work print, I plotted out the position of the island, accounting for the camera tilt, made a piece of artwork of the island which was actually only a silhouette, and photographed it on the light box. (You'll read about the light box later.)

The lab made an interpositive of both the beach footage and the island, then a dupe negative and print. The print indicated a mismatch in the tilt down of over two seconds. What a miss!

I recalculated and photographed it again. Same problem, just different timing. I did it again. Still missed. This was becoming embarrassing. I finally got the move right on the twelfth try but the island was sitting just above the horizon. I was wasting time, energy, and money. Further effort was pointless.

My wife and I had been invited for a weekend at the beach so I decided that I'd take a camera, tripod, and a couple of C-stands, and a Plexiglas with a silhouette of the island on it. This would be all I'd need to make a glass-matte shot—or so I thought.

Setting up the rig at the magic hour really looked perfect in the finder, but as I would tilt down, the island would rise. Frustrating! I knew the cause; the camera was not pivoting on the nodal point of the lens. I knew about it beforehand but it hadn't occurred to me. I was not able to make the shot.

Returning home, I took some measurements of the Bolex and built an adjustable jig in my shop to which the Bolex could be mounted to tilt on the optical center of the lens. Making it wasn't difficult; it simply required a few minutes' engineering and a half hour's work.

It also was easy to test since all that was necessary was to set up the shot and do a tilt while looking through the reflex finder.

The following Saturday, Mark, Jet, and I drove eight hours to and from the beach, having spent perhaps as little as ten minutes setting up and shooting. In editing and printing, the shot was continued by ending the beach shot with a tilt down then a pan to the right. It was dissolved to another shot made in the vacant lot next to my shop 250 miles away. It wasn't a very good transition but it worked.

We laid out six sheets of 4×8 plywood and covered them with some fine sawdust obtained at a local lumber-

A Learning Experience Making *Marley's Revenge* 19

Notice that the sawdust looks like sand. (Photo by Marie Heptig.)

yard. On the sawdust, we scattered some seashells and installed some artificial sea oats and other foliage. Starting our shot by panning to the right, a man who has dragged himself fro the surf is revealed. The beach shot and this one were joined by the dissolve. The sawdust reads like sand and nobody sees the difference.

Using sawdust was a matter of twofold economy. The use of sand would have required a heavy truck to deliver three yards at about $10 per yard plus a $100 delivery charge. The sawdust was free and, being nearly weightless, we were able to haul as much as we needed in our own trailer. Of course, we also saved by not taking a crew to the beach to do the shot in the first place.

When warm weather returned, it was time again to shoot in the woods. Except for a few pick up shots, everything left to do was to be shot in the woods, representing about 75 percent of the picture.

Of the two most serious problems Jet had, a lack of communication continued to be the greater. At the time we weren't so sure what the other was but ultimately it raised its ugly head.

Having chosen friends as his cast and crew people rather than professional actors and technicians, Jet suffered the constant fear that, because these people weren't being paid for their services, somewhere along the line somebody wouldn't show up for the shoot or simply might quit.

This underlying feeling led him to call everybody to the shoot whom he knew he needed, together with those whom he could use if one or more of the others didn't show.

He didn't quite understand at the time why that was a bad move because he always had to be there himself. People would come to the shoot and sit there for hours and then be sent home at 3:00 a.m. having done nothing but wait.

It's very important to point out that their lack of professional skills did not interfere with their professionalism. This untried crew showed up, went to work, and did their job. Sometimes it was a little strange, perhaps a little slow, but always diligent.

One night when we were doing tail slates to save reorienting the focus before the take, Lorna Walters, seeing the slate upside down, made the entries upside down on the camera log. They were odd, but we got the log entries and we got the message.

Making a call sheet so everybody would know precisely what was expected of him was suggested to Jet in vain. He accepted the comments with a nod—but no call sheets were forthcoming.

Martin, whom you remember shooting the war movie and sticking to his guns, also stuck to 50 acres in Midland, North Carolina, where he has 40 acres of woods and a warehouse full of Hollywood. The building overflows with filmmaking goodies. The back lot is a safe-guarded field of discarded 10K lamps, High-Risers and C-stands, while the really good stuff is kept inside the giant warehouse.

I asked him if we could use his woods to finish *Marley*.

"Sure," he said as if I really needed an answer. He was already familiar with the project because Jet had bought his CP-16 and Nagra recorder from him.

"You can even use one of the generators out on the lot," Martin offered. "All you have to do is level it and figure out how to make it go."

Since power would be Mark's responsibility, he chose a Mole-Richardson 600 amp generator, leveled it and figured out how to make it go. Once he did, he had to run three pieces of 4/0 feeder cable 200 yards to put power in the woods—that's about a half ton of wire. He did it by putting a couple of loops over his skinny shoulders and heading for the woods, time after time, until he had it done.

Although use of the generator was free and it performed well, it was costing $50 per night in gasoline alone. Also we had to keep it manned. After four weeks of such expenditures I asked Harry Cosgrove, who knows about such things, for some advice. He examined the power input to Martin's building and suggested tapping directly into the mains. Being a heavily serviced building, there was at least four times the power both Martin's household and we needed.

The suggestion was made to pay Martin an overage on his power bill plus a little extra and he readily agreed to allow us to tie in to the incoming power.

From Martin's first power bill we calculated that the $50 gasoline bill had been reduced to a $4.67 electrical bill. If we had bought the gasoline without tax, we still would have paid about $17 per night for generator power. The tie in was a good idea.

Mark would go out to Martin's at 2:00 in the afternoon to set up lights for a particular sequence. A strong point! Moving heavy lights around in the woods is a job, and it's slow going. But when the rest of the crew arrived, he'd be close to ready. It would invariably be midnight before we were able to shoot the first take.

There were two problems that needed fixing. Some people, as Jet had feared, would arrive late or wouldn't show at all. Jet would have to call a different shot and that, in turn, would cause the entire crew to change as quickly as possible the lighting set up for the new shot, wasting the entire afternoon's work and resetting in less time than it ought to take. It also caused the inexperienced talent quickly to rehearse scenes that they hadn't planned to do.

The second cause of the same problem was less obvious and neither of us could discover exactly what it was at first. I tried to analyze it and Jet tried to analyze it. We were nearly through with the shoot before we discovered just what it was. Mark wouldn't quit. He would continue tweaking up the lighting while waiting for us to shoot. Meanwhile, we were biding our time waiting for him to achieve his lighting goal. Ultimately, we threatened to handcuff him to a chair when the light was good enough. Set-ups thereafter progressed at a little faster pace.

The former cause was one of more concern. People not showing up is a problem that must be stopped. With no more than a month of weekends left, Jet realized that someone had to take charge of disgruntled personnel, a job which ought not be the director's.

The director must keep a good rapport with the talent and crew. Being excessively firm is no way to do it. I was, therefore, appointed to be the company jerk. I loved it.

That meant that now I could say, "Hey, you, do this," and "you, there, do that." But of course, I didn't. I too needed to keep a good relationship with everybody, and did. My newfound authority was used for the composition and institution of call sheets which, as predicted, helped immensely.

Jet and I would go over the remaining script on Monday and fill out a call sheet for the following Friday and Saturday using a Xeroxed form which had been laid out specifically to our need. On Tuesday I would have copies made of the filled out forms and would mail one to everybody, regardless of whether he was on call.

Notice that the call sheet need not be special. Ours was a single page, Xeroxed, hand done blank original, then re-Xeroxed in volume when filled out.

The call sheets went over as well with the inexperienced crew as it would have with one who expected it. Several people got an evening or weekend off when they otherwise might have been on call and they appreciated it.

A call sheet puts the communication in writing, a safeguard against anyone forgetting to bring something, or do what is supposed to be done. Those who weren't on call knew they could have some time to relax. The going is much smoother if those who are not needed are not present.

It worried Jet that someone not on the call sheet would be needed but not available. His worry was for naught. The call sheet system, on this as on all projects, worked.

Nearing the end of the shoot, two important characters, recently cast, appeared on the scene. Defoy Glenn returned from a London play date just in time to do his short but crucial appearance with Margaret Freeman who

```
Producer-Director    MARLEY'S REVENGE    Asst. Prod - Asst. Dir
   JET ELLER         CALL SHEET FOR        HARRY JOYNER
                      FRI 8-26, 1988

QUESTIONS? CALL HARRY JOYNER 9am-6pm 376-1624, nite 523-7237
IF NO WEATHER   - REPORT TO:
IF WEATHER - CALL HARRY JOYNER OR

        CAST CALL   at   7 : 00 pm  at THE PHOTO-LAB

ACTOR              CHARACTER
ALVIN              GARY            ( TO SHOOT:
DONNIE B           ALAN
DONNIE E           SLOTH           VIGILANTE BOAT
JUNIOR             TATER           INTERIORS Pg 15, 16
STUART             SHERIFF                    17
(VOICE OF COAST    GUARD OFFICER)
                                   SHERIFF IN CAR
                                         Pg 13

SPECIAL NOTE:  NO VISITORS

A MEAL  WILL / WILL NOT  BE SERVED

PROPS REQ · WARDROBE REQ · MISCELLAN
MAKING A LIST OF THOSE ITEMS YOU ARE RESPONSIBLE FOR IS RECOMMENDED.

NAUTICAL STUFF
BOAT (NT              Regular
TABLE
CANVAS OR SHEET

        CREW CALL   at   7 : 00 pm  AT 2

MARK O. (IF AVAIL)
DAVE W.                             THE PHOTO-LAB
RICHARD, LORNA,                     1424 East Independence Boulevard
TRENA                               Charlotte, N.C. 28205
HARRY J.                            704/376-1624

IF YOUR NAME IS NOT ON THIS SHEET AND YOU THINK IT OUGHT TO BE,
               CALL HARRY J.!
```

later played Whoopie Goldberg's sister in *The Color Purple*.

With only about 15 minutes of the film remaining to shoot, Jet was beginning to run out of money. We put out a sort of "silent" call for an investor. A friend, whose name needn't be mentioned here, answered the call.

A tentative agreement was reached between Jet and the new backer. A portion of his investment was made knowing that Jet still had total creative control.

He came to several shoots but was displeased with the work of one of the crew. He tried without success to pressure Jet into firing him. A couple of shoots later, he lost his temper (and at the same time the crew's respect) and stormed off the set because of his displeasure.

22 A Learning Experience Making *Marley's Revenge*

On the occasion of the next shoot, the *crew* called a meeting and collectively offered to back the balance of the production/postproduction with cash from their own pockets in order to preclude the possibility of an unwanted repeat. In doing so, the entire crew became executive producers in one fell swoop.

(In time, the offender corrected his transgression, won back the crew's approval, and continued to invest in the picture.)

Such problems point out that it is absolutely imperative that before beginning work on such a picture, everybody understand that there is but one boss on the set. He is the director and probably is the only person who has a good overview of the whole project. Nobody argues with him and any suggestions made to him are made either through the assistant director or at the preproduction or production meetings, preferably written. Those suggestions are never repeated or argued because all the options are his, and he really isn't interested in justifying why he isn't using someone's idea.

This is an important issue. Many people, seeing the obvious, will make suggestions which the director already intended to use, and later be upset because he was not paid for or credited with the idea. You will also be surprised to discover who will sulk for a year or more because his idea was rejected.

These are rules which exist on every shoot and are expected to be followed blindly by everyone who has experience in film making.

Since we were unable to shoot during the winter, we decided it would be a good time to edit the portion we had already shot. Martin lent us not one but two Movieola editing tables. We needed the machines and he needed the space they occupied.

Owning my own business gave me the option to put the editing tables where I work so I could edit during my workday and Jet could do so in the evenings. It was at the same time a good idea and a bad one. It was good in that I could edit during the day but bad because of the continual interruptions. I could not stop them because my first priority is owed to my business; it's how I make my living. Still, I made it work.

Jet had bought a Magnasync, a two player–one dubber, full coat mixing system which was not yet set up. Our tests proved however, that we could record from the Nagra to our Sonarex interlock projector and get a good recording. We dubbed all the circled takes and the rough cut began.

Fortunately, the rough cut was started before filming was finished thereby bringing attention to a number of problems and allowing them to be smoothed out by retakes or making short inserts.

By now it had become evident that, while our transfer quality was quite good, the original recordings had suffered because of the high background noise caused by a proliferation of crickets.

It's a distinct advantage to be able to edit as you shoot, especially if you aren't a veteran at what you do. A case in point was the results of the first day's editing. They indicated problems not previously observed.

Lacking a continuity person, we generally were able to maintain continuity within the set, props, costumes and so on, but while we weren't looking, the talent was being creative between takes.

Donnie Broom, for example, in the master shot was holding a cookie near his face in his left hand. In the close up, it was in his right. That's a subtle difference when you're shooting but stands out like a sore thumb when you're cutting. Polaroid shots made for continuity review would have helped to catch many such errors.

These mistakes are stupid ones only when done by a seasoned screen actor. It is simply education for someone without experience or guidance in film making. In the legitimate theater, where movement is continuous, the problem doesn't exist.

In an effort to save film, we failed to get sufficient reaction shots to bail out unfavorable cuts. (That's really what reaction shots are for anyway.) It was a lesson learned barely in time, and even so, we had to go back for pick-up shots both during and after wrapping principal photography.

It's very difficult to match a master shot long after it is made, and it is certainly more costly than doing so when you are set up in the first place.

On the other side of the coin, trying to edit in the camera to save film or time was a perfect way to cause a reshoot—expending yet more film and time—and prolonged, frustrating, unsuccessful hours at the editing table. It also requires an inordinate number of set-ups.

Having discovered the error of our ways we began to save time and money by shooting more close ups and reaction shots than we would need. Efficiency, in this case, saved our cash payout.

Rehearsal and planning yielded long master shots in which, in a single take, the talent and the camera were blocked for several moves. Such shots became much more interesting than a series of short choppy ones anyway. The planning included the option to stop or to take a note when someone miscued. So the master shot was still correctable by the editor who could use a reaction shot made specifically to cover that error.

In some cases, even though the master shot was perfect, other issues altered its useability as a single shot in editing. It was still wise to make a minimum number of reaction shots to cover for the excision of some dialogue when it was necessary. (Short takes are easier for inexperienced talent but cause the editor more work and therefore time lost. Slate shots use just as much film when doing a short take as for extended ones.)

Speaking of slates, by the way... Developing a technique coordinated by the sound man, the clapper, the cameraman and the director can save a notable amount of film and processing over the course of an entire shoot. For example, once the cameraman signals the clapper that the slate is readable, the director calls for sound; the sound man responds with "Speed"; the clapper reads the slate out loud; and the cameraman starts the camera. When the camera reaches speed the cameraman cues the clapper with "Speed," or "Mark it," at which time the clapper claps the sticks and disappears quickly.

This particular sequence of events saves the amount of film run through the camera during the period of time the slate would be read, about two and a half seconds. Multiply that by between 1,500 and 2,000 takes and you'll see how much film, processing and work print you'll save. Perhaps 2,500 feet of 16mm film! That translates to one and a quarter hours of film in any format!

Because it was going to be necessary to loop a lot of sound, Jet decided to loop it all and change some of the voices which were overbearingly Southern. There's nothing wrong with Southern accents, but in some parts of the country the locals have difficulty understanding the various Southern dialects.

We recruited some talent to replace the voices. Bob Carroll, Barry Clark, and Brooks Lindsay were veteran radio personalities while Dave Tracey and Jean-Claud Blanchard simply sounded right for the parts they were doing.

Since the editing table ran at sync speed, we simply shot a sound videotape from the screen. Using a VCR in the looping room, we would play a scene over and over for the talent to learn the pacing and inflection. Then watching the video screen, he would record the dialogue onto audiotape via the Nagra. Once he achieved a good take we would move onto the next scene in which that character appeared. The entire hour and a half picture was looped in this manner, character by character.

It really was not especially difficult, but it required patience and diligence. We were surprised and fortunate that a quality recording could be done in a simple storage room large enough that the set-up could be left until the week long endeavor was finished.

Having done this, it was necessary to rebuild the sound roll(s) from scratch, putting together all the sound takes, first in order, then in sync, just like we had the original sound track. Generally, it was not difficult since, already having a sound track in sync gave us something to match other than visual lip movement on the screen. The original sound was on sound head A while the one being installed was on B.

There were those takes which were exceedingly difficult because the original sound was missing and the lips were hard to read or because it was deemed prudent or necessary to make a minor change in the dialogue. But finally, the deed was accomplished.

Jet (right) turned out to be not only an extraordinarily good director but saved money by serving on both ends of the skill spectrum—director and clapstick whacker. (Photo by Marie Heptig.)

Having replaced the voices, of course, deprived us of the necessary ambient sounds that were recorded with them. It was necessary to go out and record such sounds as birds, crickets, traffic, and other generic sounds which we could now lay in at their appropriate levels. We also had to record a multitude of Foley sounds and effects such as running through the woods, gun shots, water splashes, monster roars, and a host of other noises you don't think of until you discover them missing.

In a month of half-days Jet did most of the Foley and edited them together the way he did the voices. In some cases, it took as few as one roll for the dialogue and two for the sound effects, but in most cases it took two for the voices and four for the sounds. There would be yet another for the music.

For a reason we couldn't understand, an occasional, isolated shot would come up out of sync while on other occasions it would not. From time to time, it would come up perhaps four frames early. We would insert four frames to compensate thereby causing it to be four frames late! Frustrating.

One afternoon while taking a break with the machine powered up but turned off, it began to vibrate—much like a person having a convulsion. Then, without missing a beat, began spewing full coat all over the room.

The culprit turned out to be a bad or dying chip. The chip was sending a crazy, electronic message that was randomly throwing us out of sync. The card was sent away for repair and that sound head was not used until it was sane again.

Harry Shipman and Dave Wilson had been working on the music by watching the same videotape that was used for looping. The music was performed on Dave's synthesizer and recorded onto three quarter inch videotape.

Doing so gave them, not one, but two audio tracks to work with and afforded them the option to lay down the music in such fashion that it would come in and out at the appropriate times without having to edit the full coat after dubbing.

Having only two full coat players and one dubber left us in the position of having the premix rolls A and B to one roll, C and D to another and then mix the resulting pair to a third. It created more generations than we wanted but we had no other option. Having one more player would have saved at least a generation, and perhaps two.

By the time we had the premixes ready, the music was done and through the efforts of Al Yelton, John Clifford, Dave and Jet, a final mix was accomplished that we felt was ready for videotape.

During the winter wait, John Boy and Billy, an unusually popular pair of Charlotte comedic radio personalities, had gotten wind of the movie and began to make wisecracks, creating a public awareness of the project.

Because of the power of the word, Jet offered them a bit part in the film—a good public relations move. While the credits crawled, the two of them did a hilarious critique of the film.

"There's nothing like a good movie," said John Boy, "and that's exactly what this was, nothing like a good movie!"

"I've got cold chills all over my body," answered Billy. "Scary, wasn't it?" said John Boy. "No," he answered, "I just dumped my cold drink in my lap." And they continued.

Now there's a critique!

As the credits came to a close, their bit ended the film. They did the most ridiculous scene which had nothing to do with the story but was tacked onto the end of the film after the credits.

Shortly thereafter, the local paper published a Sunday morning color spread, augmenting the notoriety and getting the attention of the then popular but now defunct "PM Magazine" television show, which did a story on *Marley's Revenge, the Monster Movie*! It aired locally a few weeks later and on Halloween 1988 (a most appropriate time) was rerun nationally.

We were pleased to have the publicity. In fact, we were lucky to have it since no one was in charge of public relations. All of Charlotte was ready to see it.

My plan was to make the answer print on stock with a magnetic stripe, correct whatever needed to be corrected, and run the answer print on a magnetic projector for the premiere showing.

The premiere was scheduled and some days later, I was mortified to learn that not Kodak, not Agfa, not Fuji— nobody—makes positive print stock with a mag track. It was an old technology that had died with news film.

I spent nearly a day on the phone finding someone who could put a mag track on 16mm single perf film. I found him. It would have taken two days longer than I had. We were left with no option but to do the premiere using our interlock projector. Not a good idea, but our only option.

We had seen an answer print, noted the corrections, and Jet had gone to the lab in Atlanta to make them.

Four days before the premiere, I inadvertently discovered that announcements and advertisements indicated simultaneous showings in twin theaters and we had neither time nor money for a second print. For that matter, we didn't have a second interlock projector. I wasn't losing my hair, I was pulling it out!

Knowing we could splice together the three half-hour rolls and reroll them into two 45-minute rolls, I managed to reschedule the showing at one-hour intervals; 9:00 and 11:00 p.m. in theater A and 10:00 and 12:00 in B.

Meanwhile, I was desperately trying to find a second interlock projector, all to no avail. Calling around the country, all roads led back to several broken or cannibalized machines already in my possession. Two people even suggested I call me!

I took some measurements and dashed home to my woodship and built a wooden box and threading it in an unconventional manner, once with the picture roll and once with the sound, I had a makeshift but workable interlock projector. (You'll see a diagram later to help you if you want to make one.)

Meanwhile, Mark was fooling around with the several Siemens interlock machines and got one working which precluded the need to use the homemade rig at the premiere.

The day of reckoning came much more quickly than we would have wanted. The two projectors were put in place at the theaters. Still because of bad communications, we didn't know that a regular showing was to take place immediately before ours. We weren't able to tie into their sound system until they were finished which kept us from making private preliminary tests. Unfortunately, and without dignity, we were forced to do our testing with a full house waiting while John Boy and Billy entertained the troops.

Finally, after having tapped onto the sound system and gotten our levels, we were off and running in theater A.

None of our crew could find a way to tap into the sound in theater B. Ultimately, out of desperation, one of them severed the line coming from the theater projector to the amplifier and spliced onto it. Again we were in business. While John Clifford and Dave Wilson kept a vigil over the sound from the booth, John Frazier and I shuttled the pairs of reels back and forth for the alternate showings.

The picture looked good but the sound stank in both theaters. It had an empty sound, as if people were speaking through paper cups. The audience didn't notice, or didn't care. They loved the movie. A lack of space turned away people by the hundreds. The theater (a Cinema and Draft House) had their best night ever. For days the theater was besieged with phone calls from people wanting to know when *Marley* would be run on a regular showing.

In an effort to close the barn doors after the horse had left, we put the sound track back on the dubber to analyze it and to try to find out how to repair the hollow sound. To our relief, we discovered that a few scenes needed to be remixed and the track really was o.k. The poor sound in the theater was a product of mismatched systems.

A premiere is held for two reasons, to check audience reaction for possible changes and to generate publicity. In the process, we noticed a couple of shots which just simply wouldn't do and a few places where the sound was so bad as to be untenable. In the ensuing several days, Jet fixed those sound takes.

Meanwhile, we reshot the few picture takes which were unacceptable and had them cut into the negative.

These corrections finally made, we ordered a low contrast positive from the finished negative. It arrived and Jet jetted to New York with it to make a supervised transfer to videotape.

In a five hour session at $450 an hour you expect lots of help where it will do the most good, and lots of help was exactly what we needed.

Vincent Cervone had watched it for only minutes when he announced that the print was too dirty to use as a video master and suggested that Jet go back home to arrange the making of a clean print. He was kind enough to make no charge for the abbreviated session. Not all labs treat their customers so kindly.

It was then that the nightmare—and unnerving expenses—began. Jet flew back that night and the next day we inspected the print.

Finding it dirty indeed, we inspected the two answer prints which preceded it. They too were dirty but nobody had noticed. The evening prior to the premiere we had a private showing for a local film industry association, and they hadn't noticed it either. That made us feel a little better but didn't improve the print, especially since video enhancement also enhances the dirt.

We called the lab who had processed the film and made the prints and requested they print a two-minute section of reel one after cleaning it twice. The difference, if any, was imperceptible.

We pulled a 100-foot section of outtake footage and sent it to a lab who does liquid-gate printing. The lab made a print and compared. The difference was insufficient to warrant the expense of a wet-gate print.

We decided to proceed with the print we had and the transfer was to begin at 8:00 p.m. Jet and I stayed at The Photo-Lab where we had another print available so that if Vincent had a question or problem we could quickly go to that section, check it, and give him an immediate answer.

At 8:30 he called and said he couldn't get the full coat to transport through their machine properly and that he was going to do the transfer without sound on reel one.

Knowing we could repair the cause of the problem and transfer the sound after we received the video master, we agreed and he proceeded.

When it all came we checked the full coat on reel one. Indeed there was a place which had a crooked splice—made with masking tape—a place which was machine-chewed, and, in another, a wad of transparent packaging tape the size of a golf ball stuck to the full coat!

Neither we nor any respectable lab would treat a master roll like that and the cause remains a mystery.

Having repaired the crooked splice, the chewed place, and removed the wad of tape, we effortlessly ran it through our MagnaSync and dubbed it over to a ¾ inch blank videotape.

We took our one inch video master, our ¾ inch video master, and our ¾ audio dub to Cedar Productions in Charlotte and uneventfully transferred the sound from the ¾ inch to the existing one inch master.

Being in a hurry to get some tapes in the hands of distributors, we began to make 25 VHS prints. Monitoring them in the process, we noticed one image which had not been altered according to our instructions, that the sound on reel two was out of sync, and the sound on reels two and three were overmodulated.

At this point we felt we were moving backward. We had paid dearly for the mistakes we had made, were exceeding the budget by nearly twice, and now were finishing much later than we had planned.

Dubbing from the track on the ¾ inch master, Chris Wilson jockeyed the one inch back and forth to put in the sound precisely again. The distortion was still unchanged.

Despite the expenditure involved in this resynchronising, we decided to go to an audio studio, refer back to the full coat master, and dub it over to the ¾ inch videotape master.

Unfortunately, in Charlotte, none of the video houses were, at that time, sound oriented, and vice versa. We discussed the transfer of full coat to ¾ inch transfer with Dave Floyd at Jay Howard Studio, the only recording house in Charlotte which had any video facility at all. He believed that, while dubbing from the full coat, he could sweeten up the sound which later could be transferred to the one inch.

We took a full coat machine to Dave which he tied into his elaborate audio system.

In dubbing, the two slowly drifted apart and would not stay in sync. Dave spent so much effort electronically slowing the video to keep the two in sync that he had no time to work on improving the quality. Here was yet one more problem which was costly, we couldn't control, and which we felt made no sense.

It was some weeks later that we discovered what kept the audio and video drifting out of sync. In the last few years technology has changed substantially and it is very common to shoot on film, transfer to video, then edit on video. Doing so complicates the process because the film shot on the set must be slowed down to about 23.97 frames per second during the conversion to video. Our full coat machine was running precisely at sync speed.

Here basically is the cause of the problem.

Film at sound speed runs at 24 frames per second. In order to transfer it to video, it, together with its full coat sound track, is slowed by .0025 of a second per second (23.9975 fps) and recorded onto videotape which is slowed from 30 fps to 29.97.

If the film is to be edited in the video mode, this speed-change achievement for the audio is made during the transfer from quarter inch to the multi-track system.

Our primary error lay in changing horses in midstream. Transferring the film and sound at one time was o.k. except that an audio technician had theaded it up out of sync. Trying to separately reconstitute the sound by using the 24 fps full coat machine together with a 29.97 fps multi-track audio recorder was not mechanically compatible.

Dave called Chris Wilson (at Cedar) and talked electronics with him a few minutes, primarily to discover whether, with time code, the two machines could talk to each other. As it turns out, they could.

There were several ways to do what we needed to do, but we discovered that for every advantage there was an equal and opposite disadvantage. We continued as planned. More time, more money.

The abbreviated marriage of Cedar Productions and Jay Howard Studio was a successful one. Dave performed some major surgery and minor miracles and delivered a respectable sound track made from a sow's ear. Chris put the sound on the master tape where it belonged and we began to print VHS copies that evening.

The tapes went on rental at Multi-Video, Inc., the next morning and were met with good reception. For days they were not able to keep a copy on hand from their stock of 25 prints.

We were pleased, we were finished, and we were pleased to be finished . . . or so it seemed.

A local, well respected production of commercials had seen *Marley's* and offered to show Jet what editorial excisions he could make to improve the slow pace of the first 15 minutes. He argued (correctly) that portions of the beginning were unnecessary to the story. Jet accepted his kind offer and took a look at what was suggested.

A test edit exhibited precisely the intentions the producer had. The deletions did pick up the pace somewhat, as would removing the entire opening, but there were those of us who disagreed with the selection of deletions on the grounds that important character development and sequences necessary to the story were withdrawn while other, slow-paced, less important footage was left in.

The dilemma: Who was right?

Since the picture was on a master tape it *might* have been a practical matter to go back and seek footage for bandages to support greater finesse in cutting. In any case, the making of a duplicate master would be required in which the edits would be made electronically.

The excision of those pieces reminded me of Pat Patterson's deleting the vital Open Kitchen sequence from *Body Shop*. Such problems offer the perfect excuse to refer you to all the preceding comments about planning. Certainly having a completed script before photography begins would constitute a degree of planning beyond that which we had on either *Body Shop* or *Marley's Revenge*.

In fairness to both Jet and Pat, it is important to point out that DeMille, Kramer, Hitchcock, and Lucas all have removed footage to pick up the pace—footage they planned, spent money on, filmed, and liked.

Marley's Revenge was Jet's baby; it was his responsibility, and—being writer, director, and editor—making the call was not only his privilege, it was his obligation. Right, wrong, or otherwise, his call was made solely on what he believed was in the best interest of selling the project.

For the record, the sequence, which exhibits the offshore island and the man crawling on the sawdust is missing from the release version of the videotape together with substantial portions of two other sequences.

On Mother's Day, 1990, we again trekked into the woods and shot a total replacement for the opening sequence. Essentially we simply did a daytime version of the original opening which we had done at night two years earlier. We still had to shoot wide open with a film rated at ISO 320 while using two 2K lamps. The new intro is a definite improvement from a visual standpoint and gives improved perspective of what is to follow.

Marley's Revenge was a worthwhile project for Jet because it was his first professional experience and nearly overwhelmingly an educational one. It also has allowed him to move on to other film making projects.

It was worthwhile for the crew, if for no other reason than they all had a lot of fun doing it, and for Mark Overton, the lighting man, it created a profitable business spinoff.

As the production was drawing to a close, Mark bought a step van and an abundance of lighting and grip equipment to fill it. After sending out a modicum of computer-written price lists to local and regional producers of TV commercials, Mark began to rent his truck and gear—with or without his personal services.

Even in the face of strong competition and a bad national economy, Mark has done well with his endeavor.

You will, no doubt, recall my complaint that Jet had no hammer and nail in his house or anything that I might need to enhance the execution of my simplest task. That deprivation was the catalyst which set off the enterprise of writing a simple checklist of things one needs to make a feature film.

The list later included some simple dos and don'ts and, in its expanded form, became the basis for this book. For me, too, all this has been a worthwhile pursuit.

Marley's Revenge has not enjoyed a good relationship with a distributor. In fact, agreements made with would-be agents have fallen through mostly on the basis of greed leaving the burden of sales upon the producer. You will read more about such problems in following chapters and, finishing your own projects, you'll have some first-hand encounter with such obstacles.

No international sales have been made which would create a profit for the investors. Still, if you're in the United States, you should be able to find a revised print of *Marley's Revenge* in your local video store. Those in distribution have some of the establishing scenes removed. If you are interested in buying a print of it or of the original uncut version you can get one from Multi-Video, Inc., 830 Lamar Ave., Charlotte, NC 28235 (800/289-1911).

3
Financial Considerations

Like the fruits of many industries, the making of a motion picture is an expensive proposition. The meaning of the word "expensive," of course, is a relative one. For the entrepreneur who hasn't the means to raise ten of millions of dollars, or even hundreds of thousands, the word's lowliest definition can be devastating.

Every year a few enterprising people put films on the market which they've managed to make with only a few dollars. They somehow have found a way to execute these projects with at least a pound of skill and a ton of determination. As often as not, they bring back a reasonable return of money for the investor.

The ability to make a movie is no longer a rare one. The capacity to make one on a shoestring—a film which works—is almost unique.

In fact, there are several factors which tend to increase the general cost of film making to extremes.

Photographing an image less than a square inch and blowing it up to a quality, 40-foot picture—or even a 52-inch TV image—requires precision. The primary equipment used in the motion picture industry is intensely precise. Much of that same precision exists in still cameras and consumer camcorders. The financial advantage of those still cameras lies in the fact that literally hundreds of thousands of instruments are distributed on the retail market at $200 to $2500 each. Over a several year period, only a few hundred Arriflex BL's or Mitchell BNCR's will reach the user's hands at somewhere between $25,000 and $50,000 a copy. The cost of lab and editing equipment follows suit.

Since the days of pioneer actors like Mary Pickford and Douglas Fairbanks whose popularity overwhelmed the nation, many in the acting industry who developed a high degree of popularity also developed a high level of "swollen head." They knew their demands for higher wages would be met by the executives who, in turn, knew the public would pay for it. It wasn't long until $30 a week turned into $300, then $3,000—and on to whatever it is today. "Whatever it is today" is only one of the factors that cause movies to be expensive to make.

It is not uncommon for a well known actor or actress to be paid in excess of several million dollars for a single picture, or sometimes only a small part in one. It is reported that Marlon Brando was paid over $1,000,000 for his part as Jor-El in *Superman*. The producer didn't pay it, you did.

Unions, of course, share in the blame for high expense. While there is no doubt that unions have been instrumental in keeping vast numbers of people employed and earning at the rate for a good lifestyle, they have likewise stifled segments of the industry by placing demands upon independent producers whose means are usually beneath the financial plateau which must be met in union territory. By enforcement of their own rules they have generally forbidden their members to work with nonmembers or to work on projects which pay less than the minimums they proscribe. They tend to disallow a member to wear more than one hat, so to speak.

Even though they've lightened their regulations in recent years, these attributes are all positive when and where the money flows liberally. But it surely makes it tough—for both sides—to get a start in the business, or even to continue if the successful use of minimum dollars is the goal.

In many circles there is a volume of money which, like water, seeks its own level. It is a level of cash distribution and redistribution understood by only the hierarchy of the financial industry and a few entrepreneurs who know how to tap it. That money, no matter which industry becomes its lucky recipient, is frequently abused in that it is misspent, squandered, raked off the top, stolen, paid out under the table, and dealt out in any number of secret methods, thereby skyrocketing the cost of the project for which it was intended. The $8,000 coffee pot, $800 toilet seats, and $400 hammers bought by the Pentagon constitute perfect examples, as do public expense of ludicrous lawsuits and the price of an overnight stay in the hospital. The film industry, like all the rest, is victimized by the same thumb that weighs so heavily upon the financial scales.

Last but not least is the fool who, with only the slightest bit of knowledge, money, or understanding, believes he can do almost anything but can't. It is he whom you will hear contend, "I wanna make a movie, I already have a camera." It's not just kids who say it. You'll hear 50-year-old men assert it in dead earnest. Wonder if those same people would lie down on the table for someone whom he has heard avow, "I'm going to be a surgeon. I already have a knife." These people alter the expense of film making only in that they lower the statistics of successes thereby making it difficult to raise money for low budget productions.

Incompetence, in these cases, can run rampant and nobody will know until it's too late. All industries have their traditions and their technologies. Breaking those traditions and using earlier or different technologies is how cost is reduced, but beware! There is an undefinably fine line between the dos and don'ts of film making whether you break tradition or not. Incompetence can lead to certain failure while the latter can end in a rewarding success.

You'll frequently come up with a good way to do something cheaper. It is unlikely you'll come up with a way to do something both cheaper and better. Hollywood has been making movies for most of 100 years, so if there is a better way to do it with present technologies, chances are they already know it.

If you think you have a better idea than Hollywood does, test yourself before proceeding. If it turns out you're right, it probably is because you have bad judgment and are, therefore, dead wrong anyway. If it turns out you were wrong in the first place, you just saved yourself a problem. The biggies in Hollywood simply have the money and personnel to learn instantly what works and what doesn't. Right?

If indeed you want to break tradition, try using efficiency. It will often be a better friend than saving cash and it's the one trick Hollywood, like the government, hasn't yet mastered.

Steven Spielberg surely has a movie camera but it's unlikely he'd use it for anything other than home movies or testing an idea. He subscribes to the Panavision system. Nobody owns Panavision gear but Panavision. Not even Mr. Spielberg. So taking into account that having a camera is not the issue wherein film making is concerned, consider these three basic points in proposing to yourself the making of a picture.

1. Can I raise the money to do it?
2. Once I get the money, can I successfully complete a movie?
3. Once I've got the money, what on Earth will I do with it?

It is extremely important that these questions be taken quite seriously and answered both in great detail and to the satisfaction of the guy with the bucks, even if he is you.

Backers and investors have a single mind set—"If I invest in your picture when do I get my money, how much do I get back and upon what track record may I rely to know how sound my investment is?"

If you have a money-making track record, you probably do not need this book. Though this book won't answer the aforementioned questions, it is hoped that it will not disappoint you. It will answer fewer questions than it will ask. It will bring to mind a number of factors, problems, and elements which could be excessive yet may be inexpensively dealt with.

Since you bought this book, a good probability exists that you haven't gotten past the point of having to prove yourself as a technician, a business man, or both. A hotshot businessman wouldn't need a skeleton budget anyway. But remember, no matter how good you get, just like the gunfighters of the Old West, you'll always have to prove yourself.

If you have enough money of your own to make a film, wisdom would dictate that you use it to do so only when you have satisfied the financial ramifications of question three if your purpose is to turn money into more money. Doing a picture for some humane application would achieve appropriate goals but would not necessarily fulfill an investor's financial requirements.

It is assumed you already know how, basically, to produce a feature film while never having done so, but are reading this work in order to learn how to save money in the process. Please see the Glossary for explanations of terms. What you won't find here are lessons on acting, editing, or photography.

It is generally considered unwise to make a movie just to prove you can make a movie or, if it's your first one, to prove to the world that you're an artist—even if you have the money. If you really want to do a thing, do it for the right reason. Learning how to do it well while at the same time making a profit would be a good example. Have a mentor looking over your shoulder to whom you are welcome to press for answers when the need arises and who will give you help when you ask.

Always keep in mind that any sensible investor—including you—is going to want a relatively fast, high yield return on his money because he's investing in a risky business. (The word "risky" may not be stout enough to cover the meaning. Even Alfred Hitchcock had serious money problems with his pictures both before and after production even though *Psycho* collected $8,000,000 for him alone.) Never lose sight of film making as a business. How good or bad the story, the acting, the photography, or how romantic the business may appear, is a lot less important to the investor than how much he makes. Sorry. That's not necessarily how it ought to be, or how we want it to be, but that's how it is.

Don't let the investor's attitude about money disallow the picture to have production values or to minimize an otherwise good quality. While good actors and good lighting systems may be costly, good acting and good lighting can both be free if you have someone dedicated to do so without pay. There's always another way, and always somebody else. Remember the expression, "There are more fish in the sea"? Well, there are more, and a lot of them have undiscovered talent.

When you do get rolling and the shoot is going well, it's nice to invite the backers to the set to watch a while,

30 Financial Considerations

then get them out of there on a permanent basis. Once an investor sees something go wrong, something he doesn't understand, or sees an activity he interprets as wasteful, he wants to dictate how things ought to be done. He must not be allowed! *You* must hold the budget down and *you* must make the decisions.

You must be neither intimidated nor annoyed by the continued use of the word "cheap"; cheap or cheaper is what this book is all about. If your endeavor is to reduce a $17,000,000 budget to $14,000,000, you got the wrong book. If reducing a $100,000 budget to $75,000, then you got the right one.

Remembering that business is business, the first obligation to yourself is to get educated. You will, no doubt, burn a lot of candles at both ends, rack up a high phone bill, and even higher blood pressure—not necessarily your own—in doing so.

Call film distributors and tape distributors. Read credit lines on films, posters and video boxes and call everybody whose name appears on them that you can find. Ask them every question you can think that can be considered reasonable. They usually feel that any question that has nothing to do with money or nothing to do with them is unreasonable. Ninety percent of what distributors tell you is double talk. It is necessary not only to know thyself, but to know thine enemy. There are some honest distributors, of course, but they are impossible to distinguish from the rest.

The theatrical film distributing business is a very political one and a very confusing one. Its shell is difficult to break through and upon entry you find there is little welcome and no honor among thieves, of which there are many. The audiotape distributing business and videotape distributing business are identical. Diogenes would have needed a lot of lamp oil if he'd been in the film making business.

Whether or not you have penetrated the shell and have a distributor you trust, you first must have a movie to sell, because first-timers have no track record to rely upon. Distributors, who also will have to invest some of their own money, feel much like the initial investors. "How do I know my investment is safe?" The work begins.

There are two quality levels between which you'll have to do your project. Even if you had the know-how, the lack of funds will keep you from doing a *Gone with the Wind* grade picture. Conversely, doing one which is so cheap that it's not appealing or is even unpleasant to watch will make is unsalable.

You must constantly keep in the back of your mind that incompetence is the only excuse for a poor result. It is a useless excuse and is financial suicide. Anyone can make a poor picture for $20,000 and pardon himself on the grounds that it isn't bad for a $20,000 picture. What is difficult—and imperative—is to make a picture for the amount of money you have and make it look like a good $3,000,000 picture. That's what you *must* do.

Planning, therefore, is a key. In some cases, simply putting in more money won't help while taking certain shortcuts won't hurt. Any way you do it, you alone must decide where lies that magic quality between the two extremes.

First, you need a story. Not just simply a story, but one which will be:

- entertaining to the audience
- producible within the structure described by the budget limitations
- executable within your crew's capability
- able to exhibit sufficiently worthwhile values to cause a distributor to want it.

Once you have the story, it needs to be converted into a screenplay. It's quite possible to scribble something out on a scratch pad and produce a picture from it, but the primary function of a script is to communicate. Doing it according to accepted practice costs less than doing a schlock job, or even doing a good job executed in an atypical style. Furthermore, it's easy to make changes when the time comes if it's been done "according to Hoyle." Having several copies in the formative stages, by the way, makes a conference go a lot smoother. In the long run, it's actually cheaper to write it right than to become inventive with a new style. (There will be more later about script writing.)

If you don't have a particular distributor in mind at this point, you would be well advised to find one who will read your script and comment on it. In no case will he invest with you unless he is interested in your story. He may make suggestions on how to improve marketability. You may agree or you may not, but I'd listen to him. To protect your script content, you'll need to get a document from each person who reads it *before* he reads it.

When he discovers you don't have anybody in your picture whose name he recognizes he'll profess, "We generally deal in pictures of a higher profile." That means, "Don't you have an expensive ticket-selling name in it?" Then he'll say, "No thank you," and politely hang up.

Furthermore if you have shot on tape instead of film, you're going to have to break through the video barrier. A distributor will ask, "Did you shoot on film or tape?" Being honest, you'll be obliged to tell him, "Tape," at which time you're going to get the same treatment. He'll be polite but will say no.

Some quite successful films have been done on tape. How they are sold or get a distribution agent is unique in each case, but each was done by a veteran producer. For a first-timer, it's the kiss of death.

Interestingly enough, it seems nobody ever asks, "Did you shoot in 16mm or 35?"

Remember now, we're preaching feature production here, not church projects. If you are launching an activity project or backyard movie on videotape there's still a cornucopia of good information here to help you.

The few frames you see here, extracted from *Harley's Gadget* are not poor reproductions, they are simply loosely done drawings which work well as storyboards.

While all recommendations are against feature production on tape it's worth consideration for other purposes and will, therefore, be discussed at length later.

At some point in time, all those people who will come together on the project must make some type of organized agreement, especially where money is concerned. The terms must be thoroughly discussed and put to paper. No one should be offended at the prospect of signing a contract. Such covenants are made to protect friends from misunderstandings since people don't normally elect to do business with enemies in the first place.

When the script is finished the producer, the director, the artist (if one is available), and the writer should sit down and make a storyboard—a comic book version of the script. Even if it is no more than stick figures and doodles it will do a very effective job of communicating. Having a storyboard is not imperative but, properly handled, it can save much more than it costs. This meeting will be your last best opportunity to set both goals and methods.

Whoever has the job of assistant to the producer or associate producer inherits the next obligation. On a cheap film, usually the producer wears both those hats in which case he's stuck with both jobs.

The script must be broken down into several categories. The requirements of props, crew, locations,

32 Financial Considerations

equipment along with which days they'll be needed, their budget, etc., all must be committed to paper. And the list goes on.

Once the above has been worked out to the satisfaction of all, a budget has to be worked out, then submitted to and approved by all those who have some control over it.

Even for the most experienced, this is not an easy task but it must be done. Later, changes in the film will alter the budget once again, and then again. This process will continue until the picture is finished and in exhibition. But a word of warning! The figures set down in the budget *must* be those figures discovered by research. Guessing or setting down what they ought to be isn't good enough. It is imperative to put down real costs! Then you have to budget your time by the same rules. If you don't do this with the greatest precision, you'll be in for some ugly surprises. Furthermore, you need to extrapolate a contingency amount for going over budget and for going beyond schedule.

Printed in later pages are forms which, when copied, will give you work sheets to compute and coordinate a budget. You have our permission to copy those pages, alter them, and use them at your discretion.

The agreement on the production of *Body Shop* was set at ten days. It took eight full weeks! *Hostages* was calculated to be a two-week shoot and took five. *Marley's Revenge* was guessed at about 12 weekends which turned out to be over 40. Each of these was the producer's first effort at producing and not one of them had paper documentation to back up the proposed schedule. Chances are that all of them would have saved one third to one half the production time if proper schedules had been worked out in full—and on paper—before shooting began.

The Country House, Pat Patterson's second effort, was estimated at 20 days, but took 21 in spite of a three-day setback. Pretty good calculating. Having done *Body Shop* first, he had learned well.

If you haven't produced a feature before, it is of the greatest importance that you get experienced help to break down the script into its shooting schedule because deciding that "two or three weeks ought to cover it" just won't cover it.

A plan for what scenes will be shot on what day is illustrated in the following example.

Day 1, Scenes 7, 8, 9, 11, 26, 27, 28, 44, 91 (weather permitting; if weather, then) 10, 51, 52, 62, 63

Day 2, Scenes 5, 6, 45, 56, 57, 71 (regardless); 19, 72, 73, 74, (weather permitting;, if weather then) 46, 98, 104, 110

Because the scenes are sequentially numbered in the script, the cast and crew can instantly make reference in advance to know what is expected of them and to know what questions to ask.

This continues until all scenes are accounted for.

This breakdown is generated from script content, which is scene numbered, and is devised on the basis of convenience, economy, talent availability, elemental requirements, and other variables. It is on a similar basis that call sheets also are executed, but they are recalculated and Xeroxed on a one day ahead basis as actual production progress is made.

If you have use of a personal computer with a spread sheet program, you can update the files at the end of each day or shooting session. This daily financial reevaluation can be extremely beneficial. Breaking down the script for props, locations, equipment, talent, etc., can also be more easily done with the computer.

For example, once the script is entered into the computer's word processor, the operator can ask the computer to: find and list all scene numbers for "Joe"; find and list all scene numbers for "pickup truck"; find and list all scene numbers for "ext.—night," and so on. Once printed, the operator can make breakdown sheets for any single element or combination.

Such a computer can also be used on a daily basis to alter the balance of the budget from element to element or give you a progressive overview, day by day, of those costs which are most likely to get out of hand as well as those areas which may save you enough to beef up.

For example, let's assume you have the following budget:

$1,000 for pies for the pie fight
   500 for film for the pie fight
 1,000 for four hours of talent for the pie fight @ $250
 1,000 for titles
 1,000 for paint and Bondo / auto wreck
   500 for the wrap party

Since everything went so smoothly on the pie fight sequence, you managed to finish it in two hours, saving $500 in talent fees and, using only half the pies for an additional savings of $500.

At the end of the day, you have the option to go to the computer and change the file to add the saved $1,000 to the wrap party. A more realistic approach might be to apply the savings equally to those budgetary elements which could use a boost and conversely steal it back from those which can afford a budgetary constriction with as little trauma as possible.

Every question, technical or financial, has more than one solution. Each answer will beget another question to which there will be a pair or more of answers, ultimately causing a permutation of elements and conditions unique to this project. It's not possible simply to list the dos and don'ts of making any picture.

The reason there aren't necessarily right and wrong answers is that there are choices which must be made in order to arrive at a particular end. Each choice has its pros and cons. Each decision must take into account everything that affects it and everything that it affects.

When one thinks feature film, one automatically thinks 35mm. But, for several reasons, a close look at options is in order. The greatest difference between 8mm and 16mm and between 16mm and 35mm lies in the fact that, subconsciously, the less experienced cinematographer tends to light 8mm to look like home movies, 16mm as he would news film or documentaries, and 35mm as features. To make bad matters worse, he may tend not to light for video at all.

Let's consider what format we should shoot. The choices are Super/8, 16mm, Super/16, 35mm academy, Techniscope, anamorphic, 3-Perf or videotape (which itself has a number of formats). All these are standards. Sort of. Super/8 is the only one that is cheap in the truest sense of the word. Even then, "cheap" fails once it is transferred to tape.

Let's ponder the attributes of each.

Film Format Attributes

Advantages

Super/8 is absolutely the cheapest. Can be processed by photo finishers. It records sound directly on the film and looks great for home movies. Equipment is readily available, light, portable and extremely inexpensive. Transfers well to videotape. Can be best choice for student projects and corporate safety films.

16mm is reasonably inexpensive, at least, low enough to be cost effective. Makes professional quality prints even when blown up to 35mm for release (although not nearly so good as 35mm original). Many labs work in 16mm for both picture and sound. Most emulsions, including special purpose ones, are available in 16mm. Much equipment which is obsolete but in as-good-as-new condition is available at a fraction of its original price. Well maintained rental equipment is readily available. Equipment is light and portable. It is satisfactory for transfer to video for feature release. A good choice when a high shooting ratio is required.

Super/16 is intended only for blowup to 35mm and is perceptibly better than standard 16mm for that purpose. It is substantially less costly than 35mm original. Many standard 16mm cameras can be converted to Super/16. Accordingly, Super/16 has most of the advantages of 16mm while having few of the disadvantages of 35mm.

35mm academy, that is, standard 35mm format, equipment is readily available for purchase or rental at reasonably low prices. Because 35mm has been the industry standard since before talkies, practically speaking, anything available for film making is available in 35mm. All standard motion picture emulsions are available in 35. Most special effects work is done in 35mm.

Techniscope was never popular but was a good idea when Technicolor put it on the market. Many 35mm cameras can be converted to Techniscope which is a perfect format for theatrical wide screen release. All costs of equipment and film are the same as for academy 35mm except that only half of the raw stock is required,

Disadvantages

Super/8 film is available in few emulsions. Makes poor duplicates and release prints on film. It is not handled by most professional labs. Limited market for the finished product. With most Super/8 equipment, special effects must be done in the camera in one pass or done in a larger format and reduced to Super/8. For feature release it must be transferred to tape.

16mm is less effective in the making of special effects on the optical bench than larger formats. It offers a noticeably lesser quality for theatrical prints than 35mm original negative. Sometimes a distributor won't accept it. A 35mm blowup is required for theatrical release.

Most 16mm labs cannot accommodate the **Super/16** format in their printers, although those which can generally offer a full Super/16 service. Lab rates on Super/16 are somewhat higher than standard 16mm. Not much rental equipment is readily available. A 35mm blowup is required for theatrical release.

35mm film and lab costs are roughly five times that of 16mm production, take for take. Equipment is noticeably heavier therefore more costly in terms of time and labor for each set-up.

Shooting in **Techniscope** will offer you no benefits other than the above. Techniscope work prints have become more costly since they must be made optically to conform to a standard editor. You must make an intermediate or dupe negative for theatrical prints (which is typical although not always necessary). It is not a practical format

34 Financial Considerations

Advantages	Disadvantages
therefore only half the negative processing. It can be used effectively as a supporting format for academy 35 where weight or reloading (sail plane or underwater photography) become an issue.	to shoot for video release since the usable frame area of Techniscope is the same as standard 16mm.
Anamorphic 35mm may be practical if theatrical release is your goal. The attributes of 35mm generally apply. Shooting anamorphic 16mm blows up to a remarkably good 35mm anamorphic. One simply must put an anamorphic element in front of a 16mm prime lens.	**Anamorphic 35mm** is seldom used today for shooting. It may be tricky to find a good used set of anamorphic lenses to fit your camera. It's also an expensive proposition to get good TV release prints made from a squeezed original. Using a 16mm anamorphic element usually doesn't work well with a zoom lens.
3-Perf generally offers the advantages of Techniscope wherein inter-format work is achieved. That is, it is suitable for wide screen 35mm projection while printing nearly the entire frame for TV release. Saves 25 percent on film and processing.	**3-Perf** requires special camera equipment as well as special printing equipment. One must get price quotes on camera and lab charges before deciding.
70mm (which as a camera material is actually 65 mm) is twice as sharp as 35mm. Reduction prints are readily available in 35mm. It is the best bet for background plates (matte work or rear projection) and equipment can be rented at very low rates.	**70mm** projects are generally more expensive than typical features. Fewer labs can handle 70mm projects in any of the various facets.
Videotape offers you the unique ability of seeing your scene-to-scene result right now. For those who like the look of videotape, it can be a proper medium to shoot for TV or videotape release. Excellent for student projects.	**Videotape** facilities for editing and transferring, by the time the project is finished, are generally two to 12 times more expensive than their counterparts in film for a very low budget depending upon the method used. (The preceding statement is typically untrue where a high budget is concerned.) Video can be released only as video while film can be released either way. Typically, a film negative transferred to videotape will look better than the original video will.

There are plenty more pros and cons. One must carefully weigh the elements since sometimes they tend to cancel. For example:

> Broadcast quality video cameras generally cost more to rent or buy than a film camera.
> Tape stock is cheaper than film and doesn't need to be processed.
> Using the video editorial process is costly.
> Used film-editing equipment is relatively inexpensive while second hand video equipment is both expensive and risky to use.

The result must be considered. Where will it be exhibited?

Are we starting from scratch or do we already have an impressive amount of equipment on hand?

A large TV station, for example, who is producing a movie for TV or video release, is practically home free as far as equipment and technicians are concerned. It would be essentially impractical for them to take a film approach unless they were equally well or better equipped for film operation.

Video has a proper place on the film camera set as well as its own. It too will be discussed at reasonable length.

Having read all the above you surely have gotten the message that today is not the day to order the raw stock or blank tape, hire a crew, or obtain studio space. So don't. Be sure to pay close attention now because you may be quizzed.

4
You Have to Decide...

Here's the quiz. Were you paying attention?

It is assumed you already know how to produce a film, albeit a documentary or safety film.

If you don't know how to find the answer to all the questions or don't understand one or more of the questions, you'd be wise not to do anything else with regard to producing until you do. This could be your opportunity to get details on issues that you didn't know existed. Ignoring such issues will be devastating.

What will be your shooting ratio?
What film size/format will you shoot?
Which lab have you chosen?
Will you use opticals?
If so, which optical house will do them?
What stock(s) will you select?
Does your lab transfer your ¼ inch to full coat at stock cost?
Can you do your own transfer?
Do you plan to shoot single system or double system?
Will you order timed work prints or untimed ones?
Do you have a firm checklist of camera, grip, and electrical support equipment you'll need? (That's a question relating to about 300 items.)
Will you use a caterer?
Where will you get your audio effects or who will do them?
Are the mechanical effects worked out to your satisfaction?
Will you conform the original negative or edit a video transfer?
Will you use an optical track, or will you transfer the original mix to video?
Do you plan to do any fixed matte or traveling matte work?
Where will you get your music?

All your answers done? Couldn't be. That's only about one tenth of one percent of the questions. Of course, if there is something you don't understand about a question then you couldn't answer it anyway. But let's talk about them all.

Shooting Ratio

On a cheapie it is typical to use about five times as much film as will be used in the finished film. A 90 minute 16mm movie is 3,000 feet long, therefore you would likely shoot about 15,000 feet of film if you take extra caution or settle for less than excellent takes. About 2,000 feet of that total will be used to thread up the camera and to shoot slates. The rest of the finished footage will be consumed in both good takes and unacceptable ones. Choosing to shoot them in 35mm, a 5:1 ratio would result in shooting 50,000 feet of film.

Shooting video simply will allow you to shoot more footage with little added expense for tape. Be cautious, however, because the low cost of tape stock can lull you into believing that tape is your only additional expense. The clock will be running on the whole project while you shoot more footage.

Many directors will expect to get two additional good takes after they've made an acceptable one. Some pictures, however, are done on so small a budget as to limit shooting to a 3:1 ratio. That makes it tough to do a good job but technically it can be done on any ratio greater than 1:1. Remember that rehearsing enough to get an acceptable take on the first try leaves available the film that would have been used for takes two and three, so it can be used for takes four and five on an especially difficult scene. A sensible ratio is 5:1 for a 16mm film on a $20,000 to $80,000 budget, but a greater budget sensibly demands a higher shooting ratio if for no other reason than the investment protection offered by a higher quality product. Doing short takes leaves less opportunity for error per take, but a ten-second take uses just as much film or tape for the slate as a four-minute one. Probably the best bet would be to do an extended take with the willingness to cut at an error and do a corrected pick-up where you left off, or, depending upon what the error was, simply continue in spite of it with the knowledge that it can be corrected during editing by inserting a cutaway.

Film/Tape Size/Format

Selecting a film/tape size/format is essentially easy. If you are shooting for theatrical release 35mm is the obvious choice. Likewise if you are shooting for video release. Today, 35mm is simply better than 16mm or tape from a qualitative point of view. Period. But the combination of 35mm film stock and lab services will cost five times as much as 16mm in order to get that superior quality. If it is necessary to blow up (enlarge) 16mm original to 35 mm printing negatives, that could cost about the same money you'll save by shooting in 16mm. Typically, blow-up isn't the producer's problem but that of the distributor or purchaser. Blowing up from 16 to 35 will not increase the quality of 16mm; its only purpose is to render the film usable by theaters.

If your purpose is anything other than electronic release, video is taboo.

There are occasions where the advantages of 16mm film and equipment (such as its smaller size, less weight, more running time per foot) make shooting and blowing up 16mm preferable to shooting 35. The Disney organization has done so on many of their nature series films and features on which cost was much less a factor than weight and space. Weight and inaccessibility would be paramount if the camera were rigged on the tail or wingtip of a sailplane, for example.

Labs

Unless you are shooting Super/8, photofinishers simply can't handle your work at all. Drugstore labs develop film while maintaining industry standards to provide nice slides, home movies, and still prints with absolute disregard to the client's purpose. One of the larger photofinishers will handle, perhaps, 5,000 to 30,000 rolls of still film a day, representing about that many customers.

Motion picture labs, on the other hand, keep a close eye on industry standards but at the same time control their systems, to the best of their ability, delivering their individual client a product that is engineered toward his specific need. A typical motion picture lab may develop seventy-five to a hundred rolls (of various lengths) of camera negative each day representing, perhaps, a dozen clients.

It's not our function here to recommend a lab, but the New York and Los Angeles phone books are full of them, and likewise those directories in dozens of major cities across the country. Unless there is a satisfactory lab in your own city who can do what you want, you ought to choose one on the basis of something other than location. Air shipments being what they are today, a lab in Florida is just as close as one in California even if you live in Arizona. Or vice versa.

Videotape or postproduction houses are the electronic counterparts to film labs. The greatest difference in what each has to offer lies in the video houses' ability to do the video miracles that are not expected of film labs but of optical houses.

Opticals

An optical is a film duplicate of one or more other pieces of film or artwork which is created for the purpose of inserting it into the original negative during the cutting process so that, when prints are made, the effect created by the optical appears natural. (If an effect is noticeable as an effect, it is a failure.)

Here are some examples.

Your movie is called *BOOM!* and the title creeps slowly across the screen from left to right. The word "BOOM" is red with a yellow border and a black shadow. The background for your title is a train crossing a trestle while the trestle is blown up. As the trestle falls, the letters of the title fall, one at a time until they're off screen.

Try doing that in the camera in one pass. Not likely. But if you could it would be one whale of an accomplishment. To do the optical, you must furnish the optical lab with the film of the train and trestle (best done in miniature for obvious reasons) and a simple typeset card with the word "BOOM!" Explicit instructions of the colors and activity must accompany the work, perhaps in the form of a storyboard. Chances are greater than 99 percent that it will be done wrong on the first try, and probably the next three or four. That's one of the causes of the high expense of opticals.

Let's consider another example. You have an irreplaceable piece of footage of the president speaking. Unfortunately in the background of one side of the picture is a dog scratching his ear—most distracting. You send the footage to an optical house and have them recompose it. They'll send you back an optical, that is, a duplicate, slightly enlarged and shifted to center so that the mutt is now cropped out of the shot, rendering the shot useable. You'll find this just about the cheapest kind of optical available. What about a piece of film that is scratched? If the scratch is on the base side of the original, chances are the scratch can be printed out without the need for recomposition by making a duplicate on a wet-gate printer.

Not many pictures can limit their opticals to the simplicity we've just described. Opticals can cost as little as about five dollars each with, perhaps a $20 minimum, while others can cost as much as $1,000 per foot or more! The latter is not typically discussed in the same conversation with cheapies.

In *Tempest,* the stone house on the cliff in which John Cassavedes' character, Phil Dimitrios, lived was photographed at noon on a sunny day in the Greek islands.

The churning storm clouds seen in the same shot were photographed in Midland, North Carolina, half a world away. The Optical House in New York removed stark ground shadows and replaced the sunny blue sky with those turbulent clouds. Now that's an optical! Rent the videotape and study it.

Few feature films are executed without the making of opticals. They're a necessary evil. The word evil applies only because they are generally expensive, but realistically so.

You'll be wise never, ever to guess the price of an optical. Always get a quote and make an agreement with the lab regarding your responsibilities (that is, precisely what they need you to furnish).

There are opticals you can make with your film camera. You'll read about them later.

Optical Houses

Optical houses are also called optical labs, or dry labs. Most film labs do simple opticals such as recomposition and basic titling. You'll have to find an optical house much the same way your found your lab. Your lab will recommend one to you. Ordinarily, they have little to do with videotape.

Videotape and Film Stocks

Film must be chosen upon several bases: how you plan to use it, where you'll use it, in what equipment you'll use it, and so on.

There is a number of American color film stocks available in Super/8, some Fuji color film and some black & white. All of it is reversal. The worst thing about reversal film is that it requires perfect exposure—which really isn't so difficult nor so bad, since the least one can expect from a cinematographer is proper exposure. It is available also with a mag stripe for sound recording.

In 16mm, reversal film stocks cost slightly less than negative emulsions but are slightly more expensive to process and work print. Either must be work printed for editorial purposes unless your editing will be done on video. If ultimately you need a positive image to transfer to video, reversal might be the route to take. It probably won't be, because with today's technology, an original negative transferred to video looks notably better than does a reversal original.

There is a rational argument, however, for using reversal film if you are shooting 16mm single system or Super/8. There is only one domestic brand of motion picture film stocks and, for the sake of buying American, we buy Kodak. Agfa and Fuji also make good stocks with different characteristics. You may have a purpose for using one instead of the other or to mix and match, but don't do so without purpose or testing.

Kodak gives to their motion picture films exotic names such as 5247, 7297, etc. Their names, therefore, tell you little or nothing unless you have the numbers memorized or written material to go by. For principal photography there are about six from which you can choose.

Their negative stocks are usually the same for both 16mm and 35mm and the choice of 5297, which is 35mm, would be made for exactly the same reasons as choosing 7297, which is 16mm.

In 35mm, the choices are (T means tungsten light; D means daylight):
  5247 ASA 125 T, 80 D w/ 85 filter
  5297 ASA 250 D
  5294 ASA 400 T, 250 D w/ 85 filter

The rating for 5295 is the same as 5294. This film is intended for blue screen traveling matte work, too expensive a project for a cheap film. Accordingly, that stock is not a choice. We'll discuss blue screen matte work in order to find less expensive options.

In 16mm, the choices are:
  7248 ASA 100 T, 64 D w/ 85 filter
  7297 ASA 250 D
  7292 ASA 320 T, 200 D w/ 85 filter

These films are manufactured with characteristics which allow them to be intercut. Using 7292 for interiors and 7248 for exteriors will render a result that will appear to be a single emulsion. (That capability, by the way, is a relatively recent development.)

Based on that fact, let's select only one of those two stocks. Choosing them both means we'll need both on hand, probably resulting in having more stock than we'll need. Daylight film generally is useless indoors unless your light is daylight balanced. If you have the good fortune to be using HMI lights they will be daylight balanced, but they are expensive enough that you probably will not have access to them on a super low budget.

On the other hand, using tungsten film outdoors with an 85 filter results in an image superior in some ways to that of daylight film. Therefore, we'll shoot 5294 or 7292 because it's the only dual purpose emulsion on the list which is fast enough to satisfy the requirement of light.

Take into account that some of the ISO indices listed above are accurate under ideal, if not controlled, conditions only and lose about one third to one half of their rated speed under ordinary conditions. Experimentation would indicate that those ISOs could be considered misinformation except for the disclaimer that "these indices are intended as a guide only. . . ." That's another way of saying the film's speed may be overrated. So, you had better take their advice and test it or you may get an unusable result. It's interesting that the film's ISO tends to lower itself depending upon the volume of black in the image. A normal black/white range shot in the daylight will photograph well at the published ISO of 320 while a shot with a lot of dark subject photographed in a low light level requires, perhaps, ISO 125.

Having elected to shoot Super/8 your black & white films would be:
  Plus-XR, ISO 40
  TRI-XR, ISO 160
  4-XR, ISO 400

Few labs process black & white reversal. Get in touch

38 You Have to Decide...

with Yale Laboratory, Inc., 1509 N. Gordon St., Hollywood, CA 90028 (213-464-6181).

The color film stocks available in Super/8 are:
 ELA 464 Ektachrome 160, Type A (silent)
 ELA 594 Ektachrome 160, Type A (sound)
 ELA 464 Ektachrome 160, Type G (silent)
 ELA 594 Ektachrome 160, Type G (sound)
 KMA 464 Kodachrome 40, Type A (silent)
 KMA 594 Kodachrome 40, Type A (sound)

Newsfilm Laboratory, Inc., 516 N. Larchmont Blvd., Hollywood, CA 90004 (213-462-6814) is available to process these films. The company, Super 8 Sound, can sell you the film stock. So can Bi-Rite Photo & Electronics, 15 E. 30th St., New York, NY 10016-7080 (800-223-1970).

To shoot video, your stock must be based upon your experience or upon recommendations by technicians you trust.

Since daylight or tungsten, high speed or slow, are functions of film, not tape, such issues must not enter into the choice.

Tape is relatively inexpensive, easily found in all formats, and the choice of brands or types is not likely to alter either your budget or method of using it.

Film must be chosen upon those bases mentioned earlier and, even though you are doing your principal photography in video—for reasons you'll discover later—you may need to shoot certain aspects in film that cannot be done electronically. You'll find 3M listed later. They are a supplier for videotape, audiotape, and full coat.

Full Coat

When filming double system, the picture is recorded on the film while the sound is recorded on a separate sound recording instrument; that is the typical way to make professional films. The recorder really ought to be one of those made for motion picture sound recording. These are substantially more expensive than conventional recorders. If you use a standard recorder, even a professional one, you could spend more than you have saved bailing out a problem.

Since that is a point of later discussion, assume now that you have recorded your sound properly and it resides on one quarter inch magnetic tape. In order to make use of that sound, it has to be transferred to a usable medium.

The medium in question is full coat. It is available in Super/8, 16mm and 35mm and the obvious selection is made on the basis of which of those sizes you are shooting. There is some reservation made to the issue of size which rates later discussion. In simple terms, full coat is movie film manufactured with iron oxide for recording sound instead of being coated with emulsion to shoot pictures. Its practical application lies in the fact that, when your sound has been transferred from the one quarter inch tape, the full coat sound will match the picture roll in terms of time or length, sprocket hole for sprocket hole. When editing takes place, both picture and sound are kept in mechanical synchronization allowing them to be cut precisely to the whims of the editor.

Some film labs offer the service of transferring one quarter inch tape to full coat at no charge other than the cost of the full coat stock when you get the matching picture processed and work printed. It's done simply to entice you to use their lab and is not a bad idea.

When recording double system, measures have to be taken to insure that the picture and sound stay in perfect synchronization. The most practical way to accomplish this is to have a camera whose speed is governed by an electronic pulse and a recorder which records onto the tape a pulse generated by the same source. The lab's equipment will tune in on that recorded pulse and see to it that a sync problem doesn't occur.

All this sounds complicated if you've never dealt with it, but it's something you buy and use. Like the carburetor on your car, you don't have to worry about whether or not you understand it. Mechanically, it simply takes place when the sound man pushes the appropriate button and that's that.

When you get your work print back from the lab, the magnetic sound track will arrive along with it on separate rolls so that interlock editing and later, interlock viewing, can begin. Interlock is viewing picture and sound together even though they are on separate media. Interlock is like a trailer hitch. Even though the car and the camper are on separate chassis when they leave home together, they stay together in transit, and get to the beach at the same time.

Single System vs. Double System

Single system is the recording of picture and sound on the same roll. Perhaps you're familiar with Super/8 sound; the fact that the sound is recorded on the picture roll—while the picture is being made—makes it single system sound. The same is true with a camcorder.

Knowing how some of the technology and methodology came about may help you to cheat the system and save a few bucks somewhere in your endeavors.

In the earliest days of TV news gathering, film was shot with no sound at all. Then in the mid 1960's and 70's, using cameras made 20 years earlier and converted to battery drive, they were able to shoot a picture which looked really good on the same roll with an optical sound track—which sounded like a continuing collision. Recording picture and sound on the same medium and developing them together made both JFK—who had attended "Havid Univussity"—and LBJ—who was "fum Tegzis"—sound alike because both appear to be talking through an exhaust pipe.

Single system news gathering was considered first class

television. In nonunion territory a cameraman-reporter could go on an assignment alone and do the whole job. His cacophonous sound (or racket, as the case may be) was recorded on the film alongside the picture.

Not much later, magnetic stripes were added to the raw stock, and magnetic recording heads to the cameras, causing single system sound tracks to become nearly hi-fi. Magnetic sound systems were infinitely better than optical ones for several reasons.

The fact that picture and sound are not positioned side by side on a finished film can cause the editor severe headaches. Rerecording in the station lab can shift the magnetic sound into editorial position on the film. It can then be edited and shifted back to projection position while enhancing the sound quality in the process. On the 11:00 news, that original film with a magnetic sound track was aired as if executed effortlessly, then filed away.

Many of those same old cameras, some converted for mag sound, some not—obsolete as they are—are still around shooting documentary films and an occasional feature. Documenters and feature makers choose *those* cameras on two bases only—they are cheap and they do the job. Many are still gathering dust in a corner of the news or engineering department of TV stations.

There are two drawbacks in using single system. First, few film stocks today are available with magnetic striping. Second, it's nearly impossible to find a lab who is interested in supporting your stab at doing single system sound. Using modern systems, it isn't practical to transfer the mag sound from a negative to full coat because the negative is so delicate and the machines are not. Therefore, no manufacturer makes negative stock with a mag track. The same cameras are quite useful for double system work because they run at precisely the correct speed, a critical matter in any case.

If you use 16mm Video News Film (also known as VNF) with a mag track or if you shoot Super/8 with one, you can transfer picture and sound directly to videotape in a single pass. This leaves your camera original film in almost pristine condition for possible future use.

VNF is a good choice for two reasons. It is made to exhibit a flat image that is low contrast for video transfer since flat is what electronics like. Also, it duplicates well because of the low contrast especially in the making of an internegative if one is necessary. You will have to edit the videotape rather than the film, an activity which may or may not be prohibitively expensive on a low budget project (unless you already have video editing equipment at your disposal).

While single system isn't done at all in 35mm, it is used almost invariably in videotape production.

Work Prints and Time Coded Dupes

Typically, you'll send your film and audio tape to the lab who will process the negative, make a print, hold the negative, and ship back the print. That print is called a work print, a rush, or a daily, depending upon how fast you get it back on that basis. It's a rush if you get it back tomorrow or sooner and it becomes a work print as soon as you use it for anything other than simply viewing.

If you ask the lab to *time* your work prints, they will correct both the color and the density to your expectations as described to them and their judgment of what the scene ought to look like. If you don't ask they may time it, partially time it, or set the printer on the middle number and print the whole roll, depending upon the lab. All three methods have merit.

Most cinematographers prefer an untimed work print because if they're a little off their exposures or color, they want to know it before any deviation is so extreme the lab can't correct it.

On the other hand, if they need to impress somebody else with the quality of their picture before getting very far along in the project, they can order timed work prints. Timed work prints generally take an extra half day and cost a penny or two more per foot.

You may or may not be able to save a little money by printing good takes only. Keep in mind that while 35mm work prints cost about the same per foot, there are three times as many feet per minute of running time. In 16mm, labs are prone to charge enough just to pull the bad takes that it's worthwhile simply to print the whole roll. If you have only one or two short, usable takes on a 400 foot foll, it would pay to print those takes only. In 35mm it always pays you to print the good ones (circled takes) only. You could pull the takes yourself but that requires a lot of extra time to get back the work print, it doubles your shipping if the film leaves town, and the film gets a great deal of handling that it doesn't really need. If you are doing a project which requires an enormous shooting ratio, it would be practical to remove the unwanted takes regardless of the gauge film you're shooting.

If you live near enough to the lab whose services you use, they may offer you the use of a cutting room at no charge so you can pull your own bad takes from 8 or 16mm. That'll save you a few dollars, but having done it once or twice, you may elect to do otherwise in future. If you have to pay rent for the work station then you won't save anything anyway, so why bother!

If your goal is a video production, all of which you are shooting on film and editing on tape, you really won't need a work print. A time coded video transfer from the original negative may be all you'll need. It can become your electronic editing original the use of which you'll read about later.

Edge Numbers (Coding) and SMPTE Time Code

Film manufacturers print latent footage numbers on the edge of movie film. When the original negative is printed the lab prints those numbers so they appear on the print.

40 You Have to Decide...

There's no charge for that but "print thru" edge numbers are sometimes a little difficult to read, and under some conditions, could repeat on separate rolls causing confusion or perhaps disaster. If you reserve enough film from Kodak before you start your project, they'll see to it your edge numbers never repeat.

The safer bet is to get "Inked Edge Nos. Starting at..." whatever number you choose.

Inked numbers cost a few pennies more per foot but have two advantages. You can choose the starting number based on the roll number, scene number, project number, film title or whatever you choose. They're very easily read. The time you save the negative cutter by the use of inked numbers could be a great deal more valuable than the price of the inked numbers. You have to investigate, calculate, and decide. If you want to save $600, inked edge numbers will lose out. But don't forget, negative cutters charge by the hour.

Your full coat can also be coded after it has been synchronized with the picture. This ordinarily is not useful or practical unless you are working on a musical or an unusually complicated sequence.

A music work print, that is, a duplicate work print made from an edited work print cannot be coded because, once edited, the numbers are all scrambled.

A 16mm work print will print through both edge numbers and coding only if you are working with neg/pos film. It will print through edge numbers only if reversal. In both cases, it may fail altogether if the film is torn up from use badly enough that the sprocket holes won't track properly in the printer.

Otherwise, the film must be printed from tails in order to track the good set of sprocket holes. Some printers disallow the printing through of the edge numbers in that direction. Since 35mm is tracked on both sets of sprocket holes, the problem won't exist.

The SMPTE time code does the same job for video editors that coding does for film editors. Like film coding, if the time code is not put onto the tape at the time of original recording it can be laid in by the video editor at whatever time he chooses to do so. A SMPTE time code identifies each frame on the entire tape and the video editor can instruct the machine to go find a certain frame and display it. Once a time code is placed on a tape, the numbers can be printed in the picture area and read directly off the screen on a VHS dupe.

Time code is recorded also on most 35mm camera negative stocks but can be read only by high dollar equipment.

Playing your dupe on one VCR while recording onto another, you can make your edits by using the pause button on the recording unit. You will get a substantially degraded quality on the copy, but you can easily and ponderously evaluate the cuts and remake them if you don't like them. You can still clearly read the numbers in the time code window. The poor transfer quality is not relevant since the only thing that interests the video technician will be the code numbers.

Assigning these time code numbers to paper and giving the notes to the editor, he will enter them into the computer which, in turn, will automatically find each take on the original roll and edit it into the master roll. This automation is much faster at executing the cuts than manually and decidedly more expensive per hour. If his system isn't automatic, the numbers still can be selected manually.

If you'd rather, you can sit at home and edit the time coded tape with a pencil and paper. The disadvantage lies in the inability to view the hypothetical cut when it's made with only the imagination.

Done by either of these methods, the creative editing is executed at little or no cost and the electronic editing is done in a greatly reduced time.

Director or DP?

A really sharp director can double as director of photography and even as cameraman, depending upon the type of production and volume of work. However, the greater the number of competent people you have working on a project, the more easily everyone's job is done.

A director of photography may or may not operate the camera. Running the camera is actually the camera operator's job—if you have a camera operator. Many directors like the prospect of having the DP operate the camera regardless of the number of assistants he has.

Ideally, on a tight budget, if there are sufficient personnel, a camera assistant ought to load the magazines, thread the camera, and secure its operability. Securing its operability means cleaning the gate periodically, changing lenses, and overseeing the general operation of the instrument. He could also sub as focus puller or dolly pusher if there is none other.

Having someone to do these chores makes the DP's job tolerable and maybe even doable. His function really is focused on setting a mood with the lighting, working together with the director for blocking and, in general terms, making the photography look good. (Blocking is when and where people and the camera move—all to make the picture look as it ought to.) If the DP has to load magazines, thread the camera, put the camera on the dolly, clean the gate, change the lens and put out the cat, he really won't have much time to direct the photography.

If the director has to be DP under the above conditions, he won't have time to change his underwear, let alone direct.

Official check lists can be found near the end of the book along with other lists and forms.

A Caterer!

Ordinarily we think of a caterer as serving a wedding or something like it. Well, a movie is something like it. Stopping to eat is not an inexpensive proposition. While this is not simply a social event, everybody's got to eat. Naturally there are several options.

Not all low budget pictures have the same low budget. Anything under about two million is considered low. "Anything under" also includes $700,000 and $70,000 as well as $7,000 and $700.

Therefore, if there is simply no money to cater or take the crew out perhaps you can appease them with refreshments. If they work more than four or five hours at a crack, they will have to eat fairly soon—even if they have to buy their own. Otherwise they'll do a lesser job. That's only human.

If you have the budget for it, you can have food catered in, break for lunch, and get back to work all together and efficiently. Depending upon where you are shooting, you can break, go to a nearby restaurant, then get back to work. Alternating the two might be a good idea. Taking 60 people to a local restaurant dictates that the restauranteur gets fair warning. Most places can't take a surge like that unannounced.

If the budget won't take regular meals, you can always have your spouse, sibling, child, friend, mother, or town grunt make peanut butter and jelly sandwiches at home and bring them to the set or location. This is, in effect, catering. But since spouses, siblings, children, friends, mothers and grunts generally don't charge much for their services, it's not a high dollar service and becomes affordable on the budget for any shoot. A weenie roast will lighten tensions and serve equally well as long as someone is assigned to shut it down and clean it up. If not, less professional workers and talent will hang around the fire—even in midsummer—and not get back to the salt mines until threatened or beaten.

Refreshments are also important. Many of the talent and crew on a film spend substantial periods of time just waiting. And waiting. Having a perpetual supply of soft drinks, coffee, and something to nibble on strengthens morale a far measure beyond its dollar cost. Coffee, tea, and hot chocolate are especially important when shooting in cold weather. It will keep people from getting tired, bored, and annoyed with each other, a problem which will unquestionably reduce their efficiency or the quality of their skill. To sum it up, it's generally cheaper to keep them happy than to keep them hungry.

Having a place to sit is as important a factor in keeping them happy whether it will be a log or a director's chair. If they're expected to sit for long periods, it pays to have them sit where they can watch and be comfortable but still be out of the way.

If your budget allows you to spring for director's chairs, there should be one for every executive and every actor and it should have his name printed on it. Furthermore everyone must understand that he is not to sit in a chair which does not bear his name since he will, upon the first and every occasion, be killed and publicly embarrassed.

Sound Effects—and Foley

Foley effects are the sounds of walking or running and are typically done on a stage which contains isolated areas of sand, areas of gravel, hard wood floor, wooden steps, leaves, and other elements on which a person can walk while watching the film for which he is making foot sounds. Any other sounds, whether authentic or contrived are simply known as sound effects or background, but more and more often are referred to as Foley.

Recording studios and film labs have an endless supply of sound effects (or FX). They'll take your list, pull the effects you want, dub them over to one quarter inch or full coat and charge you a reasonable but healthy sum for the service.

Remember, however, when buying effects this way that there are a hundred different crowd sounds, a hundred different traffic sounds, doors closing, keys rattling, skating rinks, drive-in restaurants, and a hundred of everything else. What the lab sends may or may not fit your shot.

Buying your sound is worthwhile if you need an effect you can't supply yourself, but a good recorder-microphone combination together with some imagination and experimentation will get you most of the sounds you'll need for anything and for almost nothing. So be prepared to take alternative action.

Furthermore, any one sound might represent any number of others. For example, the single sound of hitting yourself in the chest with your fist may sound like a log falling in soft dirt, a book falling on the carpet or being closed, a trailer hitting a bump, a shoe falling, a hamper lid closing, hitting a pillow, or dumping a shovelful of dirt. Or perhaps that original sound would not work for a single one of these. Remember that your old granny told you that the test of the pudding is in the eating. This is the test. You make a group of recordings then try each with the film to see which best fits. An effect works or it doesn't.

Knowing this, you'll understand why the sounds you see in the movies are rarely what they represent. Renting movies, videotapes, can be a good source of general sound effects although much too often a good effect is overlapped with another which will preclude its use. By the way, using generic effects is o.k. Using their music or dialogue is not!

Everyone in the business knows that crushing Cellophane sounds exactly like a crackling fire, sizzling bacon, or rain on the sidewalk. Crushing stiff paper sounds like someone walking in dry leaves—so does a recording of the recordist walking in dry leaves. Dragging your fingers down your trousers or skirt sounds like skis in the snow. Tapping your fingers on a leather chair seat sounds like a galloping horse. The list is endless. Create your own.

In *Marley's Revenge*, I can remember dropping numerous glass bottles on a concrete floor just to get the right sound of a mirror breaking. We fired a .22 caliber pistol into a stack of newspapers and recorded it for the killing of Mana. In playback it never sounded right. Finally, we played it back at half speed and it was perfect. We threw a 50-pound log into a swimming pool probably 25 times just to get the right kerploosh for Sloth to be pulled into the water by the monster. We recorded a number of buzzes to get the right one for Gary's alarm clock. We recorded a seemingly endless number of billiard strikes, glasses clinking, crowd sounds, beer can placements, commode flushes, shovel digs and dirt tosses, fist strikes, phone rings, dropped pistols, door closes and slams, footsteps in great variety, battery sparks. The explosion for the boat and the roar of the monster were noises I made with the microphone almost inside my mouth! This list, too, goes on and on.

Each take was verbally identified on the tape and logged on a sound sheet. You absolutely must slate and number each take. Otherwise, later you may not recognize them and surely no one else will.

Several good books are available on sound effects and can be found free at the library.

Mechanical FX

Mechanical FX are those special effects which take place in front of the camera, rather than inside it or at the lab. A flood in miniature (or life size, for that matter) would be a good example as would an automobile burning or a house burning. Even when the house is really burning, if it's doing so for the film, it's still a special effect.

Sometimes doing something for real is equally available as doing it as an effect. Frequently time restraints or an unfortunate lack of money will cause a mechanical effect to be less expensive than the real thing. Sometimes, an effect is the only available way.

Since this book is not dedicated to teaching how to do each element in the making of a film but rather how to minimize the cost, it would be impossible to list all the effects that can be done, then to explain how to do them cheaper than normal. Still much of that will be found in later chapters anyway.

Allowing an expert to do a dangerous effect is cheaper than being sued by someone who got hurt because he didn't know what he was doing, and $20,000 budgets don't have room for much insurance. On the other hand, if you can pay for any insurance at all, at least ask an underwriter about Workers' Compensation. It is, by far, the cheapest insurance if it's available on a short term basis from your insurance agent. By the way, he should be able to furnish you with insurance companies who specialize in the film business.

If you deem it prudent, put an accident disclaimer in your contract with both crew and talent since they'll have their own insurance anyway.

There are creative ways to do things that have a great impact. A volunteer fire department who had planned to burn down an old house for practice worked together with EO Corporation (Shelby, North Carolina), a film producer, on a shot resulting in a very strong effect for very little investment. It was easily written into the script he was already working on.

He could have burned a one fourth or one third scale model. Shooting it at a reasonably short distance would have hidden the fact that it was small. That, too, would have been relatively safe and inexpensive and would have given him a house to burn that had been constructed to duplicate a specific real house somewhere else in the script. Come to think of it, some eight or ten years later, he did.

Not all experts in burning, blowing up, falling, fighting, jumping, hanging, and you-name-it, are movie people. If you need to blow up a boat at the river, you'll need a pyrotechnist not a movie producer. When a local film maker needed to wreck a car, he hired Neal Castles, a race driver, who charged less than a stunt driver would have. Castles is now doing well as a stunt driver.

If you need a really great looking model airplane, go to a hobby shop. They'll be glad to recommend an expert hobbyist/model builder who may build what you need for materials and a screen credit. The helicopters they blow up in *Magnum P.I.* and *Airwolf* can be bought ready to fly for around $750. Certainly cheaper than blowing up a $90,000 Bell helicopter and a wino.

Needless to say, not all mechanical effects are dangerous. There are theater students and aficionados all over the place who'll work for nothing (or close to it) to build a mechanical shark akin to Jaws or an Eiffel Tower that will simply collapse as Linn Dunn's did in *The Great Race*. His was a seven dollar plastic model his daughter brought him from Paris. That model saved the studio $25,000 rendering it (the effect) a cheap entry to a very worthwhile (and expensive) film.

If you'll pay for the materials, a lot of these guys will do you a miracle, speaking of which, the local Society of American Magicians (SAM) or International Brotherhood of Magicians (IBM) are good organizations who can help to find ways to do visual effects. Contact can be made through any magic store.

Editing and Conforming

There are several options where editing is concerned, so one really needs to consider carefully which route he will take in order to preclude his dashing out dollars in money-absorbing areas.

Before *Marley's Revenge* was begun, the suggestion was made that up to $30,000 could be saved on film editing alone if it was done electronically (on tape). At the time, the proposed budget for everything was only $20,000. Saving $30,000 was improbable. For a $2,000,000 picture, saving $30,000 would have made good sense.

Whether or not paying $450 per hour for electronic editing is a justifiable expenditure is less an issue than whether $450 an hour is even possible on a super low budget. Paying such a rate for one to three weeks is hardly a consideration on a cheap film. As we've already discussed, operating that way is unnecessary anyway.

Shooting the project on videotape will require that you edit it on videotape—one way or another. You can buy a better than adequate brand video editing system for the price you'd pay for two week's editing at six hours a day—and you'll own it!

You also can buy a 16mm upright Movieola editing unit with one picture head and two sound heads for the price of an eight hour rental of a tape editing room. For a 35mm unit just like it, you'd pay about $5,500 or 12 hours electronic editing. If your goal is to make a picture for TV or videotape release, your best bet is going to be as follows:

Shoot film (with double system sound).
Make a work print.
Edit the sound to a finished master mag track.
Mix the sound to a finished master mag track.

If shot in 35mm, cut (conform) the negative to match the edited work print and transfer to a finished videotape.

If shot in 16mm, transfer the negative (circled takes) and sound mix to a video master and edit the videotape.

OR
Print the edited negative to a timed, color corrected Lo-con pos and transfer that to a finished videotape.

Each system has its merits.

Perhaps you work at a TV station who will give you free access to their editorial suite. Or if you have your own video editing system, you can edit the tape yourself at a leisurely pace after transferring the uncut negative to videotape. Editing in a videotape house goes back to a $175–$450 an hour affair while editing on the cheaper nonprofessional systems will possibly render an unsalable product. Our goal is not to raise the budget, but not to destroy the project either.

Remember, that even the transfer of the unedited negative to tape is also around $450 an hour—lab time, not running time. A proper transfer to tape is not simply a matter of putting the film on the machine and pressing the start button. Done properly, it requires a skilled technician (called a colorist) to get either the best result—or even a minimally acceptable one, for that matter.

To offer fair argument in favor of the financial ramifications of videotape editing system—if you have shot on tape or after you have transferred your film to tape, editing the VHS dupe (discussed earlier) will help keep the cost in line with reality.

If you elect to supervise the edit, it may be scheduled for any time after the numbers have been entered into the computer. Since the computer is going to find the shots and make the edits, you will probably spend your time riding gain on the sound and approving the video look. Estimate 6 to 12 hours at a rate between $350 and $450 if there are no serious problems. Then get a quotation.

Any video effects you must do such as titling, image enhancement or alteration, or digital work (page flips, squeezing, etc.) will be done before editing begins (and perhaps at a separate rate). The result can simply be dropped in at the appropriate editorial spot.

For cut edits (that is, no dissolves, fades or digital effects), some houses will rent you space for hands-on editing (without the supervision of a house technician) for as little as $30 per hour. If you need to do effects, you must have them done at whatever the rate and cut them into the matter as if they were original takes, just like a film optical.

If your end use is theatrical, you'll skip all the video steps, conform the 35mm negative to match the work and then a trial print. This is what you'll show your distributor. You may elect to make a straight video transfer from the 35mm print to send to the distributor as a matter of convenience. It will cost between $250 and $950 for an uncontrolled transfer.

Having shot in 16mm and Super/16 for theatrical release will require that the negative be conformed to the work print, an interpositive be made from the negative, and a 35mm neg made from the interpositive. The interpos can

44 You Have to Decide...

be either 16mm or 35mm depending upon the deal you strike with the optical lab.

Some will offer a turnkey rate to do the job including answer print, interpos, and dupe negative. Others do it on the basis of so much per 16mm foot or so much per 35mm foot for each element. In this case, a 16mm answer print and interpositive (Illustration A in the diagram on page 45) will serve to save you a little money with a probably-less-than-noticeable reduction in quality as compared to a blow-up Interpositive (Illustration B), and contact negative. From the 16mm interpositive the 35mm blow-up neg can be struck. C is a 16mm neg to 35mm CRI (color reversal intermediate), a single step.

Some labs still do CRIs (Illustration C) which is a less popular method but gets the job done in a single step. The 16mm negative is blown up to a 35mm reversal negative.

Most labs prefer to do B because they get to do more 35mm steps which makes more money for them and in some cases may be a little easier for them.

In the unlikely event you have shot 16mm reversal (which gives you a positive image on the original), the only sensible route to a 35mm printing negative would be a one-step blow up to 35mm dupe negative.

Optical or Magnetic Sound Track

Easy to answer. If you must have prints for projection purposes, you'll need an optical track on each print.

Putting an optical track on a 16mm print for video release is not only unnecessary and inappropriate, it's not even advisable. TV stations no longer have any interest in running film on the air. An answer print or trial print on standard print stock may be necessary for approval or correction because it looks like what the eye expects to see and gives the opportunity to check for errors.

Once done, the best bet is to make a lo-con positive and transfer it to video. It will not cost so much as the answer print, but it will make a noticeably better transfer to put a sound track on the print. If you require an interpositive for any reason, it will serve quite well instead of a lo-con for transfer to tape.

Depending upon a number of factors, you must keep in mind that a 16mm lo-con will cost between $900 and $1,500 after you've made an answer print (which will cost even more). You can make your transfer from the answer print as long as you do not scratch it during inspection. If you must make your transfer from the answer print, you would be wise to limit the use of the tape to that of a screener for potential distributors.

To add yet another fly to the ointment, some video labs swear they can transfer conformed 16mm negatives to tape. If so, it will certainly take a substantially longer transfer time than doing so from a single-roll print or intermediate. That is, you may spend an additional $2,000 on the transfer from the negative while saving, perhaps, $1,000 for the lo-con print, thereby spending an extra $1,000. Making an answer print in this case is optional—expensive, but still a pretty good idea because you will find problems that the video technician can't correct, such as the insertion of a wrong take.

Making an inquiry as to whether the lab can and will work from a conformed 16mm negative would be wise.

The discovery of an unexpected problem in video editing will probably stop progress and cause you to pay a cancellation fee. Making an answer print is still the wiser choice and would likely preclude the unexpected.

Making a chart of all the possible methods and their predicted costs is a worthwhile and educational expenditure of time and effort.

No lab will offer release prints, finished IPs, or finished lo-con positives without an answer print because invariably, an answer print will display the need for some kind of correction. Sometimes it is color, another time density, another the negative cutter stuck in a shot upside down. The corrections (if they are few) can be reprinted and spliced into the answer print rendering it useful for projection. An answer print without a sound track can be run in interlock with the full coat. Or if 16mm, the print can be struck on single perf print stock onto which a magnetic track can later be applied, saving you the cost of a sound track printing negative. You'll simply need to dub your full coat master to this print for use on a projector with a mag track capability. You'll need to consider all elements to decide whether the time and money warrants a magnetic print.

You also have the option to have an electro printed track. That's one wherein the lab optically records the sound onto the print stock before the picture print is processed, instead of printing it from a sound track negative. Few labs offer this service. It costs less than making a sound track negative to be used for a single print but is too costly for the making of more than two or three prints.

Yale Lab offers mag striping on existing prints. Newsfilm Lab offers electro sound tracks.

Transfer to videotape from your corrected sound answer print can be done well. The transferred image will not be so good as with a lo-con and, after passing the answer print through the viewing projector it is bound to have scratches. Therefore, investing in the lo-con is advisable if it's affordable.

If you have uses for a film print other than transferring it to video, there's no reason not to put a sound track on the answer print using the most appropriate method.

Releasing your picture on videotape only, the sound track can be laid onto the video master using the master sound mix, whether you shoot in Super/8, 16mm, Super/16, or 35. Transferring from the full coat will sound better than an optical track and will save the thousand or two the optical track negative would cost. Doing so as a double system technique requires you to do so, if not simultaneously with the picture transfer, at least with equipment which syncs with it.

THREE WAYS TO THIS 35MM PRINTING NEGATIVE FROM 16MM ORIGINAL NEGATIVE

16mm Interpos

35mm Interpos

16mm Answer Print

Original 16mm Neg.

5
Techniques for Making Screen Titles

Remember "BOOM!" in front of the train and trestle? If "BOOM!" has to move, come apart, and fall, it will require a travelling matte; maybe, in this case, a $5,000 investment. If "BOOM!" simply pops in over the train and trestle, sits there a few seconds and pops away, a fixed matte will do the job at around $100. If someone on your staff does it, the cost may be ten dollars worth of materials plus processing and printing.

Here's how to do it yourself.

First, shoot and process a film of the toy train going over the trestle at the appropriate slow motion speed.

Then on paper do the artwork; that is, draw a black "BOOM!" on white field. Make a litho negative (**A** below). From **A**, make the contact litho positive, **B**. Combine the two, with **A** slightly to the right and an equal distance lower and register punch them while together. Print this **A/B** combination onto a pre-punched litho film. This will result in a registered negative of the shadow only and will be labeled **C**.

A B A/B C

The litho films will look like these. **A** is the negative of the main title, **B**, whose positive image is shifted up and to the left, when laid over **A** exposes only the shadow area, and **C** is the resulting negative of that combination.

Thread your camera with the original film of the train and trestle bi-packed together with the duplicating stock. Using a paper punch, be sure to indicate a start mark on both the camera original film and the print stock so that later you can rethread in exactly the same position.

Counting frames, run-up the camera to the beginning of the shot, then continuing to the piont where the title is to pop in. Now, in the HJ reflex box, insert both **B** and **C**. Together, these block all of the printing light where both the title and shadow appear.

Continue shooting long enough to complete exposure to the title end, then fade out. Remove both lithos from the HJ reflex box, cover the lens, back crank the film to the beginning of the fade, and fade back in. Continue shooting until the shot ends. (You'll have to know where the shot begins and ends by frame counting.)

Cover the lens and back crank your camera leaving the print stock at the start mark but remove the original film.

Insert into the HJ reflex box the litho of "BOOM!" that is, **A**. Cover the camera lens and advance the film to the frame where the title pops in. Put a filter on the lens, perhaps a K-2 (yellow) and shoot to the frame where you must begin the fade out of the title and repeat the fade. Remove the film and have it processed.

The result will be the train wrecking in the background while the title appears—and fades out in the foreground, yellow with a black drop shadow. Had you decided to make the drop shadow deep red, you then would make a third pass using the **A/B** combination and a deep red filter.

Whether the "BOOM!" on the HJ reflex box reads right or must be backwards will depend which intermediate stage you begin and end. Knowing that the image reverses or "flops" each time you print it, you'll have to stop and consider exactly where to start.

The final result of the fixed matte.

There are three ways to achieve a proper exposure. Put a good color transparency (4 × 5, or bigger) on the glass and take a "reflected" reading from about two or three inches. Or with nothing on the glass you can set the meter for "incident" reading, put the meter directly on the glass, and take the reading. The third—and best—way is to do a film test at a number of f/stops, taking or slating notes, and let your lab choose the best density.

Is this the cheapest way to do your titles? No, it's an inexpensive way to be classy. A cheaper way would be to include the titles and credits in the principal photography, perhaps the way Linn Dunn did in *West Side Story*. The credits were painted on old doors, brick walls, fences, and sidewalks. (Rent the tape and check it out. Of course, being in Hollywood, their title budget was $100,000.)

In our case, a lot of effort could be saved by painting the separate titles and credits on the sides of the train cars and let the last title car pass before blowing up the bridge. This would be easier but which of the two would be better? You must decide or ask your art director.

You could simply photograph handwritten or typeset cards. These can be done with transfer type bought at the local art supply store, cheaper than paying to have type set but quite time consuming. Today every third individual has a personal computer that could be used to print titles.

If such titles are designed to relate to the cinematic subject, they can be very effective at very little cost. When the subject revolves around school, for example, doing the titles on the blackboard with chalk would be appropriate. Titles made with crayons on white paper might work well for a film set in a kindergarten class.

If your release goal is for video only, there's a better than even chance that titling for almost any type of result can be more cheaply done by the video lab than by a filmed method.

The worst possible option is to generate your titles in your video camera. Even those cameras which have nice fonts never seem to have the one you need and variable placement of the words is usually not possible.

If you are not able to use some of the techniques described, you can at least have litho negatives made, stick them on the kitchen window, and shoot either film or video that way. Carefully done, it'll work fine.

The design of your titles would figure a great deal in your decision about which technique to use. For example, if you wanted the titles to appear painted on a wooden fence, you'd probably be wise to paint them on a wooden fence. If, on the other hand, they simply need to be a typeface appearing "in space" in front of a wooden fence, shoot enough film of a frence for editing purposes and let the lab or optical house superimpose the type.

It is understood that in using the former method, the title

is seen to be painted on the boards of the fence while the latter displays the titles in space in front of the fence with no relationship to it.

If you're editing on tape, a short piece of tape, enough for a freeze frame, will suffice for the video man to lay in the titles using a character generator. It'll look better if he has sufficient footage for the entire title with tape rolling, even though there is no movement.

Like any creative enterprise, the design of titles and credits is an art. If done well, such work can enhance the quality of your film because the viewer's attitude is altered by a subconscious interpretation of what he sees first. This effort is justified by the premise that you get only one chance to make a first impression.

Typically, anyone making a circus film would automatically choose "P.T. Barnum" as his typeface. The movie *Superman* used the same typeface as the comic book, eliciting memories 50 years old (for some of us).

Poorly thought out art may serve the purpose but obviously won't do a proper job. While the main title and executive credits on *Body Shop* were bold and easily read, they were done simply in a contemporary typeface rendering them legible but unimaginative. The tail credits, in contrast, were red type on a black field and too tiny to read on a theater screen, let alone on a TV set.

When the time came to do titles and credits on *Marley's Revenge*, we carefully decided what to do. The decision was to do straightforward, bold yellow letters with a red drop shadow on a black field with action in the periphery or background.

Having chosen an appropriate typeface, we made litho negatives and photographed them on the HJ reflex box twice—once with the red drop shadow and once without, just to compare. The yellow with the drop shadow was favored and therefore used.

We had by now a set of titles and credits that looked good but we still needed to film a background. In several skull sessions we bounced around a number of ideas. One began with a very tight shot of several kilos of dope (flour in plastic baggies), an arm hanging from the top of the screen dripping blood on white packages. (The blood was two parts white syrup, one part water, one part red food color.) As the camera dollies back, a black background is revealed leaving the packages at the bottom of the screen. The blood continues to drip. We hold this image for the duration of titles and credits which appear in the center of the black area. When it was done, it looked good—but it just didn't fit the content of the picture.

We regrouped and rethought, and conjured up this idea. We'll have voices of several sheriff's deputies talking on their police car radios about discovering footprints, bodies, and clues germane to the story. The background would be extremely out-of-focus images of police car lights, buoy lights, and flashlights that also are relevant to the story. It looked good, but the director didn't like the confusion of the voices behind the printed titles, so he wrote a completely different opening.

A hunter in the woods (with full foliage) hears a strange sound. He investigates and discovers a gigantic footprint. As he looks up, he is greatly startled and we cut to black. First title appears.

While the new opening is not relevant to the script, the viewer isn't aware of it. He doesn't yet know the story anyway. Also, hunters don't hunt in the summer but nobody noticed the incongruity. The startling ending of the introduction together with the bridge music worked well to introduce the titles.

When the picture was ready to release, the distributor agreed to accept the picture only if we revised the title sequence since it didn't make sense.

On Mother's Day of 1990, we reshot the original opening segment of our very first shoot. We shot negative stock which was transferred directly to videotape, friend John Autry edited it electronically, and inserted it into the master. It was a distinct improvement.

Knowing we were going to crawl the tail credits, I had already used some of my scarce spare time to build a motorized frame to do so. It was quite simple. It basically was a motor-driven roller which would wind up a long strip of eight-inch wide film as the film was pulled through a frame attached to the HJ reflex box. It worked fair, at best.

A name had been left off the credits, so it had to be typeset, photographed onto litho film and spliced into its proper place. That caused a tiny jump as the splice passed through the frame. Before we filmed the credits, it was discovered that two other names had also been overlooked and another misspelled. The corrections were made and then other errors and omissions were found. Each time we made a discovery and a correction it cost more money.

By the time we had all the credits correctly in place, there were dozens of splices in the strip of litho film. The patches were so abundant that the film would jiggle and snag and refuse to go through the frame properly.

Two options were open to us. One was to remake the litho negative. It was about nine feet long and was made of 20-inch sections. Even a perfect one would have several splices. The other option was to make a rotating drum around which we could wrap the strip and light it from the inside. We opted for the latter. Since I had a shop and the materials on hand to build the rig, there would be no cash investment. It could be used in the future for such work.

Since the rig did not have to be pretty, it required a minimum amount of engineering and only an hour or two to build. Once done, we simply wrapped the litho negative around the drum and taped the negative down with black electrical tape. Turning on the motor rotated the drum. We timed its rotation and continued making adjustments in the voltage regulator until it took exactly two minutes to rotate once.

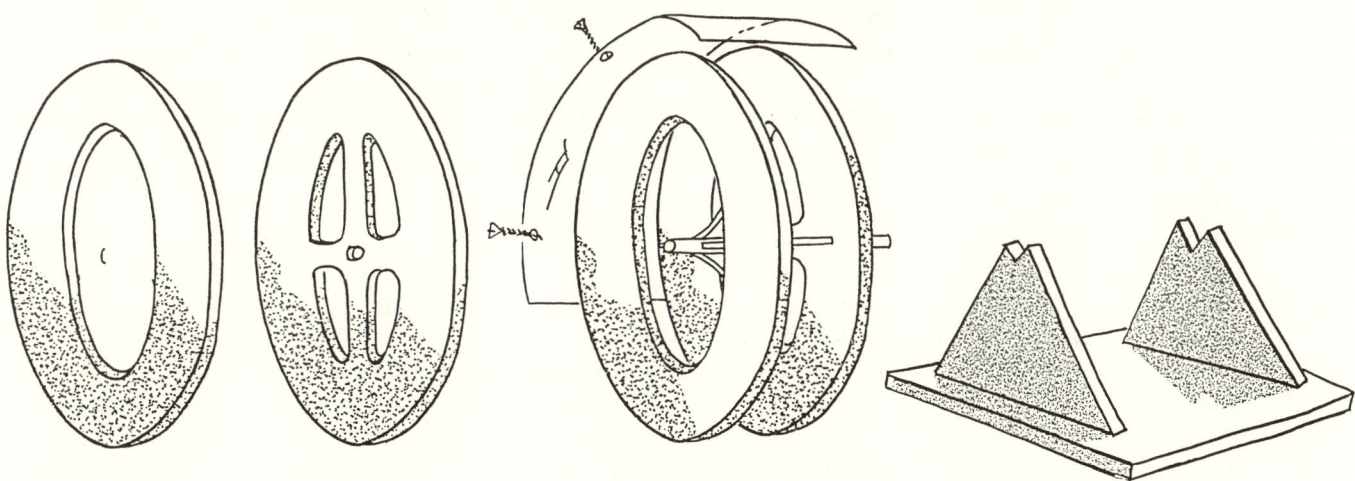

Above: A homemade gadget designed to crawl the tail credits. *Below:* A diagram explaining the construction of the rig above.

We covered the inside of the Plexiglas with diffusion material in order to get even light dispersion, then set a 1000w quartz unit on the inside of the drum and evaluated the exposure. We were ready to shoot.

Whoever makes your wooden gadgets can also make this one for you very simply. This person will have to cut two three-inch-wide rings from three-quarter inch plywood, each having a three-foot diameter. One of the two must have four spokes. A one-inch dowel becomes the axle which must be buttressed to the spokes since there can be no support on the other side. A thin strip of Plexiglas is heated and bent around the two rings, then drilled and attached (gently) with wood screws.

This "Ferris wheel" gadget must rest in the forks of a stand onto which is mounted a slowly rotating motor (like the one in your rotisserie). We put protruding brads on the "wheel rims" about six inches apart, wrapped nylon string (the drive belt) around the outside of the brads and step-down motor shaft and it worked like a charm. A voltage regulator controlled the speed.

Using the Ferris wheel required us to use our standard camera which had only a zoom lens. Setting it at the most advantageous distance did not allow us to focus without taking extraordinary measures.

There are two ways to resolve such a problem. With a conventional lens, you can use extension tubes or a bellows to move the lens further from the focal plane. The extension allows you to focus closer than the lens mount is designed for. This doesn't work with a zoom lens since, once you focus, you can't zoom without instantly and totally losing focus. A close-up lens (also known as a plus diopter) will solve the problem with either type of lens and allows the zoom lens to zoom.

None of us had a close-up lens but Jet, who works at an eyeglasses factory, resolved the problem for us. I had him pick up a +1 and a +2 lens. Since the lenses were not yet cut to fit eyeglasses, which are about 2½ inches in diameter, they were more than big enough to cover the front element of our zoom lens. These new lenses made our job a snap.

While we're on the subject, allow me to tell you that such lenses at a camera store are about $20. The price from an optician—if you can talk him into selling you one—is about three dollars.

Plus diopter lenses are positive supplementary lenses, usually of a weak meniscus type, which may be positioned in front of a lens to permit sharp focusing at very close distances. Plus diopters shorten the focal length of the normal lens permitting closer focusing. A few super/8 cameras and nearly all camcorders are equipped with a macro range zoom lens. This allows focusing as close as the front surface of the lens in some cases, while the majority of professional zoom lenses require a plus diopter supplement for focusing closer than five feet.

Plus diopter lens power is expressed in metric values and is quite easy to understand. The plus sign indicates a positive or converging lens. The power of a plus diopter is the reciprocal of its focal length expressed in meters. A +1 lens, for example, has a focal length of 1 meter (40 inches) and will focus the image of an object at this distance unaided. When positioned in front of a conventional lens or zoom lens set on infinity, it will project a sharp image of an object one meter away (measured from the front of the lens, not the focal plane). Focusing the camera lens closer than infinity will deliver sharp images at closer subject distances.

A +2 diopter has a focal length of one-half meter (the reciprocal of 2) which is 20 inches. A +3 focuses at one-third meter or 13 inches. A +10, therefore, has a focal length of 1/10 meters, a little over four inches.

When using diopters, one should remember that putting any object in the light path diminishes the quality of the image to some extent. It is sometimes necessary to do so. You should establish your light level to allow you to stop down two stops for every diopter you use if possible. Typically, this will reduce the degradation caused by the optical obstacle.

Plus diopters can be stacked thereby adding the sum of their powers. You could buy a +1, a +2, a +4, and a +8 giving you a complement exceeding a +10—more than you'll ever need. Anything greater than a +3 is impractical, but when used in combination the greatest power should be put closest to the camera lens.

The container you keep the diopters in ought to be marked indicating their focal lengths and the distance range at which they apply with the lenses you have. The greatest distances are formulated above. The shortest distances will have to be determined by experimenting with your particular lenses since some are manufactured to focus closer than others.

The power of a diopter remains fixed regardless of the prime lens with which it is combined. Furthermore, the diopter will have no effect on depth of field since all the lenses at a given distance and f/ stop have the same depth of field when the images are projected or printed the same size.

Subject magnification depends upon the focal length of the camera lens and makes the distance from the subject. The plus diopter simply makes it possible to focus at much closer distances. A somewhat longer-than-normal focal length (or a zoom lens positioned at the same focal length) will deliver the same size image as a shorter focal length lens positioned closer to the subject, but will give you a little more working room.

There are minus lenses, too, which don't apply here. It would pay you to investigate their uses.

Now, back to our titling. Knowing the trouble, frustration and the man hours that were required, the most efficient choice would have been to do the titles when doing the video transfer, since the film was intended for video release anyway. But it might have cost about $500 to set and enter them into the computer. The mistakes we made originally would also have been entered and corrected at still more expense.

In retrospect, it is good that we had the titling experiences. In spite of the problems, we probably spent less cash than we would have spent had we done the titles electronically. It's interesting to note, even if you shoot video, shooting the titles on the wheel will look as if they were done on film whereas doing them electronically will somehow be quite different.

It is important to consider ancillary markets when the opportunity to do video elements arises. Doing video elements looks fine when viewed electronically, but if there will ever be need for film print-making from the original—such as foreign release—those elements must be in the negative at printing time.

6
Advice for the Director

In today's market, a low budget picture is one whose working capital is less than five million dollars. In the Hollywood parlance, this type of film is in the minority.

The director for such a picture has usually worked on pictures with a higher budget. The director will probably alter the style of thinking for the purpose of getting more out of the crew and talent for the money spent. This director may well work harder for less money because of pride or a conviction about the project.

It has been reported that Steven Spielberg directed *The Color Purple* for the minimum fee allowable by his peers. He did so as a favor to a friend. While its twelve million dollar budget cannot be considered low, it is substantially less than most of his works and attests to the fact that the preeminent must also, from time to time, engage in budget-cutting strategy.

I have never directed a feature. I have directed specific sequences for various reasons and have a working knowledge of what the responsibilities are. I measured my own success on whether I was reproached or complimented.

To teach directing is not within my purview, nor is reminding the seasoned director how to do his job. However one of the goals of this book is to pass on to the novice some of the techniques generally known only by those who have paid their dues through experience or education, or known by those of us who have watched them gain their experience.

Earlier chapters have commented in passing on how a director may save a few feet of film here or there, what cutaways may serve the editor, or how to bail out a bad take. Discussing some of these same techniques in greater detail should bring to mind specifically how these procedures work and why they can save money.

As a point of contrast, I'm going to describe the methodology of a particular director on a specific low budget picture. I won't name him or the picture simply because I am pitting his technique against those which are about to be recommended. More important, I don't want to break a confidence.

This fellow was a bright, good-natured, seasoned part-time director—a medical doctor by profession—who had shifted from stern drama to a lighter, slightly comical type of work. It was my perception that he was "covering his tail" so to speak by shooting full front with a 50mm lens to a good take. Then move three quarters to the right, 50mm lens to a good take. Then to profile to the right, 50mm lens to a good take and continuing until he had shot full circle. Then he would repeat the whole thing with a 25mm lens, then a 75mm. Following that, he would repeat the scene doing reaction shots for each of the talent, going through the whole sequence again.

The producer later confirmed my suspicion confidentially. The producer felt encumbered by a myriad of useless good takes and, like the talent and crew, became frustrated with the monotony. There were plenty of good takes, but what a waste!

On standard or high budget pictures, most directors will move to the next scene only when he has two good takes of a given scene number. Furthermore, he may do so only when he has two good takes of several different interpretations of the actors' work. Having plenty of time and money to doodle with, this is a valid method and not much different from the one described above. On a two-million dollar low budget, time spent in repetition is a great deal more costly than the film, processing, and work print. On a budget of a few hundred thousand or less, not only the time, but also the film, processing, and work print involved with repetition can take a more notable percentage out of the coffer.

For example, if you do a page and a half of dialogue and maneuvers in a single take then move in for a half dozen reaction shots, you might pull it off with one or two hours of rehearsal while lights are being set up. This assumes that your talent come in already having memorized their lines and understanding the motivation of their parts. The camera follows through its blocking as the logic of the rehearsal develops.

If the director has given a great deal of thought to a scene beforehand, he may come in with the ideal moves on a loosely drawn storyboard. Going through the scene with the talent, blocking both them and the camera from move to move, this team effort will require the above mentioned hour or two of rehearsal and blocking, then be photographed in real time—perhaps a three-minute take plus another pair of three-minute run-throughs for reaction shots and inserts.

Using this contemporary technique—shooting several

lines of dialogue, first wide, then close up, and ultimately the reaction shots; moving on to the next set of dialogue shooting wide, then close, and the reaction shots—can offer assurance in getting good takes fairly quickly from low or unskilled talent and crew. However those dollars saved by few takes may be greatly offset by spending the extra time required to do it a piece at a time.

The simpler, piecemeal approach may be more adeptly handled by practiced professionals than by the inexperienced. That is, those who have less experience in this method of acting have a greater opportunity to damage continuity from shot to shot. The problem may be so subtle that it will not be noticed until the editor has it on the bench and is pulling out his or her hair.

A case in point is the murder by Pat Patterson (the mad doctor in *Body Shop*). He killed his victim on the operating table by stabbing at her with a scalpel in his right hand in the wide shot and making impact with the scalpel in his left hand in the close up. The error went undetected until it was being edited. The editor was unable to use either shot in its entirety. Fortunately he found the only frame in each of the two shots where an apparent match could be made and repaired the faux pas. (Not all the blame goes to Patterson. Every picture has one or two such problems.)

Novice talent frequently misunderstand the purpose of the director's command "Let's see that one more time," or "Let's do it again from the top."

The director is saying, "I want to see it again exactly the way you did it to confirm what I already think."

The rookie talent is hearing, "I didn't like what you did. Do it again but do it differently."

It is imperative that newcomers understand that if the director wants to see it differently they will be told what didn't work and what improvements are desired. In the absence of such direction, exactly the same action, dialogue, expression, timing, and blocking is wanted for 50 consecutive repeats, if necessary.

The director ought not to be considered a fool on this basis. This course is being taken because there's a problem. If you discovered this course is taken because the director is a jerk—and many are—then you are welcome to consider the director to be a fool.

You'll most likely find that the great majority of directors have long since discovered you can catch more flies with honey than you can with vinegar.

They also understand that if you (as talent) have to do the same thing 50 consecutive times without a change there is a problem that needs to be discussed. After only a dozen or so tries it makes the most sense to stop, do something else, and come back to it for sanity's sake, since it will just get worse, not better. This applies to crew as well.

It's important to understand that continuity is the director's responsibility with reasonable prompting from the script and continuity clerk. Maintaining continuity is possibly the single toughest job the director has. If either of them is being fooled by traces of variation then continuity is doomed.

On the following pages you'll find a short piece from a fictitious script, one made up just for you and me to play with. First, read it through and make notes on how you would direct it in order to get the most out of it from a budgetary standpoint. Then you and I, together, can direct it twice, once by each of the above mentioned techniques, giving you the opportunity to see the merits of both.

Backstreets

by
Tweedle Dee and Tweedle Dum

The characters in order of appearance:

DETECTIVE FRANK CORN is a tough, bright, reasonable cop from Florida.

CAPTAIN PHIL COB is his boss. Also tough, perhaps a little more street savvy, educated, a nice guy.

SILKY, a lithe, sexy redhead is the dispatcher. Needs no character development.

114. INT.—Day, FRANK CORN's office

It is early morning when FRANK CORN and PHIL COBB enter the office together. They both are obviously tired and cold.

          FRANK (shivering)
I'd give my sanity to get back to Miami.
          PHIL
Seems to me you gave it up to come to New York.
          FRANK
You're probably right. Of all the things I've ever lost, I guess I miss my mind the least—the calories I lost coming up those damn stairs is what I miss the most.
          (Now serious)
You know, I sure thought last night was going to be productive. It just doesn't make sense that our happy little killer didn't hit last night after the pattern was set up.
          PHIL
Do you suppose he established that pattern just to set us up?
          FRANK
It's a possibility I hadn't considered. Why would he care? It should be obvious to him from the newspaper insults that we're not making any headway.
          PHIL
I don't necessarily agree. What if he had access to some inside information? He'd know what alleys we were watching. That would keep him from those particular ones or keep him from operating altogether.

54 Advice for the Director

> FRANK
> Yeah, well, great! All we've got to do is have 14 cops tied up every night forever just to keep a nut from killing indigents and putting their shoes in mailboxes. You know what I think? I think he's not a nut at all. I think he's putting their shoes in the mailboxes so we'll believe he's a kook and go off to the far corners of our fair city looking for somebody who doesn't have good sense. I think he's as sane as you or I and that he's got access to information that we wouldn't want him to have.
>
> PHIL
> You can't be serious, FRANK. He's probably...
>
> SILKY (entering and interrupting)
> I've got the news you've been dying to hear, boys and girls.
>
> FRANK
> Break it to us soft and gently, sweetheart. Our feet are tired and our buns are cold.
>
> SILKY (holding up a pair of old shoes)
> Need I say more?
>
> PHIL
> They find a body?
>
> SILKY
> In the Village. Want to hear the punch line?
>
> FRANK
> Make it a good one.
>
> SILKY
> The dead man had his hand stuffed in his coat pocket. It had a badge in it still pinned to some blue cloth.
>
> -FIN-

There you have it. How much of a mental picture did you get while reading it? Could you bring FRANK, PHIL, and SILKY into that office and direct them and the camera crew into a scene which would entertain the audience but also inform them? Remember, it's necessary to keep the scene visually interesting. If you don't, the viewer's mind will pick up on some pointless detail and ponder it while missing all the ensuing dialogue.

Consider doing the scene for radio. Would you need to explain anything other than what is heard in the dialogue? Probably not. The sound effects of stomping snow off shoes as they slam the office door, a file drawer opening and closing, the sipping of coffee, and striking of a match might well be all the information a listener might need to establish a mental picture.

In any case, we are not directing radio but the same psychology will perform the same mental miracles.

Let's look at the script again but this time we'll write notes to follow while directing.

EXAMPLE 1

114. Int.—Day, FRANK CORN's office.

It is early morning when FRANK CORN and PHIL COBB enter the office together. They both are obviously tired and cold.

CAMERA is on a MS of the half-glass door as they enter together in single file, FRANK first. He is removing his hat as he enters the room and nonchalantly tosses his hat over the CAMERA as he disappears CAMERA left. PHIL has his hat in his hand. He carefully places it on the file cabinet (CAMERA right) as he comes through the door. PHIL stops at the door pushing it shut behind him. He is holding a cup of coffee.

CUT TO:

Wide TWO-SHOT. Screen right, PHIL is leaning on the file cabinet. Screen left, FRANK is just passing the hat rack where his hat is still swinging from the successful toss. He opens the file drawer and pulls out a pack of cigarettes and matches.

> FRANK (shivering)
> I'd give up my sanity to get back to Miami.

He strikes a match and lights cigarette. PHIL puts down his coffee and takes off his overcoat while talking.

> PHIL
> Seems to me you gave it up to come to New York.

CU of FRANK throwing his match into the trash can and puffing on his cigarette as he takes off his coat.

> FRANK
> You're probably right. Of all the things I've ever lost, I guess I miss my mind the least—the calories I lost coming up those damn stairs is what I miss the most.

[insert] Shot of small flame flaring in trash can, then dying.

> Frank (continuing, now serious)
> You know, I sure thought last night was going to be productive. It just doesn't make sense that our happy little killer didn't hit last night after the pattern he set up.

He takes a puff.

CUT TO:

PHIL, hanging up his coat on the same rack that FRANK's hat is on.

> PHIL
> Do you suppose he established that pattern just to set us up?

He crosses his arms and stands back on his heels as if he plans to stay a while.

CUT TO:

FRANK, cigarette in his mouth, still holding his coat.

> FRANK
> It's a possibility I hadn't considered. Why would he care? It should be obvious to him from the

newspaper insults that we're not making any headway.

FRANK sits on the corner of his desk.

CUT TO:

PHIL, same as his last shot.

PHIL
I don't necessarily agree. What if he had access to some inside information?
  (Shaking his pointing finger)
He'd know what alleys we were watching. That would keep him from those particular ones or keep him from operating altogether.

CUT TO:

TWO-SHOT. FRANK twists to his right to reach an ash tray, flicks his ashes.

FRANK
Yeah, well, great! All we've got to do is have fourteen cops tied up every night forever just to keep a nut from killing indigents and putting their shoes in mailboxes.

CUT TO:

CU of FRANK, shaking his finger back at PHIL.

FRANK (continuing)
You know what I think? I think he's not a nut at all. I think he's putting their shoes in the mailboxes so we'll believe he's a kook and go off to the far corners of our fair city looking for somebody who doesn't have good sense. I think he's as sane as you or I and that he's got access to information that we wouldn't want him to have.

CUT BACK TO:

PHIL reacting before FRANK finishes talking.

PHIL
You can't be serious, FRANK. He's probably...

CUT TO:

MS of SILKY as she enters

SILKY (entering and interrupting)
I've got the news you've been dying to hear, boys and girls.

CUT TO:

CU of FRANK

FRANK
Break it to us soft and gently, sweetheart. Our feet are tired and our buns are cold.

CUT TO:

MS of SILKY—quick zoom in on the shoes

SILKY (holding up a pair of old shoes)
Need I say more?

CUT TO:

CU of PHIL

PHIL
They find a body?

CUT TO:

CU of SILKY

SILKY
In the Village. Want to hear the punch line?

CUT TO:

CU of FRANK

FRANK
Make it a funny one.

CUT TO A THREE-SHOT:

SILKY
The dead man had his hand stuffed in his coat pocket. It had a badge in it still pinned to a patch of blue cloth.

BOTH MEN put on their hats and coats. FRANK drops his cigarette into PHIL's coffee. PHIL reacts as they all walk out the door and close it behind them. CAMERA stays on them through the glass as they walk away.

-FIN-

What we just shot was the dialogue takes of the entire sequence. We might have shot each several times in order to get a take acceptable to the director.

Most likely, we would have shot all of the two-shots first, all of FRANK's business second, all of PHIL's, then SILKY's. This would require fewer camera and lighting set-ups than doing them in sequence.

Next we would redo the entire piece shooting a close up and, in some cases, a medium shot of the listener instead of the speaker. These are called reaction shots and become a tool for the editor to give a substantial amount of latitude which may or may not be required. Of course, using them can very well enhance the psychology and the timing of the scene even if they are not needed for a mechanical bail-out (which we'll talk about later).

Scripts are difficult to read no matter who you are or how many you have read. However, surely you got a more detailed mental image from the second reading than the first. You can see how the director's instructions to the talent to do these certain things will impress upon them not only the need to do them but to do each on cue.

Frank's staring at the burning trash can was not mentioned. But he'll do it and there is only one place in the entire script that it would be the natural thing to do.

His turning to put away his ashes, being noted, now becomes part of the business. It will all work except, invariably, some tiny detail which will be discovered inoperable during rehearsal. That's one of the purposes of dry runs.

Let's shoot the whole thing again, but this time we'll do the entire script in a single take. You first will want to

56 Advice for the Director

briefly study the drawing of the set to see how it is designed and where the dolly moves take the camera.

Example 2

114. INT.—Day, FRANK CORN's office

It is early morning when FRANK CORN and PHIL COBB enter the office together. They both are obviously tired and cold.

*CAMERA (sitting in position **A** is on a MS of the half-glass door as they enter together in single file, FRANK first. He is removing his hat as he enters the room and nonchalantly tosses his hat over the CAMERA as he disappears CAMERA left. As CAMERA dollies back to position **B**, PHIL, with hat in hand, enters close behind FRANK and carefully places it on the file cabinet (CAMERA right) as he comes through the door. FRANK continues to other file cabinet (CAMERA left) and opens the drawer. PHIL stops at the door, pushing it shut behind him. He is holding a cup of coffee which he sips and puts on the file cabinet. As FRANK opens the file drawer (CAMERA left), he pulls out a pack of cigarettes and matches.*

FRANK (shivering)
I'd give up my sanity to get back to Miami.

*He strikes a match and lights cigarette as CAMERA dollies to a MS then to position **C** including PHIL in an over-the-shoulder shot as FRANK sits down on the corner of his desk.*

PHIL
Puts down his coffee beside his hat and takes off his overcoat while talking.
Seems to me you gave it up to come to New York.

As FRANK (facing CAMERA, his back to PHIL) drops his match into the trash can, he takes a puff on his cigarette, then takes off his coat and watches the smoke rise. Zoom in tight as he speaks.

FRANK
You're probably right. Of all the things I've ever lost, I guess I miss my mind the least—the calories I lost coming up those damn stairs is what I miss the most.

(Becoming serious, he hands his coat to PHIL who hangs it up beside his own.)

FRANK
You know, I sure thought last night was going to be productive. It just doesn't make sense that our happy little killer didn't hit last night after the pattern he set up.

He takes a puff.

PHIL
Do you suppose he established that pattern just to set us up?

*As PHIL crosses his arms and stands back on his heels as if he plans to stay a while, CAMERA dollies back to **B**.*

FRANK
It's a possibility I hadn't considered. Why would he care? It should be obvious to him from the newspaper insults that we're not making any headway.

*FRANK still on the corner of his desk, CAMERA dollies to **D** and drops below FRANK's eye level, composing them in a tight TWO-SHOT.*

PHIL (shaking his pointing finger)
I don't necessarily agree. What if he had access to some inside information? He'd know what alleys we were watching. That would keep him from those particular ones or keep him from operating altogether.

Zoom back as FRANK twists to his right to reach an ash tray, flicks his ashes. His face is to the camera as he flicks and speaks.

FRANK
Yeah, well, great! All we've got to do is have 14 cops tied up every night forever just to keep a nut from killing indigents and putting their shoes in mailboxes.

*Zoom to CU of FRANK, shaking his finger back at PHIL as CAMERA dollies back to **B**, still fairly tight on FRANK, but slowly zooming wider.*

FRANK (continuing)
You know what I think? I think he's not a nut at all. I think he's putting their shoes in the mailboxes so we'll believe he's a kook and go off to the far corners of our fair city looking for somebody who doesn't have good sense. I think he's as sane as you or I and that he's got access to information that we wouldn't want him to have.

Recompose to PHIL reacting before FRANK finishes talking.

PHIL
You can't be serious, FRANK. He's probably...

Off CAMERA we hear the door open. FRANK turns in reaction, pans and zooms wide to include SILKY and PHIL, then tightens on SILKY.

SILKY (interrupting)
I've got the news you've been dying to hear, boys and girls.

Zoom and pan to CU of FRANK.

FRANK
Break it to us soft and gently, sweetheart. Our feet are tired and our buns are cold.

Dolly and zoom back to a wide shot.

SILKY (holding up a pair of old shoes)
Need I say more?

PHIL
They find a body?

SILKY
In the Village. Want to hear the punch line?

Advice for the Director 57

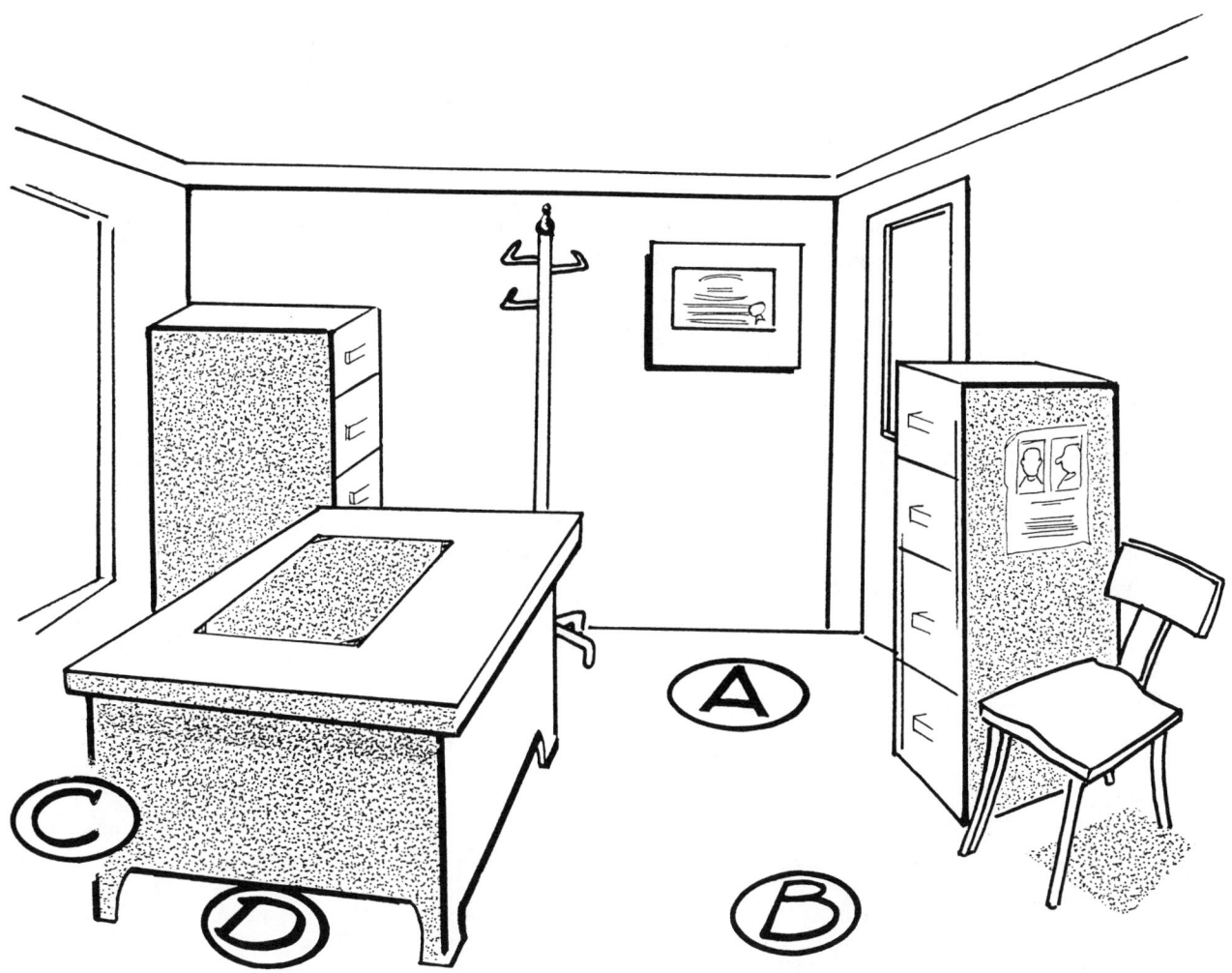

The set.

FRANK
Make it a funny one.

SILKY
The dead man had his hand stuffed in his coat pocket. It had a badge in it still pinned to a patch of blue cloth.

SILKY tosses the shoes on the floor near the hat rack. BOTH MEN put on their hats and coats. FRANK drops his cigarette into PHIL's coffee. PHIL reacts as all three walk out the door and close it behind them. CAMERA slowly zooms to the shoes. We hear small talk through the glass as they walk away.

-FIN-

Now, having shot this entire sequence in one take, we are going to play a little game of pretend. Because of something that is said in an earlier scene it will be necessary to remove the dialogue:

FRANK (continuing)
You know what I think? I think he's not a nut at all.

How can that be done if the scene is shot as a single piece? It can't. After shooting it as a continuous shot you then go back and shoot the same reaction shots you would have done for the first example. Here is the one you would use:

CUT TO

CU PHIL reacting while FRANK is talking. Hold this shot just long enough to delete the two sentences.

Then, cut back to the master shot.
This little bit of corrective surgery takes place just before the dialogue:

PHIL
You can't be serious, FRANK. He's probably . . .

In doing this second example, any one of the actors might have bungled his lines, missed his mark, or made any of many errors. The dolly grip or camera operator also might have goofed. If such errors are few and minor,

58 Advice for the Director

the director may have them regress one sentence and continue. By cutting to a reaction shot, the editor can excise the bad footage and use the overall scene as a good take.

To enhance it still further, the director may have shot it employing both methods although he probably would have executed our second one first.

Understand also that the lighting for the second one will have to be more skillfully accomplished because that single set up has to look good for the duration of the shot. It will take substantially more time to get the shot ready—but only once. And that time can be used to rehearse.

Having filmed both techniques, then shot MOS reactions, the editor can use the continuous shot for the primary scene repairing or enhancing it. This can be accomplished if necessary, by cutting either to dialogue inserts (from example 1) or the MOS reactions that would be the same from either example.

7
Visual Effects

Traveling Mattes and Miniatures

The making of traveling mattes really seems to have no place in a book on budget cutting. But a matte shot will invariably either cost less than the real thing or will be possible when the real thing is not. Since you may require the use of one or more inexpensive versions of mattes or substitutes, and are willing to take a crack at doing so yourself, the subject does deserve to be addressed.

One of many types of opticals, traveling mattes are made exclusively in 35mm and larger formats. Making and using traveling mattes is an expensive proposition and seldom finds its way into cheap movies. Even so, it's not out of the question.

While it's possible—even feasible—to make traveling mattes in 16mm, optical houses refrain from doing so. But there is hope!

If you are producing and have a shot which simply has to be done with a traveling matte, consider this possibility. Beg, borrow, or steal a 35mm camera, perhaps an Eyemo. Thread the camera with the 35mm version of the film stock you are using. Shoot both the principal shot and the background plate using the appropriate techniques we'll discuss later.

Assuming you have the matting method under control, have the lab reduce the 35mm original with matte to a 16mm CRI dupe negative in one pass which will allow you to do the process in a single generation. (The lab you use may make an IP and a dupe neg, two generations.) Using 35mm original upholds sharpness to a maximum, as does the one step generation. Be sure the service is available from your lab before you invest your time and money. The alternative method would be to use VNF in the 35mm camera and make a 16mm reduction internegative—still one step. You must check with your lab to find out if they process 35mm VNF. Most labs don't. They'll probably be able to recommend one which does or have it done for you.

Since any respectable lab will inform you that you've lost your mind when considering an Eyemo or other 35mm camera without registration pins, simply don't tell them your plan. It won't improve your work but it'll avoid an argument that leads nowhere.

You'll simply have to take a chance on whether the camera offers a steady enough image for matte work. It'll either do or it won't, and a steadiness test short of actually doing a matte probably will not tell you anything you haven't already guessed. The bipacking and printing of the boy and then the female matte onto the print stock in one pass, then doing likewise on the same print stock with background and the male matte on the next pass, will render a composite image of the boy standing by the train (see the following pages).

The train used for the shots on the following pages.

The making of a custom traveling matte is tricky, precise, and time consuming. Those traveling mattes which are used on very low budget pictures probably will be simply moving split screens, wipes, and other generic effects that require movement but don't have to follow the finite contours of the subject.

To understand precisely the pros and cons of that statement look at the illustration of the train in the background

Traveling Mattes and Miniatures 61

Opposite, top: The boy in front of a matte screen. *Opposite, center:* Hold back matte. *Opposite, bottom:* The background plate. *Above, top:* The counter matte. *Above, bottom:* The composite.

62 Visual Effects

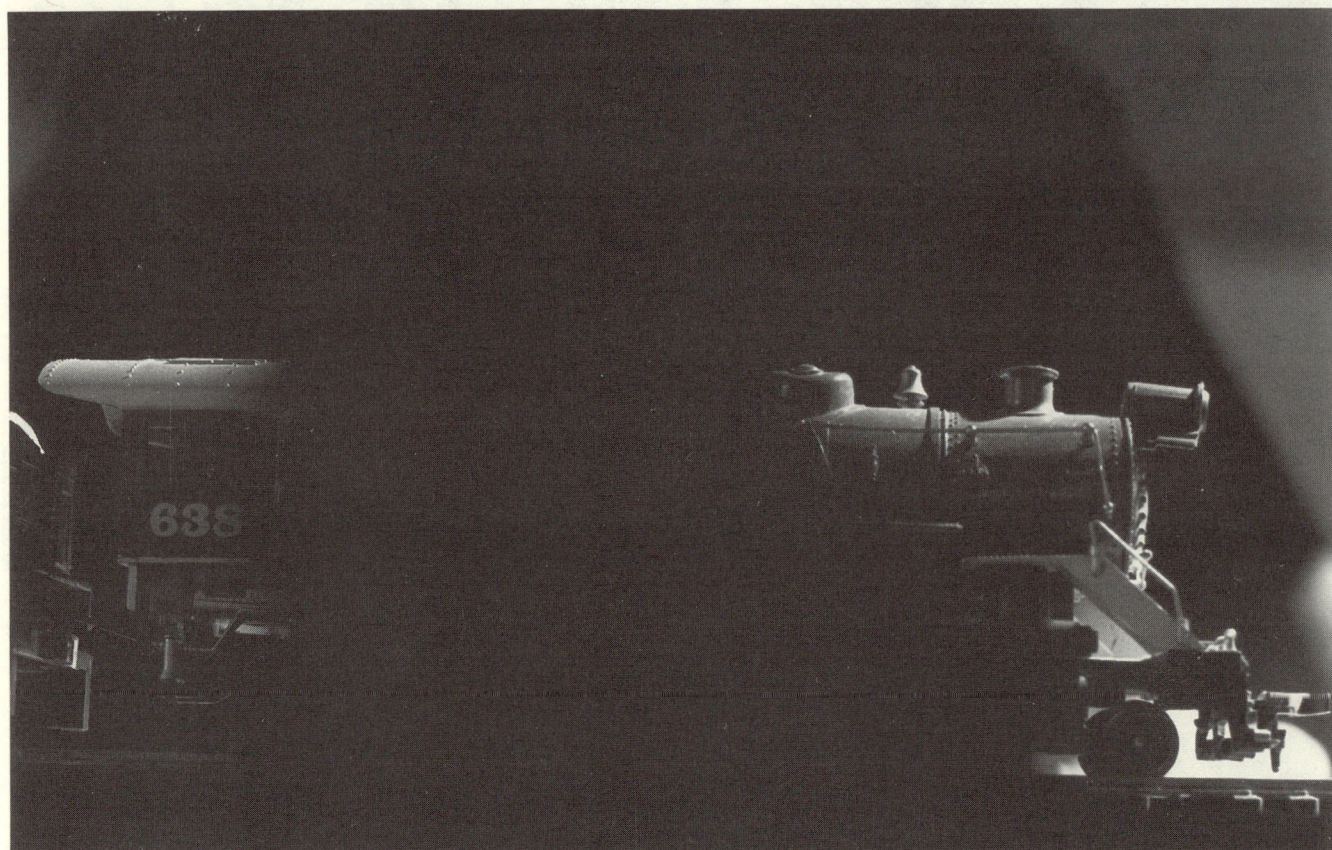

Above, top: **The kids in black limbo.** *Above, bottom:* **The train, lit for effect.** *Opposite:* **The composite.**

Traveling Mattes and Miniatures 63

while the boy stands on the platform, moving around in the foreground.

The only thing that makes this expensive is original 35mm photography of the boy in front of a background that offers the capability of making a matte by photographic means (usually a blue screen of specific color value and brightness) and of having the lab actually execute the six or more stages of matte making and printing them, often over and over until they are acceptable.

While no other technique will replace the fine, moving edge of such traveling mattes, there are some less expensive options which may be acceptable substitutes. You may have to redesign those shots before shooting them though by recomposition, different lighting, or both.

Of course, shooting the kids in front of a real train would simply be a matter of setting up at the station platform both at great dollar expense and time consumption.

The shot above could be rewritten as a nighttime shot. By keeping the kids in "black limbo" they can easily be inserted in a black area of the background image, either the broadside of the train or the darkness of night.

The train and part of the ramp being models, you can get the same effect by lighting both train and kids as described and, if necessary, slowly moving the model as it approaches or departs.

Both the kids and the train are shot on reversal film. Because the kids are standing in black limbo, and because the train is lit so that it is black or unlit where the kids are seen, then both shots are self matting. Accordingly, the two shots can be double-printed onto internegative or print stock in one step to render the composite without the need of a matte.

Knowing that only one step occurs between the camera original stock and the double printed master, it would pay you to shoot through a mirror to reverse the camera image since a single printing pass will reverse it again.

If principal photography is done as a negative then doing this piece of matte photography on reversal film and shooting through a 45 degree mirror will laterally reverse (flop) the image so that making a contact print onto an internegative stock will leave the emulsion in camera (B wind) position, offering the advantage of cutting correctly into the original negative and of being a one generation dupe. VNF is probably the best choice of reversal stock since it can be bought in several ISO speeds, exhibits a generally flat image suitable for duplication, and is available in S/8, 16 and 35mm.

What makes all this work is that reversal film is self matting in black areas, either in the printing stage or in the camera.

64 Visual Effects

For double exposure in the camera, black areas are self matting *no matter what film is used.*

Being quite careful to count frames in the camera so that the film can be back-cranked to the starting point, after exposing the kids, you can expose the train (or vice versa). All elements appear on the original film with no monkey business required at the lab. This approach was once Disney's favorite, but it does require great care since getting a single take wrong also destroys its counterpart.

The technique was used in *Marley's Revenge*. On the HJ Reflex box, a short roll of negative was shot of the moon and a starlit sky. This was actually a photographic film positive of the moon stripped onto a black piece of litho film with pin holes for stars. The same film was re-wound and taken to the beach where it was again used to shoot the surf day-for-night. The result was the moon and stars over the surf at night.

The same effect can be achieved by the printer using negative camera stock, but interpositives must first be made from the original negatives. Since this adds one printing pass (for a total of three), you wouldn't shoot through the 45 degree mirror. (You would shoot through a mirror only when you have an even number of passes and are making the "optical" by contact printing.)

These separate interpositives are double printed (as was our reversal stock) to a single dupe negative where the composite image appears for the first time. The main disadvantage here is that it adds a generation of degradation and you pay no more to the lab for doing more printer passes. Still, you'll have spent a lot less than a traveling matte would have cost.

Negative film is self-matting in white areas, but only if you intend to print A and B negatives to the interpositive or CRI. White matting (which can't be done in the camera) is less often successful, or at least more troublesome, than its counterpart but still worth an experiment or two.

By using the latter lighting approach the above can be done in video if the editorial system has a split-screen capacity.

The Schufftan Shot

Perhaps doing a Schufftan shot would be convenient. Schufftan shots are done in any one of several ways using carefully cut mirrors, partial mirrors, beam-splitting mirrors, painted mirrors, and mirrors from which portions of the silver have been removed. The chief advantage is to accomplish what we've already described, but in a way that the cameraman can see the resulting composite while it is being photographed in a single shot.

The basic set-up is the same as for the shots made individually except that both shots can be made simultaneously because of the mirror.

The lighting would be identical to those self-matting shots we've discussed as would the result.

Top: A Schufftan box setup. *Bottom:* The result.

Imagine a tree-lined street, perhaps a little moving traffic and a spaceship flying past overhead while a couple moves around in the foreground.

While looking through the finder, you or a helper would paint out the street area and trees (leaving spots of clear in the trees through which to see the passing spaceship).

The saucer will appear through the trees, then above them, as it flies by. How you fly the model of the saucer will be left up to your own ingenuity. (Using a video camera and monitor may be helpful in painting the glass. Once done, remove the video camera and replace it with the film camera—unless, of course you're shooting video.)

Straight edge division can be accomplished with a mirror cut to suit. For example, removing the two-way mirror from the box and replacing it with a thin glass of the same size upon which is glued a small, carefully cut mirror of appropriate dimensions, you could get a "doll's eye view" of a little girl peeping through a window. (Both epoxy glue and silicone caulk do an excellent job of gluing glass.)

If you can satisfy the depth of field problem, the illustration can be a real room or simply a dollhouse, making the little girl appear as a giant or the people in the room to be Lilliputian. See the original King Kong.

THREE WAYS TO MAKE A TRAVELING MATTE

METHOD NUMBER 1

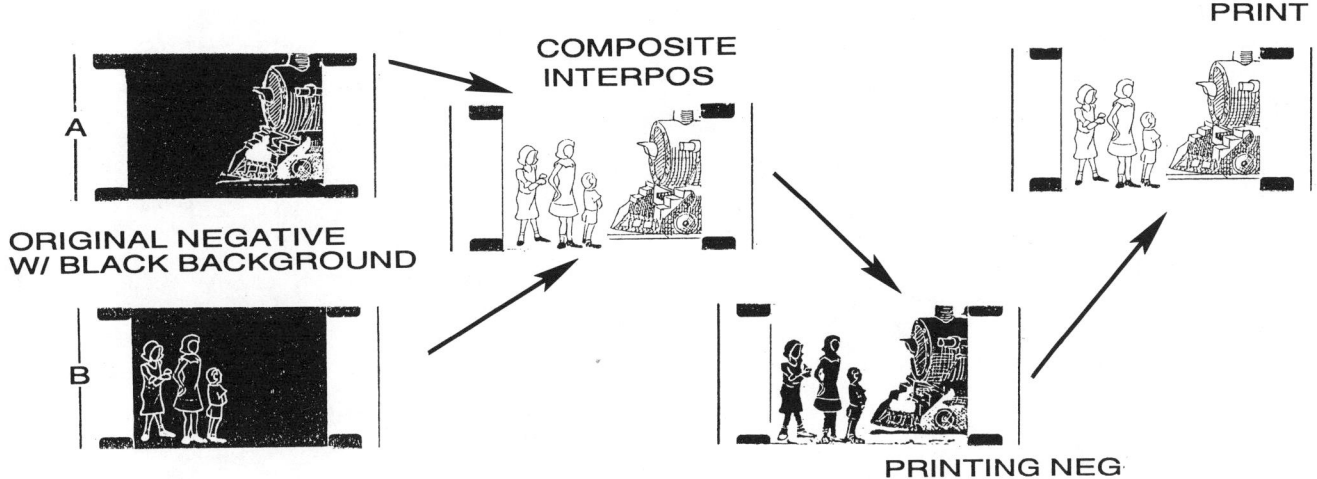

METHOD NUMBER 2

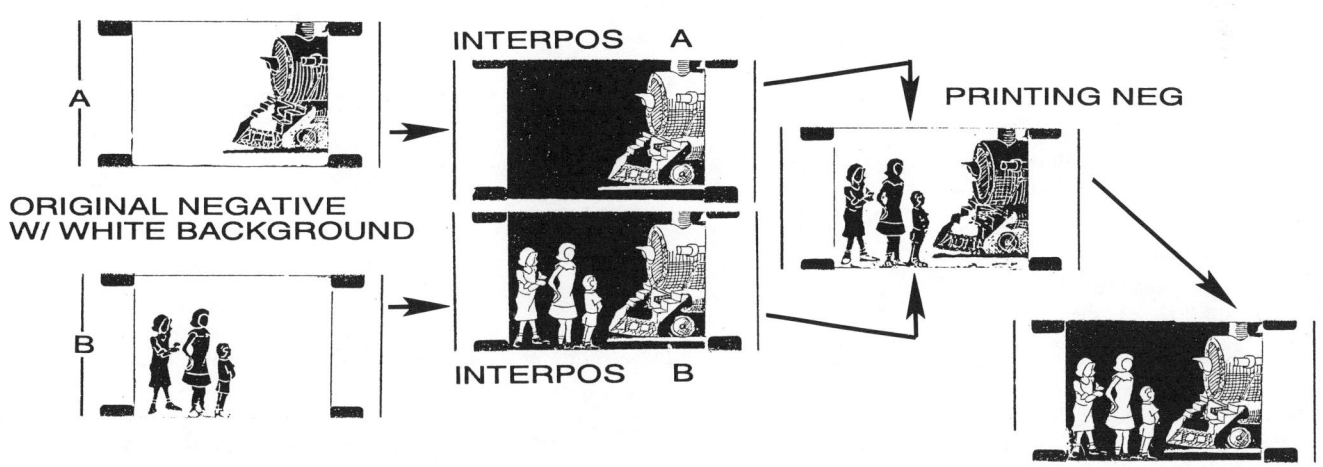

METHOD NUMBER 3

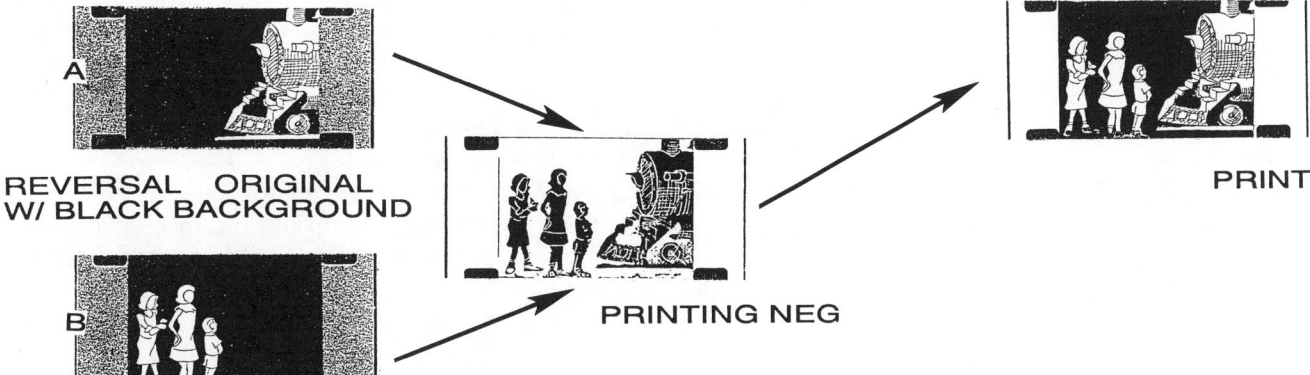

66 Visual Effects

Rotoscoping

Rotoscoping is a technique in which you draw your matte on white paper and photograph it, as if it were artwork, while your developed camera original is in the camera, bipacked together with duplicating stock.

To do so, you must have a camera so designed that a light can be placed behind the gate temporarily, enabling you to project the original image as a single frame and using the camera as a slide projector.

For example, a shot in which you have a house that you want to replace the sky, would be projected onto white paper. The roof line and chimney would be carefully tracked twice, once on each of two separate pieces of paper. On the one sheet, the sky would be painted black leaving the rest white. The other is painted the reverse and used as a counter matte.

Threading the camera using the original developed film bipacked together with duplicating stock. Photograph the first paper matte—with the black sky—and you will have actually printed the house onto the dupe stock, leaving the sky area unprinted. Rewinding the print stock and replacing the original film with, say, a picture of a volcano, and reshooting using the counter matte, will result in a picture of the house with a volcano behind it when processed.

Unlimited motion can take place on either or both

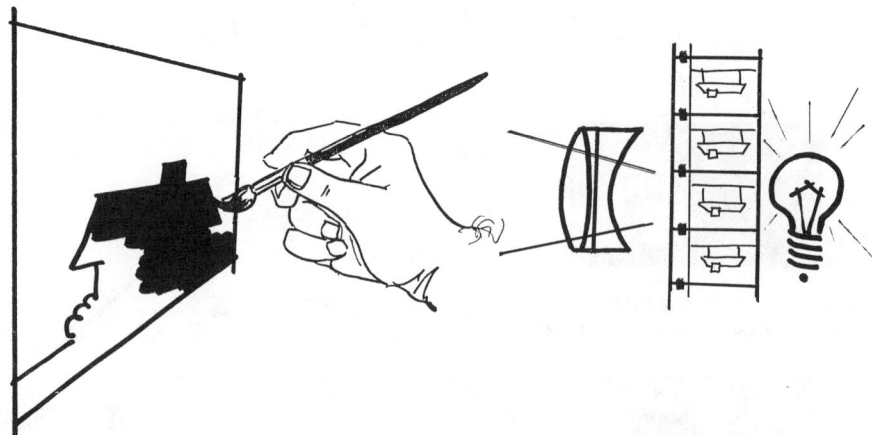

The background must be painted black.

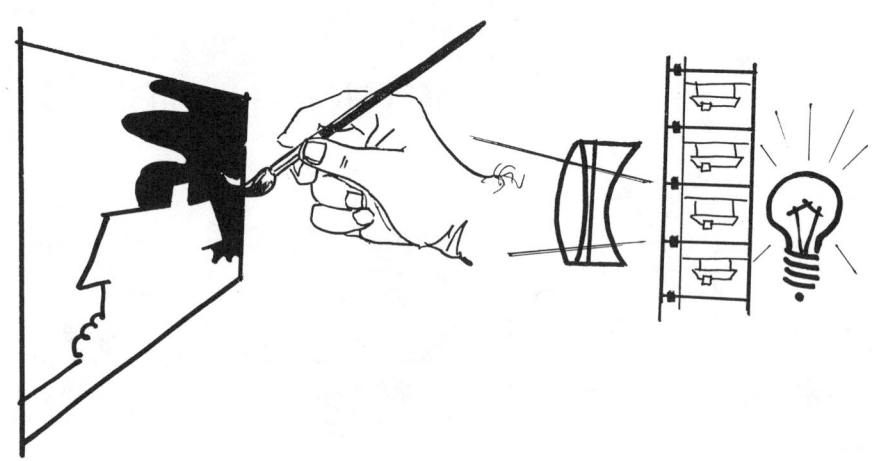

On a separate sheet, the foreground must be painted black. The film is developed film of the house.

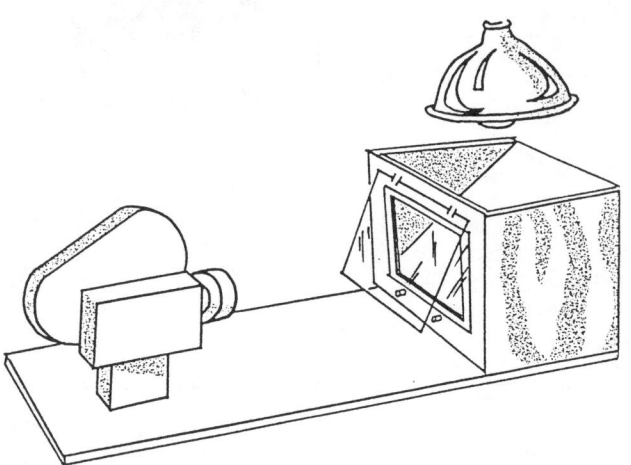

sides of the matte line as long as the matte line itself is not breached. The paper must be register punched so that each time you remove it and replace it, it will be in exactly the same position. Furthermore, the camera must be mounted in a fixed position from the time tracing begins until the job is completed.

You can buy a register punch and pins for $200 to $300 through a dealer. Or from a printer's supply house you can buy the pins for around two dollars each and pay ten dollars for a two-hole punch at the office supply house. They do the same job.

If you aren't handy making things, ask someone who is to build the following doodad and camera mount. (We'll call the doodad the HJ Reflex box for lack of a descriptive name.)

It is simply a box (my first one was cardboard) with a sheet of white paper at 45 degrees behind a glass-covered hole. The white paper evenly distributes the light through the glass.

Once this device is built, establishing exact location of your frame parameters is no problem with a reflex

Rotoscoping 67

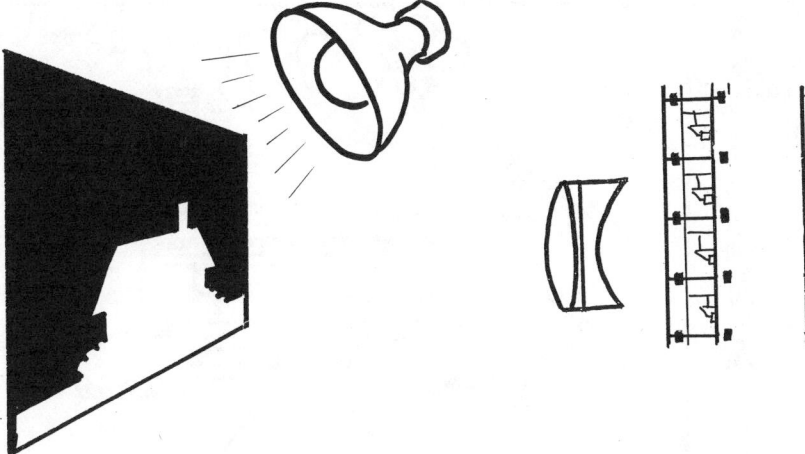

Note that the house is black. The film is raw stock of the volcano.

Note that the house is white. The film is of the house.

camera. If yours is not reflex, you'll have to determine where your frame parameters are by photographing a comprehensively numbered grid.

Taking into account that internegative/interpositive stock is rated at about ISO 2, as are most intermediate and print stocks, it takes a lot of light to get a proper exposure. Instead of front lighting your paper mattes, it may be prudent to have a precision, register-punched same-size litho negative and positive made from your single paper drawing and backlight them for greater intensity.

Even though you may not be able to rotoscope, there is a limitless number of matte and printing effects you can do with this device. Let your imagination be your guide.

Marley's Revenge called for a sequence in which a flare gun is fired, narrowly missing the main character and the monster. The flare bounces off a tree and returns to its source. A second character ducks, allowing the flare to hit a bell on the bow of the boat. It rebounds back and hits the windshield, boomerangs and hits the bell again, ricochets forward and strikes the paddle which the character is holding, causing the flare to bounce into the mouth of the monster who swallows it and sinks into the water, mouth smoking.

We filmed the sequence using flares made for 12 gauge shotguns. (As it turns out, the flares are high-powered, directionally inaccurate and therefore dangerous. If you use something like this, experiment before the fact and be careful. Roman candles might have been a better bet.)

We would cheat the position of the characters by several feet, but the flares didn't ignite until they were some 20 feet outside the muzzle of the gun. The shooter had to back up and much care was taken for safety sake.

Although much slower than bullets, the flares were still quite fast. We weren't sure whether a flare would actually be photographed during a fly-by or whether the shutter would be closed for that brief period. As a safety measure, we did a number of good takes for each shot.

Of all the shots we made, two outtakes had good flares. The others either had weak flares or none at all. We edited the work print as if the flares were apparent.

The sparks emanating from the wheels of the mine cart in Steven Spielberg's *Temple of Doom* were animated and inserted as an optical effect. We decided that if animation is good enough for him it's good enough for us.

We brought up the appropriate flare shots on the screen of the editing table. Dividing the screen into quadrants with a China marker, we positioned the fly-by or impact of each flare one at a time. Not a single one had to be positioned in an exact place. For example, the bell took up about a fifth of the screen from left to right and about a third of the screen from top to bottom. It was satisfactory for the flare to hit any part of the bell and still work.

By making such divisions, each fly-by was drawn as a ragged, black line with a comet-like head. The first exposure showed less than a third of a frame while the second extended the fire line by at least two thirds, giving it the illusion of movement.

The impact frames showed the position of the flare shortly after impact, but a splatter of sparks emanating from the contact point. Each splatter was comprised of three frames.

All this art was photographed onto litho negatives

68 Visual Effects

Projected frame of the house for effect shown on previous pages.

The resulting composite of the effect on the previous pages.

which were weakly colored with red and yellow markers. Putting them on the HJ Reflex box, we counted frames to the appropriately calculated points and photographed each cell on VNF which would render a positive image. When photographing the flare traces, we put frosted acetate over the head of the flare to give it a slurred or fuzzy look.

We had the lab cut the negative of the flare sequence to match the edited work print and make an interpositive. The interpositive and VNF were double printed together to render a composite negative—effectively an optical. The illusion, which required little precision, was visually perfect when printed.

The Camera as Printer

If for whatever reason, you simply need to print (A) a negative to an interpositive, (B) a positive or an interpositive to a dupe negative, (C) a negative to a print, or (D) a reversal original to a reversal print, you can use the HJ Reflex box with your camera to do so.

The camera is threaded with the original film together with the duplicating stock. The HJ Reflex box becomes the light source, and simply running the camera prints the shot. In this case, your camera is being used as a step contact printer.

Getting a proper exposure is achieved by experimentation and having your lab make an evaluation of each take. A good starting point for doing so would be to set your meter for ISO 2 (assuming you're using a lab stock) and taking an "incident" reading by putting the meter right at the glass on the HJ Reflex box. If you are duplicating onto a regular camera stock, you would set your meter on the film's normal tungsten ISO and reading by the same method. You'll want to repeat the operation several times bracketing f/stops and making notes.

Doing this sort of work is time consuming and a little delicate to do well, but it can save a ton of money while the accomplishment can be quite rewarding.

Even when done by your lab or optical house, fixed mattes are used frequently in 16mm and larger formats and are neither expensive nor difficult. Carefully planned and skillfully handled, a fixed matte may do at little expense what a traveling matte would have done at a much greater cost. Even with a fixed matte, you may want to use VNF in either 16 or 35mm in order to get from original to dupe negative in a single step.

Glass Shots

Since we've already breached the subject of mattes, let's consider one of the simplest-to-use types, the glass shot. In case you don't know what a glass shot is, it is a piece of glass in front of the camera upon which is painted a portion of the set or subject. That portion doesn't have to exist in real life because while photography of the set is taking place, the painting is being photographed in exactly the right position to fill in what's missing.

The advantage of such a glass shot is an enormous savings of cash. The disadvantages basically are two: very limited camera movement and talent cannot appear in front of the matted portion of the glass.

Typically, glass mattes are painted on the set or location where the shot will actually be filmed in order that the artist has a constant opportunity to check the blending of the art to the real thing. Artists paint these mattes because they are fine art in the truest sense.

Judicious choices can eliminate the need of an artist. In one cheapie, a silhouette was cut out and pasted on a glass. The glass and the camera were taken to the nearest beach where both were properly positioned at the seaside and the shot was made offering the illusion that

Glass Shots 69

Creating sparks at the light table.

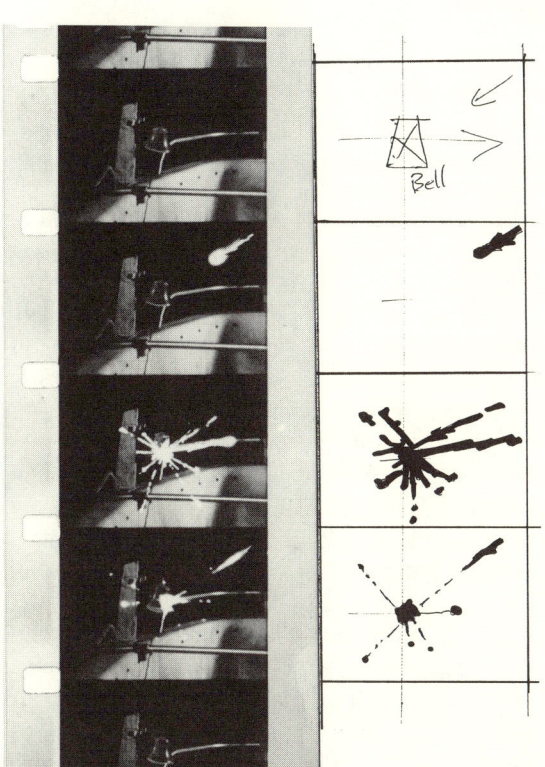

there was an island just a few thousand feet off shore. You've read about it; the cheapie was *Marley's Revenge*.

A shot in an all nighttime picture displayed the moon in the sky where it stayed in one position for the entire time filming took place. A four-inch photograph of the moon was affixed to the glass in the appropriate position and was front lit by a small spotlight with a straw gel to make it yellow. In this case, the camera could pan and tilt since the moon did not actually blend into some element. It was used only in the shots which required it but it was always available when it was needed. That's total control.

Since the glass is usually only two to six feet in front of the lens, measures must be taken to insure sufficient depth of field. You must make sure that both the matte and the background into which it visually fits are equally sharp, or equally fuzzy.

Don't be embarrassed to use a technique like this. It goes back to the classics like *Ben-Hur*, *Cleopatra* (both silent versions and the CinemaScope remake) and *The Abyss*.

Use your imagination. The procurement of any number

Opposite: **Frame blowup of the flare (left) and paper sketch of the finished film (right).**

of props or sets may be avoided by the use of glass shots. It simply requires sensible planning and execution. Don't belabor the prospect, however. Forcing yourself to use a matte or glass shot could be limiting because, more often than not, you can get only a single angle, can move the camera only slightly, and you have practically no latitude with the lighting.

Using miniatures also can save money for several reasons. For example, it may be necessary to use the same impressive mansion or commercial building throughout a picture. Unfortunately the mansion or building either is not available for the entire shoot, or exercising control over it would be too costly or problematic.

Hanging Miniatures

In the above scenario, the logical substitute would be to build a miniature three dimensional facade of appropriate size. Then place it in front of the camera so that it visually is in its proper position and perspective. Or you can place it in forced perspective behind the subject. Remember, you don't have to build all of it, just the part that'll be seen.

Always remember that a miniature is any size smaller

Top: The Steerman PT-17 under construction. *Bottom:* The "miniature" was stuck in the house like a dart. (Photo by Robbie Joyner.)

than the real thing. *The Great Balloon Chase* and *Hit the Road Running* both used a real airplane (flying) which had to be duplicated to be crashed. In order to do a convincing job, it was needed to build the miniature as small as possible but as big as necessary. It was 90 percent scale because it had to be crashed into a real building. The real airplane had a 26 foot wing span while the miniature's was 23. Big enough to be convincing (and to be proportioned with the house it crashed into), it still qualified as a miniature and was certainly cheaper than crashing a real plane. Actually two such planes were built, about a year apart and for separate pictures.

You may assume that building such a plane would be out of the question on a tiny budget, but maybe not. Material costs were under $500. Man hours and shop space are what made the two cost about $5,500 each.

I called the Library of Congress in hopes of getting some cheap plans for a PT-17 airplane and was stunned to find out that the plans for air frame planes were $100 and the engine $300. I called Modelers Hobby Shop in Charlotte who recommended I contact Sterling Models. They had a comprehensive set of Steerman model plans in my hands the next day at a cost of only eight dollars.

After shooting close up slides of the plans, I projected certain details, such as wing tips and ribs, on the wall and traced them on paper. Other dimensions such as the cord (the distance from the front to the back of the wing), I extrapolated mathematically and took notes.

We ordered several sheets of Luan and FoamCore to make wing ribs, alternating them for strength and to maintain a light weight.

My son, Robbie, helped me construct both planes. For the airframe, a small saber saw, a hot glue gun, a screwdriver, and a pair of pliers were the only tools required. The engine was assembled as a stack of Luan rings, glued and wired together, for each of nine cylinders.

The assembled airplane was covered with muslin (the least expensive material we could find) and painted to match a real plane—dirt, grease, oil stains and all.

Using the iron plumbing pipe through its center, the plan was to hoist the plane up a cable attached to a crane and allow it to slide down the cable and into a building. Since we had no practical means to make its propeller turn at a realistic speed, it was written into the script that the plane ran out of gas—that way, we would have no need to make the propeller turn at all.

On the first occasion, the plane was dropped into a barn and was destroyed. A year later, Earl Owensby called me, said another picture was under way, and told me that he'd like me to repair the plane for another shot. I had to tell him that it had been reduced to rubble. "Build me another one," he said, "but make it strong enough to repair."

We did, and it was. We slid it down a cable as before.

Hanging Miniatures 71

The center of the plywood engine is a plastic salad bowl.

On impact the wings and landing gear collapsed. It was definitely repairable, but it was stuck in the house like a dart.

E.O. Studios also built a one third scale model of a local building and set fire to it, while the actors performed in front of it. It was indistinguishable from the real thing in spite of the reduced size, which was still pretty big. Imagine making a one third scale model of the front of the house you live in. It would be small as houses go, but it would still be a pretty big model, wouldn't it?

The original *Ben-Hur* (the silent one) required so many spectators for the chariot race that miniature stands of people were constructed. The tiny four-inch people were made to wobble slightly, creating the impression of living individuals. The miniature was hung in front of the camera and the illusion was the presence of numerous people who weren't really there. Of course, there were real people in the full size stands near the camera. It was something like this: Perspective caused the miniature stands to fit between the full size stairways.

The design of hanging miniatures is limited by only the imagination of the cinematographer or effects designer. They can be used to shoot over, under, around, through or any combination extracted from the four.

One might redesign a city block of an existing town by altering the store fronts as was done in *The Color Purple*. Then one could use a miniature tree close to the camera to block a statue in the middle of an intersection. Depending upon how the miniature tree was situated, it could appear to take the place of the statue or it could appear to be a full size tree closer to the camera.

In *The Abyss*, a camera placed at a high angle photographed an emergency raft which was dropped through a hole in the sea platform. The raft fell about 40 feet to the ocean while several people around the periphery of the hole looked down as it fell. In fact, the people stood around the periphery of a chalk line drawn on the floor while a miniature raft was dropped down into a small tank above their heads. The illusion was perfect.

Photographing the Bataan Death March of World War II required thousands of extras. Thousands of extras cost thousands of dollars, so they used the same ones several times in sequence on split screen shots. At great distances the repetition of people can't be recognized, so putting them on the same screen in several places will not draw anybody's attention.

This is a split screen technique which is done with a fixed matte. It can be done in the camera during original photography by putting a black card of appropriate size, shape, and position in the camera's matte box. Then you back-crank the film, change the matte and shoot the second shot. If shot without the mattes in position, the lab can composite the shots as an optical.

If the lab does it, it will be a safer bet. If you do it in the camera, you'll save the price of an optical, and you'll get to see it as a work print a week or two sooner.

Still, it can be easily done in the camera, using a matte box and carefully setting up each shot. Remember, if you ruin a single shot, you'll have to start over. If shooting video, you'll have to shoot separate shots for the video lab to split screen together.

Whether you plan to make the optical union of these images or have a lab do it, it would be a good idea to place a matte line on a natural vertical line, such as a lamp post, door jamb, tree, or room corner. That way there will be less chance it will be noticed.

72 Visual Effects

Doll house setup.

The resulting picture.

Hanging Miniatures 73

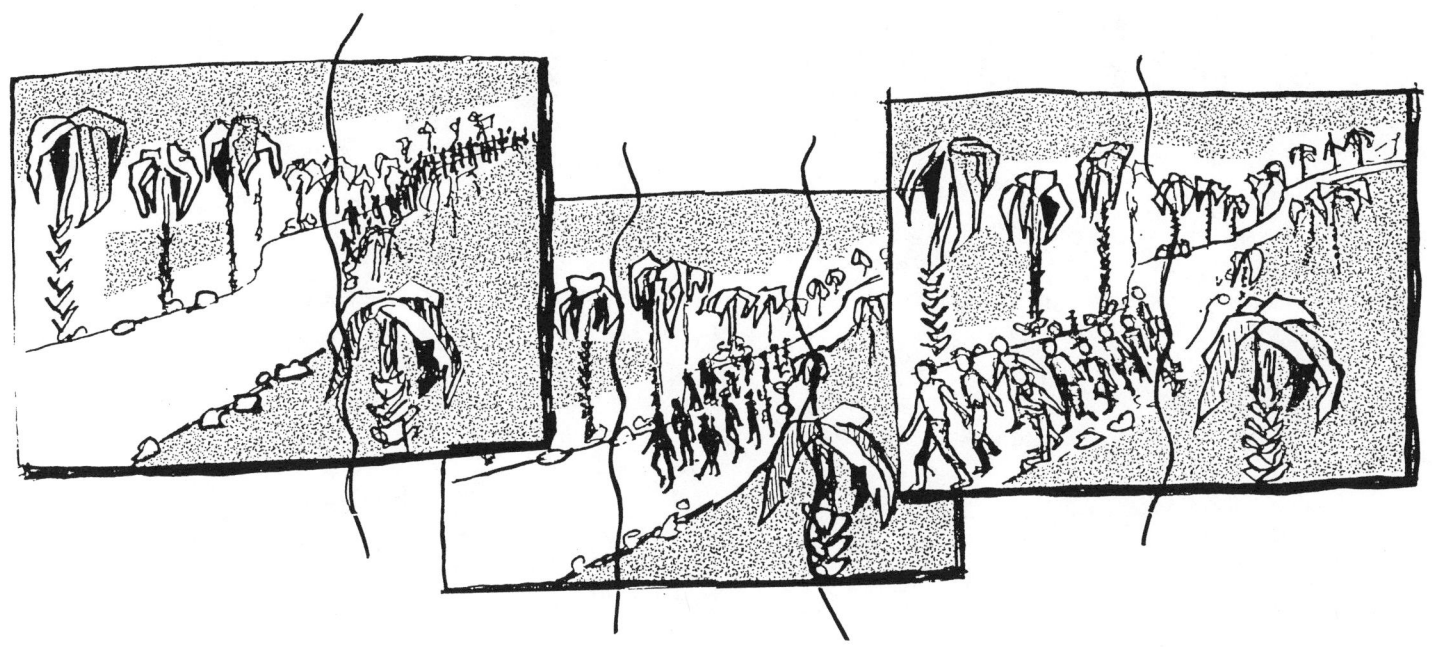

The elements.

The illusion.

74 Visual Effects

The miniature.

The illusion.

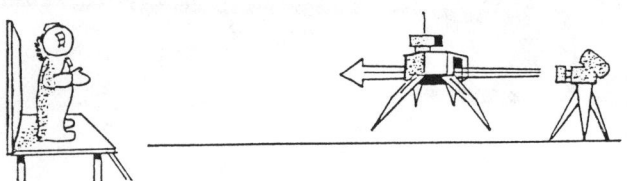

The set-up.

A different treatment was used for the grandstand in *The Natural*. Some of the fans were real people while a high percentage were cutouts. While they weren't real people, they weren't exactly miniatures either. But they were certainly cheaper than mannequins or extras would have been.

Any good magician will tell you that it is the effect that counts; how he attains it is unimportant.

For *Marley's Revenge,* a real boat was chosen to be filmed. Then a one third scale miniature of it was built to blow up. A nighttime shot, it was acceptable that the finished model be a little loose (basically accurate but lacks pizazz and detail). Unlike the airplanes which were crashed in broad daylight, the model boat was seen at a distance, in the dark, for three frames (one eighth second), and then blown up. It cost $28 in materials, required only loose design and roughly 20 man-hours of work. Certainly cheaper than blowing up a $40,000 cabin cruiser. The same model could have been built full scale for daytime use—at only a little more expense—and destroyed on the ocean instead of a pond—at a lot more expense. The producer of a big budget picture may well have opted to buy a stripped down cabin cruiser which had problems too expensive to repair, fix it up cosmetically, and blow it up. Even a stripped one with problems could cost several thousand.

A real boat would be full size and could be shot with film or video. On the other hand, a miniature has to be shot on film because it moves in real time. As a small object, it must be shot in slow motion to appear realistic. Video cameras cannot shoot in slow motion.

Take into account that a real car falling off a cliff will fall three feet in exactly the same time that a miniature car will fall three real feet. Therefore you have to slow down the miniature car enough that it will appear to fall one miniature car length in the same time that the real car falls one real car length.

There are formulas for calculating precisely the camera speed needed, but inverting the fraction and multiplying the camera speed usually works fine. If your model is one half size, multiply your camera speed by two. If it is one sixth scale, multiply by six. If you do one sixteenth scale, you may be in trouble because few cameras will run that fast.

Doing effects at night hides a multitude of errors. That means that the script must be written for nighttime effects but frequently that can be arranged. If not, you simply have to find another way.

One would not always consider some of these examples to be effects because they represent something typical. They are effects because an artificial means has been used to represent something natural.

Sometimes it's difficult to distinguish between what are props, miniatures, sets, and effects devices. Miniatures, of course, are props—unless they are miniatures of the set

How to set up for front screen projection.

Hanging Miniatures 75

Top: **The set-up.** *Bottom:* **The illusion.**

itself, in which case they are . . . what are they? It really doesn't matter what they are. If using some of these tricks or other ones will cut the budget and still look good, then what the heck, go ahead and do it.

One sadly overlooked money saver is front screen projection. Too many small film producers reject the premise of using this technique because interlocking the camera with the projector is problematical.

Here's the basic set up and how to avoid the problems. Buy enough material, that is ScotchLite, from a silk screen printing house. (It's the same stuff on stop signs, license plates, and safety vests that is reflective.) Mount it onto your studio wall. The camera should be set up so as to photograph something less than the entire ScotchLite area. Put a two-way mirror in front of the camera at a 45 degree angle. Project your chosen image into the mirror with a projector on an axis perpendicular to that of the camera.

Two-way mirrors can be bought and cut to size at your local glass dealer. It comes in 50/50 transmission, or 40/60, 30/70, and so on. The 50/50 transmission is usually preferable. It will require some serious adjustment, and a little education that you'll need to get from another source and from experimentation, but the system can be made to work for you.

The value in this technique is threefold. First, the additional space required for rear screen projection is not needed since the projector and camera theoretically occupy the same place in space. Second, the key and fill lights intended for the subject but spilling onto the ScotchLite have little effect, if any, on the projected image since ScotchLite is designed to reflect light back to its source. Third, a low intensity light is all that is required for projection, such as that of a standard projector.

But what about flicker? Who said anything about a movie projector? A slide projector will do nicely for many backgrounds. In fact, you could put a real door and window in the flat, put ScotchLite around them and project the building on the set while actually using the real window and door. There are a million and one backgrounds that have no reason to move and would be good subjects for front screen projection from a slide. The bigger the original slide, the better.

Of course, the actor in front of the camera casts a shadow onto the ScotchLite. Since both camera and projector are on the same optical axis, his body blocks his own shadow. But beware! If the projector and the camera are not carefully aligned, a telltale rim (a matte line) will be seen around the actor.

Don't forget to take into account that the mirror will steal a great portion of your light. A 50/50 mirror will deprive you of one f/stop. A 40/60 will cost you 40 percent of your light turned one way and 60 percent turned the other. Getting a balance between the projected background and the subject is done by eye, looking through the finder. Looking through the finder is the only practical means to see the projected background since it's almost invisible from any other angle.

Some tests have been successfully run using a conventional film projector. That is, one with a butterfly shutter, together with a camera with a 180 degree shutter, and manifesting no flicker at all. The prospect is worth at least some research and a test with your own equipment. Plenty of good information on front screen projection is available.

Bran Ferren, who did the effects on *Manhattan Project*, had a neat brainstorm. He had the sets built in miniature and put a medical video camera (which is about the size of a Zippo lighter) on the tiny set. The camera output went to a video monitor which was stationed in front of an 8 × 10 inch camera equipped with a Polaroid film back. When he saw the angle he wanted, he photographed the monitor. Drawing a cartoon of the characters onto the 8 × 10 Polaroid photograph provided the background for an almost instant storyboard. The result wasn't used in the movie but was used as a tool to make it.

Enough, already! The goal was not to teach special effects but to remind you that from time to time the use of an effect, a miniature, or something "unreal" can save a few, if not a lot, of bucks. You simply must be innovative in your thinking.

A subscription to the quarterly magazine *Cinefex* (P.O. Box 20027, Riverside, CA 92516) and the monthly *American Cinematographer* (P.O. Box 2230, Hollywood, CA 90078) will bring you numerous interesting and valuable reports on how the effects in many first class movies were done. So will buying the video, *Amazing Special Effects You Can Do with Your Camcorder*. It is available from Multi-Video. The video has practical special effects you can execute in a single shot in any gauge film or video with little or no money.

8
Communication

There's a better than even chance that most of the businesses that fail in this country fail for the lack of proper communications.

Good Instructions

"Ya'll come tomorrow morning," really won't cover it on a professional commitment. The cast, the crew, sponsoring agencies, outside support companies and organizations, the police, the press, the company guards and watchmen—everybody who has the remotest need to know—all need to know. They need to know in no uncertain terms: where to go, when to go, what to take with them, what to wear, whether they'll be fed, and so on.

Not all of the above need be stated to each person since "dress warmly" will cover what to wear for everybody but the talent. "Mecklenburg County Court House" is precise enough a location for everyone to know where to show up. Knowing they'll be fed five hours after first call, everyone can calculate whether they will be fed about the normal time or whether to smuggle in a cheeseburger and a bag of chips.

If this communications business sounds as if it doesn't have anything to do with the budget, it will become painfully obvious how costly it can be when the prop master comes in without the fog machine because he rented it out having forgotten you mentioned needing it a day or two earlier.

On *Asimov's Probe*, one fool failed to bring his jacket on a night which was misty and cold. He cut a hole in an inverted plastic trash bag big enough to stick a head through. This made a satisfactory poncho. (Don't ask who the fool was.)

It is unfortunate that even the best educated of the world's population are generally poor listeners, and even those who listen well are prone to misunderstand. The big business tycoons (and the successful little ones, for that matter) have always relied on memos and other forms of *written* communication because they know that verbal communication is not likely to be retained. Even if it does, verbal communication can easily be misunderstood, misquoted, or left open for argument.

Writing a Useable Script

The bar scene script (see page 86) was badly formatted, even though it was done on a word processor. The scripts were stapled at the top because there was no room at the left to hole-punch them. The following is a rewrite of the same in proper form. Notice how much more easily read it is, and what information you find that you can't find from the preceding.

24. INT. BAR—DAY

Sloth, Tater and Howard are shooting pool. Roll focus to entrance as Brent walks in.

[INSERT]

Reaction(s) of Tater and friends as Brent sits at the bar and orders a beer.

25. INT. BAR—DAY

As Brent turns on his bar stool to watch their game, all three men noticeably try to avoid eye contact with him.

26. INT. BAR—DAY

Tater slowly takes his shot which he misses badly. He reacts angrily, then returns Brent's stare.

>> TATER
>> I'm taking that shot over!

>> SLOTH
>> The hell you are!

>> TATER
>> Hell, I can't shoot with somebody staring a hole through me.

>> BRENT
>> (grinning)
>> What's the matter, Tater, you're acting like a brat with a guilty conscience.

Tater slams his stick on the table and turns towards Brent as if to pounce. Sloth quickly grabs his arm.

>> SLOTH
>> Y'all just hold on a minute, now.

>> —etc.—

78 Communications

MEMO

```
DATE:  NOVEMBER 25, 1988
  TO:  ALL CREW MEMBERS
FROM:  LOCATIONS
  RE:  SATURDAY'S LOCATION - INTERIOR IRONSBORO AIRPORT
```

Our location for Saturday, the interior for the Ironsboro Airport, is located at the new City Government Building at 600 East Fourth Street (ACROSS FROM THE OFFICE). The building is brand new and the City is quite particular about its use. As per the City's request, please remember the following for Saturday:

1) No smoking is allowed in the building at all (This is a City code and not just a rule for us).
2) No food or drinks are allowed in the lobby area.
3) <u>ALL EQUIPMENT</u>, if staged inside on the lobby floor, must have something under it to protect the floor. To avoid any hassles, try to stage most of your gear outside on the sidewalk near the equipment trucks.

NOTE: Even dollys, when rolled into the lobby, must be on some type of runner. We will provide something for you.

Thanks

Goldcrest Films & Television Ltd.   Goldcrest Films & Television Inc.
City Hall Annex, 600 East Trade Street, Charlotte, NC 28202
Phone: 704-334-9221 -:- FAX: 704-333-2630

In March of 1987, *Asimov's Probe* was filmed. It was the pilot for the 1988 television series *Probe*. This and the following pages show you to what extent Goldcrest Films and Television Ltd. went in order to insure thorough communication.

When a script is not all jammed together, it's simply easier to read, even if the format is wrong. Doing it right is just as easy, just as fast, just as efficient, and just as cheap.

The half-page of script, simply called BAR SCENE, showed no scene numbers which makes reference an absolute nightmare. In this case, the director had no problems with it since he set up the slate himself, using scene numbers such as "B-6, take ONE." That means, the sixth shot made in the bar. The scene number R-4 means the fourth line in the residence sequence. Made sense to him, but what about the poor editor. How does he know that R, in this case, comes before B? The script girl also would have preferred something sequential, such as scene one, scene two, scene three. As it was, the script girl had no concept of what was going on with her unnumbered script and was obliged to ask questions of the sound man,

CHARLOTTE GOVERNMENTAL BUILDING
600 E. FOURTH STREET
(INT. IRONSBORO AIRPORT)

DIRECTIONS FROM THE ADAM'S MARK

*Go west on 2nd St. (towards downtown).
*Turn right on Davidson Street.
*Crew parking entrance on 3rd Street.
*Governmental Building on Davidson between 3rd and 4th Streets.
*Entrance to work area on 4th Street.

SPECIAL INSTRUCTIONS

*Crew parking in lot behind First Baptist Church.
*Base camp on Davidson Street between 3rd and 4th Streets.
*Equipment parking in circle driveway off 4th Street.
 EQUIPMENT TRUCKS PLEASE TAKE 4TH STREET (ONE WAY WEST) FROM HOTEL.
*Catering at First Baptist Church.
*Extras holding in Governmental Building.

****MONTAGE SEQUENCE****

1. Fountain at McDowell Park (McDowell and Third)
2. First Union Tower Clock (Third and College)
3. Civic Park (Trade Street between College and Tryon)
4. Flagpole (corner of Trade and Tryon)

DIRECTOR: MIKE HODGES   BLACK RAINBOW   Goldcrest Films
                                                City Hall Annex
PRODUCERS: JOHN QUESTED   600 East Trade St.
           GEOFFREY HELMAN   Charlotte, NC 28202
                                                704/334-9221

DATE: Sat., 11/26/88   COURTESY VAN LV HOTEL: 8:50A
DAY #: 18   CREW CALL-LOCATION: 9A
                                  (except where otherwise noted-other side)
LOCATIONS: 600 East 4th St.   WEATHER: Mostly sunny & breezy; highs in
           (across street from Prod. Ofc.)   low 70's
           Charlotte   WEATHER COVER: Rain or shine

                                  SUNRISE: 7:09A   SUNSET: 5:13P

SET	SCENES	CAST	PAGES	D/N	LOC #
INT. IRONSBORO AIRPORT - CONCOURSE Opens locker, takes package	92	5,x	1/8	D	
INT. IRONSBORO AIRPORT - ARRIVAL LOUNGE Still watching, gives up	94	3,x	1/8	D	
INT. IRONSBORO AIRPORT - ARRIVAL LOUNGE Harley passes Gary	91	3,5,x	2/8	D	
INT. IRONSBORO AIRPORT - CONCOURSE Harley gets bag, crosses Weinberg	103	3,5,7,x	2/8	D	

---MONTAGE-SEQUENCE---
1. Park opposite Adam's Mark
   Fountain comes on
2. Civic Park
   Garbage & leaves blow
3. Near Radisson Plaza Hotel
   Raising "Old Glory"					

CAST & DAY PLAYERS		CHARACTER	P/UP	WDB/MU/HR	ON SET	REMARKS
1. Rosanna Arquette	H	MARTHA				
2. Jason Robards	H	WALTER				
3. Tom Hulce	W	GARY	8:45A	9A	9:40A	
5. Mark Joy	W	HARLEY		9A	9:30A	Court. van lvs htl 8:50A
7. Ron Rosenthal	W	WEINBERG		w/n	w/n	Court. van lvs htl @ w/n

ATMOSPHERE / STANDINS

75 Travelers
 4 Pilots
 6 Stewardesses   } Rep. to loc. @ 9A
 5 Skycaps
10 Clerks

ADVANCE SCHEDULE

Mon., 11/28/88
EXT. GARRISON HALL - D Sc. 11 2/8 1,2,11
INT. GARRISON HALL - D Sc. 12 1-0/8 1,2
POSSIBLE REHEARSE & LIGHT
If time permits:
Martha walks past rubble @ demolished Charlotte Hotel
Tues., 11/29, Weds., 11/30, Thurs., 12/1
INT. GARRISON HALL - N Sc. 20 9-0/8 1,2,11,14,17,28,29,x
INT. GARRISON HALL - DRESSING RM - N Sc. 21 2-6/8 1,2,14,17
Prep fuel plant

1st Assistant Director: Jay Tobias   UPM: Robert E. Warner
2nd Assistant Director: Paula Brody

Any questions/problems call: Paula 372-4100 Ext 305

COURTESY VANS LV. HTL @ 8:50A
DATE: Sat., 11/26/88   CALL SHEET

STAFF AND CREW	@ LOC.	STAFF AND CREW	@ LOC.	EQUIPMENT	@ LOC.
Director	P/U as per Mike	Craft Service ready @	9A	Insert Car	
				Low loader	
Production Manager	o/c	Property Master	9A	ALL TRUCKS @ LOC. 45 BEFORE CREW CALL	
1st Asst. Director	8:30A	Asst. Prop	↓		
2nd Asst. Director	9A			Set Dressing Truck -1	
Set PA's -2	8:30A	Set Decorator	o/c	Prop Truck -1	
Set PA's -1	9A	Leadperson	o/c	Camera/Sound Truck -1	
Location Manager	o/c	Set Dressers (5)	per Barbara	Grip/Electric Truck w/Genny -1	
Asst. Location Manager	per David	Set Dressers			
Train Coordinator				Hair/Makeup Trailer - 1	
SI/PA's	9A	Standby Scenic	9A	Wardrobe Trailer -1	
Script Supervisor	9A	Greensman			
				Crew Vans -2	
Visual Consultant	o/c	Costume Designer	o/c	Pickup Truck	
Art Director	o/c	Costume Supervisor	9A	Mini Van -1	
Art Dept. PA	per Patty	Set Costumer			
Construction Coordinator	o/c	Set Costumer		Cars -3	
Carpenters	per Tommy	Seamstress	per Clifford		
Construction Foreman		Wardrobe PA/Driver		Water Truck -1	
Chargeman Scenic		Asst. to Cost. Designer	↓	Special Effects Truck -1	
Painters		Makeup Artist	9A		
Construction PA	↓	Add'l Makeup		Honeywagon (1)	
Special Effects (3)	9A			Motor Homes (4)	
Modelmaker		Hair Stylist	9A	Generator	
D.P.	9A	Add'l Hair		Walkie-talkies (15)	
"A" Camera Operator					
1st Asst. "A" Camera		Transportation Coordinator	o/c	Crane	
2nd Asst. "A" Camera		Captain	per Lee & Bubba		
"B" Camera Operator		Drivers (12)			
1st Asst. "B" Camera		Driver		Train	
2nd Asst. "B" Camera		Driver	↓	Picture Vehicles	
Still Photographer	↓				
		Editor	o/c		
Sound Mixer	9A	Asst. Editor	per Malcolm		
Boom Operator	↓	Apprentice Editor			
Playback Operator					
		Production Office Supvr.	o/c		
Gaffer	9A	Production Secretary	per Eileen		
Best Boy		Production Auditor	o/c		
Electrics (3)		Asst. Auditor	per Barbara		
Electrics Dimmer (1)	↓	Office PA	per Eileen		
Genny Operator	w/trucks				
Key Grip	9A	First Aid/Paramedic			
Best Boy		Nurse		BREAKFAST ready @	9A
Dolly Grip		Firemen		LUNCHES for 65 ready @	2:30P
Grips (2)	↓	Policemen (2)	per David	DINNERS for ready @	
Grips					

NOTES

PROPS: Message board
Envelope w/key
Harley's overnight bag & umbrella
Travelers' luggage, newspapers, briefcases
Skycap luggage carriers
Baggage lockers
Package for Harley
For montage: Leaves & garbage

LOCATIONS: Fountain to turn on in montage (1)

FX: Wind machines montage(3) and wetdown(2)

TRANSPORTATION: P/U Director as per Mike
P/U Tom @ 8:45A
Courtesy vans lv. htl @ 8:50A
Courtesy van lvs. htl @ w/n (Ron Rosenthal)

82 Communication

PAGE 2:

DAY 6 - SATURDAY - MARCH 21st (SEE DAY 11)   -CHARLES HOTEL-
                                                                 (LaFayette, Warren, Shelby)
    3 5/8 - INT. HOTEL BASEMENT   (D) sc. 74 thru 78

    ---------- COMPANY MOVE TO: OLD STAR BUILDING, SHELBY) ----------

    1/8 - EXT. BROWNSTONE   (N) sc. 141
    6/8 - EXT. BROWNSTONE   (N) sc. 167,168,169
        (4 4/8 TOTAL PAGES)

DAY 7 - MONDAY - MARCH 23rd   -MECKLENBURG COUNTY COURT-
                                                    HOUSE ANNEX - (E. Trade
                                                    Street, Charlotte)
    2 5/8 - INT. MORGUE CORRIDOR   (D) sc. 57 thru 61
    2/8 - INT. MORGUE CORRIDOR (VTR) (D) sc. 82pt. from sc. 61
    1 5/8 - EXT. CITY MORGUE   (D) sc. 61A, 62pt.

    --------- MOVE TO COLLEGE & 9th, CHARLOTTE ----------

    1 1/8 - INT. CITY MORGUE   (D) sc. 55,56
    2/8 - INT. MEDICAL EXAMINER'S OFFICE (D) sc. 53,54pt.
        (5 7/8 TOTAL PAGES)

DAY 8 - TUESDAY - MARCH 24th   -DISCOVERY PLACE, CHARLOTTE-
                                              (Tryon Street)
    6 - INT. SHOWROOM   (D) sc. 106 thru 120
    3/8 - INT. SHOWROOM   (D) sc. 220.
        (6 3/8 TOTAL PAGES)

DAY 9 - WEDNESDAY - MARCH 25th   -DISCOVERY PLACE, CHARLOTTE)
                                              (Tryon Street)
    1 4/8 - INT. SHOWROOM   (D) sc. 199,205,209,210,
                                                     213,215pt.,216,218
    1 5/8 - EXT. SHOWROOM/STREET   (D) sc. 200,201,202,208,219
    4/8 - INT. STATION WGN/EXT. SHOWROOM (D) sc. 204,207,212,215pt.

    --------- MOVE OUTSIDE ----- 6TH STREET ----------

    1 3/8 - EXT. CITY STREET   (N) sc. 170
        (5 TOTAL PAGES)

DAY 10 - THURSDAY - MARCH 26th (SEE DAY 5)   -6TH STREET & CHURCH-
                                                   (Charlotte)
    3/8 - INT/EXT. STATION WGN/STREETS (D) sc. 64,65,66
    1 3/8 - INT. STATION WGN.   (D) sc. 67 thru 71

    --------- COMPANY MOVES TO MOREHEAD & MINT ---------

    1 - INT/EXT. STATION WGN.   (N) sc. 123 thru 129
        (2 6/8 TOTAL PAGES)

DAY 11 - FRIDAY - MARCH 27th (SEE DAY 6)   -MOREHEAD/MINT, CHARLOTTE-
    1 - INT/EXT. STATION WGN (Towed)   (D) sc. 62pt.
    5/8 - INT. STATION WAGON (Towed)   (N) sc. 121,122
    3 - INT. STATION WAGON (Aftermath) (N) sc. 130
        (4 5/8 TOTAL PAGES)

Shown above is page 2 of the One Line Shooting Schedule covering day 9. The opposite page shows a Call Sheet. Both of these documents were used for *Asimov's Probe* and may serve as a model for your own communications.

    These two sheets, together with a copy of the shooting script, communicate everything the participants need to know as a general overview. Anything an individual might not know will surface and remind him to ask appropriate questions of those who do know.

    It also should be noted that, like script rewrites, these sheets are passed out daily to everyone. When they show revisions, it is customary to Xerox or print them on paper of a different color—and if possible, a color which has not yet been used on the project. The color change is itself a communication.

F/X PRODUCTIONS
CALL SHEET

PROD OFFICE 482-0611

DAY 9

Producer: WAGNER / LEVI	Date: WEDNESDAY – MARCH 25, 1987
Prod. #: 87001	Shooting Call: 930A
Title: "ASIMOV'S PROBE"	Director: SANDOR STERN
Crew Report To: MAXWELL'S FURNITURE – MAIN ST. – GASTONIA	PRODUCTION MANAGER: DODIE FOSTER
Crew Call: LEAVING E.O. @ 8:00A / LOCATION @ 9:00A	1ST ASSISTANT DIRECTOR: JUDITH VOGELSANG
	2ND ASSISTANT DIRECTOR: ALAN CONNELL
	LOCATION MANAGER: MIKE ALLEN

IF NOT ALREADY COMPLETED:
- 9/8 – INT. SHOWROOM sc. 199, 205, 209, 210, 213, 215, 216, 218 AND [220] (D2)
  (AUSTIN, MICKEY, ATMOS.)
- 15/8 – EXT. SHOWROOM / STREET sc. 200, 201, 202, 208, 219 (D2)
  (AUSTIN, MICKEY, ATMOS.)
- 4/8 – INT. STATION WAGON / EXT. SHOWROOM sc. 204, 207, 212, 215 PT (D2)
  (MICKEY, ATMOS.)
- 13/8 – EXT. CITY STREET sc. 170 (N)
  (AUSTIN, MICKEY, ATMOS.)

233 MAIN STREET
GASTONIA

3 7/8 TOTAL PAGES

CAST	CHARACTER	LEAVING	MAKEUP	SET READY
PARKER STEVENSON	AUSTIN	PU @ 8:30A	9:00A	9:30A
ASHLEY CROW	MICKEY	PU @ 7:30A	8:00A	9:30A
JOHN PLESHETTE	BLAINE	PU W/N		
STEVE KELSO	STUNT COORDINATOR	HOLD		
WILLIAM PHIPPS	SMILES	HOLD		
RAY COLLINS	CUSTOMER	TRAVEL (F)		

CREW: EXTERIOR NIGHT FILMING – DRESS WARMLY

ATMOSPHERE
- 3 STANDINS (TODD, SANDI, DAN) W/CARS → REPORT TO LOCATION 9:00A
- 35 CUSTOMERS / STREET ATMOS (10 W/CARS) → REPORT TO LOCATION 9:00A **RECALLED**

TRANSPORTATION	SPEC. EQUIPT.	MISCELLANEOUS
1 - CAMERA TRUCK LOC @ 9A	PRACTICAL COMPUTER PROGRAM	10 - WALKIE-TALKIES
1 - SOUND AMBULANCE LOC @ 9A	T.A. – HARRY JOYNER 9A	
1 - GRIP / ELECT. TRUCK LOC @ 9A	AUSTIN'S STATION WAGON	
1 - GRIP TRUCK LOC @ 9A		
1 - GENERATOR LOC @ 7:30A	SFX: WET DOWN (PER RAY)	1 - SET DRESSING TRUCK – O/C
1 - HONEYWAGON LOC @ 7:30A	CITY BUS 9A	1 - SET DRESSING VAN – O/C
1 - MOTORHOME LOC @ 7:30A		1 - SPECIAL EFFECTS TRUCK – LOC @ RIG
1 - MOTORHOME LOC @ 7:30A		1 - WARDROBE VAN – LOC @ 9A
1 - VAN (PROPERTY) LOC @ 9A		1 - 15 PASSENGER VAN – LOC @ 9A

CREW CALLS

DIRECTOR OF PHOTOGRAPHY: DIXON	LOC @ 9A	SOUND MIXER: HENSON		BOOM MAN: JONES	LV 8A
CAMERA OPERATOR: SMOOT	LV 8A	(2) SPECIAL EFFECTS: HUGGINS /			RIG
1ST ASSISTANT CAMERA: FISHER		PROPERTY MASTER: BIVINS	ASSISTANT: HOLLER	LV 8A	
2ND ASSISTANT CAMERA: KNEECE		WARDROBE: MENS : NATIONS		LV 8A	
GAFFER: GOFORTH		(2) WOMENS: BUNDY		LV 8A	
BEST BOY: PEACE		MAKEUP : ELWOOD		LOC @ 7:45A	
3 - LAMP OPERATORS		HAIRDRESSER: KENNEDY		LOC @ 7:45A	
KEY GRIP: SMITH		CATERER: COFFEE & DONUTS READY @ 8:30A			
FIRST GRIP: ALDRIDGE		(O/C) LUNCHES READY @ 2:30P			
DOLLY GRIP: FORNEY		CRAFT SERVICE: PER RAY DURHAM			
3 - GRIPS		SCRIPT SUPERVISOR: MCINTIRE		LV 8A	
GREENSMAN		PRODUCTION INTERN: JIM SHORES		W/N	
4 POLICEMEN: TRAFFIC CONTROL	8A				

THURSDAY – MARCH 26, 1987
- EXT. WAREHOUSE sc. 79, 184, 185, 186
- EXT. CITY STREETS sc. 1, 3, 5 THRU 8
- EXT. STREET / BAR (N) sc. 2, 4

GARDNER & MORGAN
SHELBY

COVER CALL – MORGUE (CHARLOTTE) & HOTEL BASHA (S.H.)

✱ SEE MAP ON THE REVERSE SIDE ✱

84 Communication

You'd have to see some scripts to believe how badly they're put to paper. The script form of *Body Shop* was not the worst in form, but it was certainly in the running. What you see here is an exact copy of the original script, page 7A—notes, dirt, fingerprints, brevity, and all. If it weren't for the notes, dirt, and fingerprints, page 7-A could be deleted.

cameraman, and director at every take. That's distracting for all four.

Notice on the rewrite that there is plenty of space to take notes. For example, you might want to break up TATER, SLOTH and BRENT into 26, 26A, 26B, and 26C, then yellow them out as they are successfully filmed.

Instructions on script form may be found in many books, but the following abbreviated instructions may be helpful in doing your next script. Reading an appropriate book on the subject will be more helpful when you have the time.

Script Form

Proper script is important because it will help you to communicate economically. You measure success on content and brevity, not eloquence. No reader is favorably impressed with excess length or elaborate descriptions.

It is recommended that a script be at least 90 pages and not more than 130. The following describes the expecta-

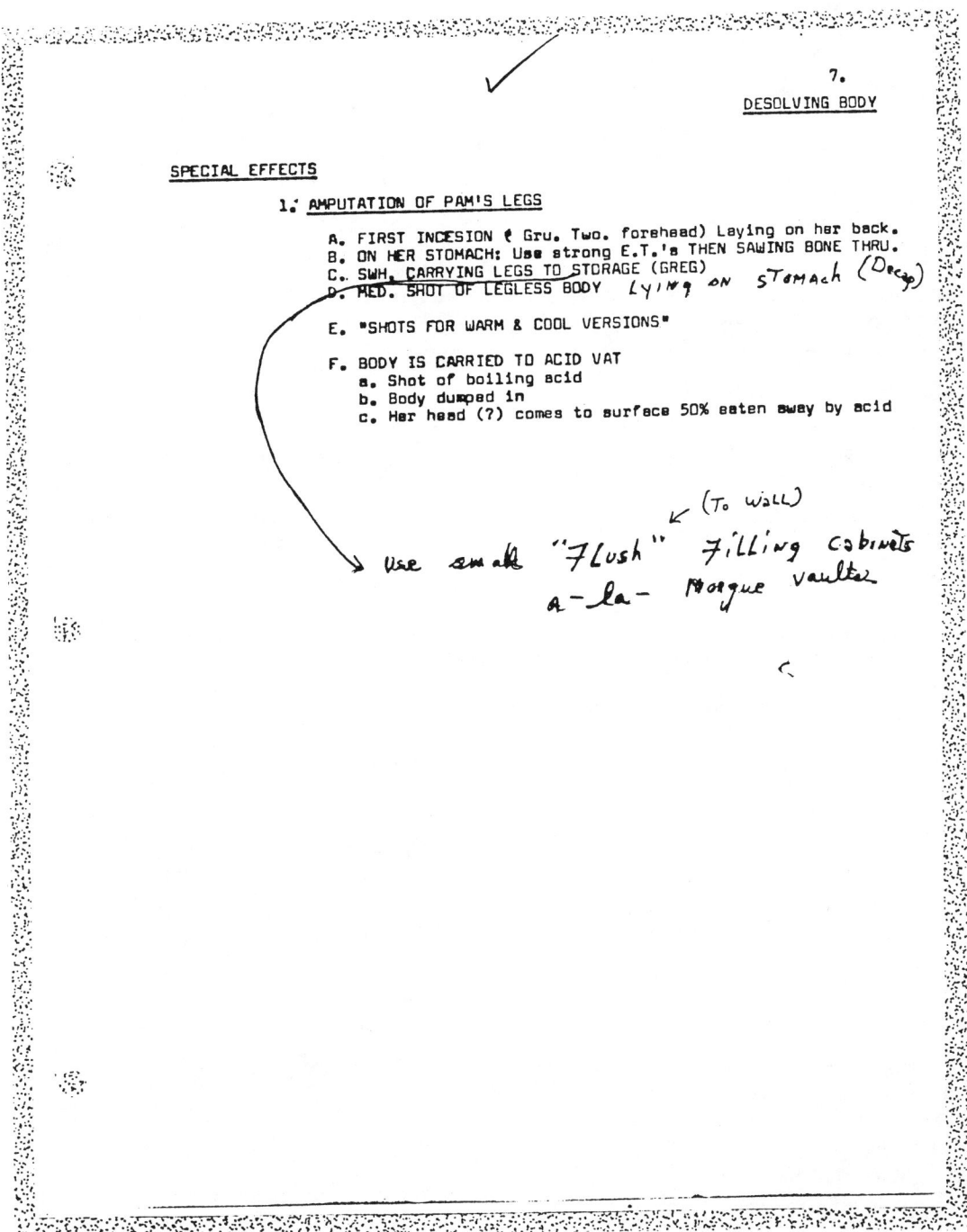

This is a copy of page 7 from *Body Shop*'s script. Many of the pages were this brief and exhibited poor form. The entire script was about 28 pages. Not enough for complete and proper communication. The director was also the writer. The relationship between writer and director is often an adversarial one. If the writer and director had not been one and the same person on this project, a difficult task would have been an impossible one. These comments are not intended to be a reflection on the quality of the story line which, by the way, was a pretty good one.

tions of any cast or crew member regarding the script. Nobody wants to figure out the cute techniques of a newcomer.

The first page should have the story title one fourth down from the top. In the bottom left or right corner should be the name of the author and the copyright date. It is perfectly legitimate to put ©1993 at the top of each page if published or used as a loose leaf document. The second page should be a one page synopsis of the story. Next, the cast of characters is described in order of appearance. One or two lines for each is sufficient. Not all characters need be described. This page can be omitted leaving descriptions to be inserted on the first occasion of the appearance of that character.

86 Communication

```
                              BAR SCENE
                              ─────────
    1  Shot opens in bar showing Sloth, Tater, and Howard shooting pool.
       Roll focus from pool ball to front entrance of bar.
    2  Brent the reporter enters.
    3  Reaction shot of Tater and friends as Brent sits at bar and orders a beer.
    4  As Brent turns on his bar stool to watch their game, all three men noticably
       try to avoid him.
    5  Tater slowly takes his shot which he misses badly. He then turns angrily
       and returns Brent's stare.
TATER   "I'm taking that shot over."
SLOTH 6 "The Hell you are."
TATER   "Hell; I can't shoot with somebody staring a hole through me."
BRENT 7 (Grinning comfortably) "Whats the matter Tater, you're acting like a Brat
                                with a guilty conscious."
      8 Tater slams his stick on the table and turns towards Brent as if fixing
        to pounce. Sloth quickly grabs Tater's arm and says:
SLOTH   "Ya'll just hold on a minute now."
```

On *Marley's Revenge,* the director was also the writer. He made the script a workable one, but it is laid out in such incorrect form so as to be very distracting. Such a problem makes it almost impossible to follow the story line while reading it, even if you already are familiar with the plot.

Read this page and see how confusing it is and how difficult it is to read because of poor design.

EXAMPLES:

ROB KENNY is a special agent of the FBI. He is intelligent and pleasant, and has every intention of achieving the goal of knowing just what is going on.

OFFICER PALMER is a black policeman and has a strong sense of humor but is a serious policeman.

BETTY is a girl scout, has one line and requires no character development.

Pages should be numbered with page 1 being the page bearing scene one. Scenes (if numbered) should be numbered in whole numbers beginning at one and the word "scene" is no longer used. (See following example of scene 34.) A single scene number applies to the entire sequence unless it is interrupted by another sequence. Once a scene has been left, it will be assigned a new number upon return. The writer may choose to say, "57. EXT. BARNYARD—DAY (continuation of scene 43)."

The scene number appears as far left as any copy on the page and is followed by a period, then a space, then the upper case set/location/description.

EXAMPLE:

34. INT. PAT'S BEDROOM—DAY

If a scene is interrupted by another which is simply a cutaway, the latter can be inserted simply by putting the lower case word "insert" in brackets and positioned as far left as any other copy. It will not be numbered until the director or A.D. does so on the set. (See [insert] under 24. INT. BAR—DAY.)

The line bearing the scene number and description is followed by a blank line. The blank line is followed by a description (each line indented) if one is necessary. Names are all caps in descriptions as are special or unusual props.

EXAMPLE:

40. EXT. HOSPITAL—DAY

HARLEY is pushing PAT in a WHEELCHAIR. Her arm is in a CAST. JANICE is walking alongside.

The name of the character who speaks follows a blank line. The name is centered and typed in all caps. The name can be followed, if necessary, by a parenthetical instruction.

71. INT. PAT'S KITCHEN—DAY

PAT is pressed against the ceiling.

PAT (muffled)

Get me down! Get me down! I'm stuck up here!

The direction "(muffled)" could also have been centered under PAT or could have been placed in the middle of her dialogue if that's where the muffling begins. Note that (muffled) could have been (excited), (horrified), (depressed), or any other adjective or adverb which may not have been obvious. Notice also that the dialogue is compressed to approximately three quarters of a page width and is centered. It must be flush on the left. The right side may be justified, that is, flush like this paragraph or ragged, like the next one.

When a sequence continues onto the next page, the parenthetical word (continuing) or (continues) must appear alone on a line. It may be either centered on the page and above the page number, or in the bottom right of the page, still a line above the page number. The following page begins with a repeat of the scene number and (cont.) or (continued).

The writer ought not feel obligated to direct, act, and edit the work. The simpler he can communicate to the reader, the better. The director must be allowed to direct, the actors to act, and so on. Today's screen writers do not usually state camera directions. It is sufficient to say in the scene description CU (for close up) *only if it is imperative* that the shot be made as a close up; (O.C.) goes beside the character's name if he is off camera and it is not obvious by reading the script; or (enters camera left) is used if that order is dictated by a shot occurring later but isn't obvious now.

In scene descriptions, nothing is abbreviated except those things which are *always* abbreviated. Mr., Jr., and Inc., may be abbreviated but never Jan, Feb, Mar,; 2nd, 3rd, 4th; N.Y., D.C., Col.; St., Ave., Blvd. These must be written out. "Dr. Jones" is O.K. but never, "It's time to call the Dr."

While writing the script and entering scene numbers in whole numbers it may be convenient to pull scene 24 and put it between scenes 6 and 7 by assigning it the number 6.5. Later, scene 86 may become 6.75. This is not an acceptable finished technique but will hold your sequence together long enough to finish the work. The original numbers 24 and 86 will say, "24 - deleted," and "86 - deleted." The final draft will be renumbered to eliminate both the point system and the deletions.

Take into account that with the open pages in our rewritten example, there is plenty of space for the director and talent to take notes. Xeroxed rewrites are briefer and 130 pages isn't very much writing when each page has so much white space.

Harley's Gadget (no kin to *Marley's Revenge*) was written by a first timer on a word processor. The writer didn't know the proper form for a script nor did he know how to use his word processor.

BEFORE

CUT TO:
SCENE 78-G (the montage)

EXTERIOR. DAY. IN FRONT OF AN AIRPLANE HANGAR. Several airplanes can be seen inside. Several older fellows are sitting in folding chairs outside the hangar.

GENTLEMAN:
"FELLOWS, IF I HAD A BICYCLE LIKE THOSE FAA FELLOWS WERE JOKING ABOUT I'D GET RICH FLYING FOLKS AROUND TOWN." Flies his hand around like a kid playing airplanes. "VOOOOOOUUUUUUM! HA!"

DISSOLVE TO:
SCENE 79

INTERIOR. DAY. Pat is sitting on a dining room chair talking on the phone.

PAT:
"HONESTLY, BECKY. IT'S JUST RUMORS. I MEAN REALLY, WHEN'S THE LAST TIME YOU SAW ANYBODY RIDING A BICYCLE UP IN THE AIR?"

After seeing the mess he made of putting a really neat idea on paper, his agent sent him a couple of books on script writing. He improved the work a lot. (I am an expert on the foolhardiness of that writer because, indeed, it was I.)

AFTER

78. EXT. IN FRONT OF AIRPLANE HANGAR—DAY.

Several airplanes can be seen inside. Some older fellows are sitting in folding chairs outside the hangar.

GENTLEMAN:
Fellows, if I had a bicycle like those FAA fellows were joking about I'd get rich flying folks around town. (Flies his hand around like a kid playing airplane.)
Voooooouuuuuum! Ha!

79. INT. PAT'S DINING ROOM—DAY.

Pat, slightly flustered, is on the phone talking to a friend.

PAT
Honestly, Becky. It's just rumors. I mean really, when's the last time you saw anybody riding a bicycle up in the air?

What a difference!

The script that takes the cake was the one for *Night of the Cat*. The producer made it up as it went along. Not even the director knew what was next. In fact, none of the script was even put to 3 × 5 file cards until the whole project got in financial trouble. A superior court judge told him to put it on paper or go to jail. All night long it was peck..., peck..., peck..., because he couldn't type. Couldn't write either.

So, you see? Communicating well isn't just a good idea, it's absolutely essential.

While we're on the subject of scripts, let's consider briefly the creation of one which is intended for a really low budget picture, a really cheap one. The sequence of events will differ from picture to picture. More often than not, some first timer will have a story in the back of his head before he has the idea to make a movie. The question is how to film the story inexpensively.

When the prospect of making a movie comes up, it is frequently easier to first invent an idea which can be done cheaply. Horror movies generally win out as subject matter in this scenario because it is quite easy to get a strong horror effect with two dollars worth of beef and chicken fat. Furthermore, there is an audience for horror shows of good quality, bad quality, and anything between.

It is not an overwhelmingly large audience. But the fact that they've made multiple sequels of *Halloween*, *Nightmare*, and *Jaws* is a clear indication that it is large enough to get you your money back with a little profit.

Once the writer—or whoever creates the general story line—puts down on paper his notes and organizes them into a synopsis of one or two typewritten pages, an additional draft or two will tighten up the story a little and make it more easily read. Those additional drafts really ought not be any longer.

When he's basically content with what he has on paper, it needs to be reviewed by the cinematographer (in order to be sure that it is cheaply photographable); by the special effects man (to insure that the effects can be done within budget); by the wardrobe master, set designer, greens keeper, company pilot, police or chamber of commerce liaison, and absolutely anybody else whose job will have a bearing on the budget. All these needn't be different people, but if they do wear more than one hat, they must observe the problems from all points of view.

When making a picture with a serious budget, it is not typical to include anyone more than the writer, producer, director, and optical house rep in this first meeting. They are pretty savvy on all fronts and have a reasonable amount of latitude in the disbursement of funds. When a super skinny budget is called for, it is necessary to consider initially all the angles on a point-by-point basis in order to preclude undercutting or forgetting some budgetary element.

When the synopsis has been passed around and everybody agrees that they can do their part within their part of the budget, the writer can go ahead and compose the shooting script.

As the first day of production approaches, a production meeting should take place wherein all production staff and crew attend and discuss the script from the first scene to the last.

When the meeting is over, everyone understands what will be shot when, where, and how. It is a time that all known problems are brought out in front of everyone. That's important because it may be the telephone receptionist who has the solution to how much water the main character used brushing his teeth (if the script demands it), when actually it is the technical adviser who is responsible for the information.

As an example, look at this overview of *Marley's Revenge*, and see how the style of the story had direct bearing on the budget. Over 75 percent of the picture was shot in the woods at night. Not being able to shoot until dark (which comes at about 9:30 P.M. during the summer) and having a 700 amp generator which guzzles gas, it becomes obvious how costly a night shoot can be. That cost cannot be calculated precisely in terms of money or of having to begin the session with late-hour fatigue. When you can't start until late in the evening, you simply have to grin and bear a certain number of problems and frustration.

Shooting in the woods at night—or any other single location for long duration—can also cut some costs considerably. There is a distinct advantage in being able to go to the same clearing in the woods and establish a set-up identical to the previous session, day in and day out. While the expense of the generator continues, there may be a need for fewer set-ups because the camera can be panned 45 to 90 degrees, the lights readjusted a bit, and the location has become an apparently different one without the need to break down the gear, move everything, and then set up again.

The producer exercised a good idea in the preproduction of *Marley's Revenge*. He shot it first as an amateur in Super/8 at about a $400 expense, painting for himself a vision of the potential problems he would have to overcome when he shot the "real" picture. It also gave him a great deal more insight for his script rewrites and an opportunity to see how it would cut, or edit, along with the bonus of using it to communicate specific ideas. Today the same would be done with a camcorder.

Being a horror film, the woods sequences called for a considerable number of zombies. Being cognizant of the need for money-saving ideas, the producer had the make-up crew make several universal wounds and rotting flesh prostheses which would fit anyone. Then anyone who could walk could be used as a zombie offering the production a source of free talent while doing a good job of public relations. Lots of investors' daughters, police, neighbors, press, crew, and other associates got an opportunity to be in a movie in spite of having little or no talent. While not all films require zombies, a sequence designed with such prospects in mind is a more exciting enterprise for these people than being an extra, because they can enjoy the experience of having make-up put on and of following direction.

When in make-up, zombies should be accounted for judiciously since, as any boss can tell you, it is hard enough to distinguish dead employees from the live ones anyway.

In contrast, it is not worthwhile to write in a sequence

for the gratuitous insertion of relatives, friends and neighbors simply to appease them. The trick is to find valid and needed sequences which they can handle realistically either as an actor or as an extra.

You could very well antagonize people by shooting them in a sequence and cutting them out in editing, even though such exclusions may be necessary. You simply have to use good judgment anytime you're dealing with people, either living or . . . undead.

9
Location, Personnel, Financing and More

Let's begin the preproduction on a movie—right here on paper—just to see how it goes and how we'll resolve some of the problems. We simply consider everything we can think of that will save us some money beyond those things mentioned in earlier chapters. Having checklists to go by is imperative; you simply can't remember or think of everything necessary without help. We must consider all possibilities in order to have a good overview.

Jewel in the Crown and *Brideshead Revisited* brought such success to Granada Television Productions that they were awarded the BBC contract to produce the series, *Sherlock Holmes*, which was aired in America in 1988 and again in 1991-92. All were done in 16mm, which was indistinguishable from 35mm on the home TV set. (The former two titles are available in video stores in the United States.)

Knowing this, the script for *Eyes of a Scarecrow*© was written specifically to produce as a 16mm feature for release as a videotape, making it a perfect example for us to use. A short supply of money is expected and the project is intended to be the initial effort for a group who is experienced at making features but has never produced one.

Since video release is the primary end, and producing as cheaply as reasonable is a primary goal, 16mm is the obvious choice for the shooting format. Be constantly aware that cheaply as "possible" is not the only goal nor should it be. Too cheap will mean no good . . . and no sale.

The writer, J.B. Clark, Jr., was commissioned to synopsize a story which had limited interior locations, a small number of exterior locations, only a few characters, just a handful of expensive props, and very few costly effects. It was to be a slasher because such films have a built-in audience. Those are very demanding limitations, especially if you have to keep it interesting at the same time. He was expected to offer some degree of progress within a couple of weeks. (Remember *The Twilight Zone* series of the 1960s? This production and others like it followed these criteria.)

Knowing that the judicious use of shortcuts is the key to low budget production, Mr. Clark's fertile mind came up with the following in no more than a weekend:

Eyes of the Scarecrow© 1988

CAST

6 Primary Characters: JOHN & ANN, JESSE & MARY, JUBAL & PAULINE

5 Secondary Characters: SHERIFF, DEPUTY, 2 STUDENTS, PAULINE'S FRIEND

1 SCARECROW—sometimes a person, sometimes a prop.

LOCATIONS

Exterior—front of Jesse & Ann's house, fairly nice—rural
front of John & Mary's house, quite poor—rural
farm field—plowed
farm field—stand of corn
country road
swamp

Interior—Jesse's porch
Ann's kitchen
Mary's living room
Pauline's bedroom
Sheriff's office

Set Dressing—
typical furniture & fixtures

Props—pickup truck
tractor with disks
police car
shotgun
pistol
axe
pitchfork
flashlight

90

scarecrow
fog machine

Wardrobe—uniforms for sheriff & deputy
　　work clothes for John
　　street clothes for everybody else

Live stock—
　　pit bull dog
　　kitten

The use of only ten people in the picture would obviously limit the expenditure of money for talent. The script called for all but two characters to be killed, one at a time. Having only a few people is quite beneficial financially. Getting rid of them helps the budget even more.

The two houses actually are a single, full size facade with the front of one house on one side and the front of the other house on the back. Building such a prop is a less expensive and less demanding proposition than finding two houses that meet the needs, particularly since that would require moving set-ups back and forth between them. Such a structure has the added advantage that it can be built to face in the preferred direction—even built to rotate for that purpose, if necessary. On the other hand, the cost of building the structure can be avoided if two houses that meet the requirement are easily found.

Modern warehouses make excellent temporary sound stages for various reasons. Foremost, they are spacious in terms of both floor space and ceiling height. A high ceiling is an absolute requirement to produce proper lighting that can be set up quickly. Plenty of floor space which is nice and flat—preferably concrete—is equally important for good blocking and camera moves. Warehouses are usually located in low noise areas. Even if insufficient power is readily available, the local power company will quickly install a power drop in an existing building on either a short or long term basis.

Warehouses are customarily very secure buildings, generally cool in the summer, although seldom warm in the winter. Most of them have plenty of storage area. Offices, film loading rooms, and dressing rooms can be quickly and cheaply built in if they're intended to be temporary.

The porch, kitchen, living room, bedroom, and office of the interior locations list are easily constructed in the four corners and center of a warehouse "stage area." Striking those sets is also economical. They can be built during the night for daytime filming since the building has usually been rented for only a short period. This arrangement will make the most efficient use of time quite important, if not vital.

Such construction ought to be safe, but need not meet building codes. Both construction time and materials can be saved by skimping. Often such materials as fireplaces, door frames, bannisters, and stairways can be found intact at house wrecking companies. These materials are often cheap and exhibit the character of age and use.

If construction continues after shooting begins, you might want to have a partial night shift of carpenters or set dressers on call. This strategy may preclude having to rent the warehouse for an additional month to cover only a single day's work for a couple of shots you didn't quite have time to shoot. Working at night might also save the expense of guard.

Set dressings (that is, props) for the rooms as described can be procured at the local Salvation Army, AmVets, or Goodwill stores at extremely low prices. It is altogether possible that they would lend or rent them for a reasonable donation or small fee.

The police car simply needs to be a car of proper vintage and suitable color. It also ought to be a Chevrolet, Ford, Dodge or Plymouth because most police cars are. For only $15 a bumper-mount whip antenna can be bought, or for $0 it might be borrowed. You'd need a bubble gum machine (flashing light) for the top which can be rented for $10 a day.

The siren, of course, is a sound effect which can be dubbed in. The sheriff's department logo on the side of the car (either one side or both, depending on the shots required) can be quickly made. Put stick-on or rub-on letters (from the local art supply store) onto a paper or show card and coat the back with rubber cement. Then with the same cement, coat the car door. (Don't worry, it will rub right off.) Let both surfaces dry. Cut the card to appropriate size and shape and affix it to the door. Then rub off the excess cement. It'll stay for the entire shoot if it doesn't get wet. Then when you're done, it'll easily peel right off with no damage to the paint. Now, you've got a sheriff's car. (Caution! Don't use spray cement; it may refuse to come off.) In metropolitan areas, police supply houses can sell you a decal for three or four dollars. It, too, will be hard to remove.

(The executive producer of *Marley's Revenge* called the local sheriff's department and they were delighted to furnish a car—provided it was driven by a county employee. That was no problem since no stunts were needed. Being a public servant, the deputy sheriff made no charge.)

The pistols can be a problem in some states so be cognizant of the law where you are or where you shoot. (If you actually shoot the pistol you may require a whole, though brief, education for yourself and crew. Remember, a mishandled gun can be as dangerous as a car!)

The rest of the props are easily procured and require no discussion here, as is the case with wardrobe and livestock.

The effects of the people being killed are a blending of the ideals of the writer and the director. They can be bloody if you choose, or they can be handled with taste and propriety (at least to the degree that violence can be handled with taste and propriety). It is knowing your

92 Location, Personnel, Financing and More

target market which must dictate how gory your picture is or isn't.

Read this brief synopsis and you'll get an idea of how cheaply the picture could be done.

CHARACTERS: John, whose legs are crippled, and Ann are a nice, married couple around 30.

Ann is pregnant; John, who is crippled, farms Jesse's property.

Jesse and Mary are married. Mary is o.k. but Jesse is a real jerk who drinks too much. They have two children:

Jubal and Pauline are around 25 years old. Both are as rotten as their father. An incestuous relationship is implied between brother and sister.

The sheriff is an efficient but "good old" country boy.

The deputy is likewise, but a little crooked.

The two teenagers are just that and are used only in passing.

Pauline's friend is a married man whom we see briefly only once; needs no character development.

The scarecrow sometimes is a prop, sometimes a live figure, but is ominous.

As the story opens, the two couples are out front talking. Jesse, who owns the farm, is arguing with John and verbally abusing him.

Pauline and her friend arrive and make a small but disgusting scene. Her friend leaves.

Jubal then arrives in the family pickup truck and, just having fun, nearly runs over Mary. When John tries to defend her, Jesse sics the pit bull on him while the family laughs. Just to show her arrogance, Pauline kills Mary's kitten with the pitchfork.

Later that day, John goes back to talk to Jesse who, by now is drunk. In his stupor, Jesse kills John. He hides the body in the scarecrow in the field until he can find a better place. When Jubal comes around, Jesse tells him what he's done and they both have a good laugh. They hear a noise outside. Upon inspection, they discover that their dog has been literally torn apart.

The deputy arrives and investigates, then discovers John's body. He tries to blackmail Jubal who runs over him and throws him into the swamp. Later, Jubal enters the house and finds that Pauline has just gotten out of the shower and is naked. He starts to make an incestuous pass at her but is interrupted by a noise outside. When he investigates, he is run over by the tractor pulling disks.

When Jesse investigates, he discovers Jubal dead. Returning to the house in a frenzy, he finds Pauline pinned to the floor with a pitchfork lying in a pool of blood, dead or dying.

The sheriff arrives, startling Jesse. He draws on Jesse but too late. Jesse shoots him with a shotgun. Jesse, outside again, is pursued by the scarecrow. The scarecrow catches up with Jesse and kills him the same way he killed John, by evisceration.

—FIN—

Now, mull over this treatment. It doesn't matter that this type of story is not your cup of tea. You can see that a great deal of effect—that is, stark emotion—can be drawn from it with little effort, little talent, little money, and no music at all. (Music is in order anyway.)

A little travel with a minimal crew is necessary to go to the nearest swamp where Jubal and the deputy argue. Otherwise, no travel is necessary except to one fixed interior location and one fixed exterior location.

No one talent is used for more than 25 percent of the shooting schedule. Everybody has such a short bit of business that he's got plenty of time to get it right and do it well even though he may not be a professional actor.

Nighttime interiors make sound stage work much simpler. Except for the aforementioned daytime exteriors, the remainder are shot after dark. Wind and weather notwithstanding, you have total control. You put the lights and the fog in the appropriate places and don't worry about having to match daylight shots.

The goal of writing a script for minimal financial outlay was clearly met, so now that you've mulled it over, take a look at how the budget was calculated and a summary of the budget that was proposed for it.

The producer, director, and writer collaborated on this project before it was a project. Having a tremendous number of hours invested before anything existed other than a glimmer of hope, they equally get a choice piece of an unusually small pie at $4,000 each. If not enough money is raised to pay *everybody,* then at least these three will take theirs in additional shares in the amount of eight percent.

The crew *all* will have to be paid in cash or *all* will have to accept shares. Otherwise you will have dissension among the crew that cannot be easily overcome. It is paramount that, whatever the method, they understand *they are being paid* for their services. If they are not, or if they feel they are not, you simply will be unable to make demands upon them and will have lost control of the project. But by no means should you fall for the "Please let me help, I'll work for nothing just to work on a movie" line.

Pay them somehow, and be sure they understand that they too are to uphold their end of the bargain. If they are willing to work for nothing, that is probably what they are worth. If they work only for the experience, then charge them for it. You'll discover that paid labor is much cheaper than free labor.

Those who work for points of the profit are being paid in full. It simply means that they are being paid with something of value other than money but they don't collect until their obligation is satisfactorily met. You will have to deal with the fact that when paying with points—just like paying with cash—if you buy it, you pay for it, even if you don't use it. Even if the picture is a bust and everybody loses, everyone was paid in full. They invested their money in a loser and you owe them nothing. Sounds cold, but "facts is facts."

Likewise with the talent. On an extremely low budget, there is no room for prima donnas. The leading man (or lady) is no more important than the sound man, and he (or she) should know it. There is no option for limos or drivers, caviar or lobster. The talent are just like the crew—except the crew doesn't wear makeup.

Having extreme nighttime exteriors could be used to expedite start up, if the lighting doesn't change from the night before. If it does change substantially, it will slow start up.

After each evening's shoot, the lighting units are lowered but left in place. After they cool, the lamp heads are covered with plastic trash bags. The aluminum stands, being weatherproof, present no problem. The C-stands are also left but the nets, gels, and flags are moved under cover. Electrical unions and junction boxes are also covered with trash bags, tarps, or wrapped in polyethylene sheets and disconnected at the source. All camera and sound equipment is stored indoors. The exterior location must be left with a guard.

By leaving the equipment, each evening's shoot can be set up quickly, saving more than half the normal set-up time. Furthermore, each individual lighting unit will be in the same place as before insuring more nearly matched shots from session to session.

Having considered all the foregoing and resolved to do the project in 16mm, let's put together a budget and see how it works.

The following summary generalizes the expenditures as well as underestimates them from a typical budget standpoint—even for 16mm. It is a rational budget however. Many a picture has been done with less money.

Eyes of a Scarecrow
Budget Summary

Value in $	Item	Rate		Expected Cash Cost	Percent of Ownership
$4,000	Producer	$4,000		$ 0	8 %
$4,000	Director	$4,000		$ 0	8 %
$4,000	Writer	$4,000		$ 0	8 %
$1,500	Cinematographer	$ 150	per day for 10 days	$ 0	3 %
$1,250	Camera asst./gaffer	$ 125	per day for 10 days	$ 0	2.5%
$2,500	Editor	$1,250		$ 0	5 %
$1,500	Dolly/grip	$ 125	per day for 10 days	$ 0	2.5%
$1,500	Recordist	$ 125	per day for 10 days	$ 0	2.5%
$1,500	Sound grip	$ 125	per day for 10 days	$ 0	2.5%
$1,000	Gaffer grip	$ 100	per day for 10 days	$ 0	2 %
$1,250	Wardrobe/Prop master/ Script-cont./Makeup	$ 120	per day for 10 days	$ 0	2.4%
$ 500	Spec EFX			$ 500	

CAST

$1,250	3 characters @	$ 400		$ 0	.8, .8, .8%
$ 750	3 characters @	$ 250		$ 0	.5, .5, .5%
$ 300	2 characters @	$ 150		$ 0	.3%, .3%
$ 300	3 characters @	$ 100		$ 0	.2%, .2%

PURCHASES

$ 6,561	Film stock, dev. work print (15m ft. @ .55)			$ 6,561	
				$ 600	
$ 600	Meals (120 @ $5)			$ 2,000	
$ 2,000	Tests & preprod.			$ 2,000	
$ 1,325	Music			$ 0	3 %
$ 1,260	Negative cutter			$ 0	2.5%
$ 2,000	Sound X-fer (from orig. to mix & fx rolls)			$ 2,000	

94 Location, Personnel, Financing and More

Value in $	Item	Rate	Expected Cash Cost	Percent of Ownership
$1,000	Sound mix (to full coat)		$ 1,000	
$ 300	Sound mix (to master roll)		$ 300	
$ 500	Livestock (kitten, dog)		$ 0	.5%
RENTALS				
$1,000	Studio space (15 days)	$1,000	$ 0	2 %
$1,500	General location exp.		$ 1,500	
$2,600	Props		$ 2,600	
$ 250	Truck (5 days @ $50)	$ 250	$ 0	5%
$2,000	Camera, record., lights	$1,500	$ 0	3.5%
$ 500	Edit equipment rental	$ 500	$ 0	.5%
ADDITIONAL PURCHASES				
$ 200	Camera and edit supplies (misc.)		$ 200	
$ 744	Miscellaneous (LD calls, post., etc.		$ 744	
	Legal		$ 0	
$1,000	Contingency (by agreement		$ 0	
	Insurance		$ 0	
$40,440			**$18,005**	**60.9%**

Accepting points over cash, the talent, staff, and crew own 60.9 percent while the investors own 39.1 percent. Based upon your contractual agreement, the backers may demand more.

Ignoring the points-for-pay system, the term "the package" does not necessarily mean the whole pie. For example, you may put together a project for which you will need $75,000 to finance. If you declare it to be worth $150,000, then the backer is buying only half interest at $75,000. You'll own the other half. Perhaps you'd prefer it to be 40:60, maybe 70:30. You'd be wise to discuss this with a corporate lawyer or a CPA, lest you innocently do something dishonest or even illegal.

You also want to be sure your backer understands exactly how you are calculating his return, clearly stating so in the contract.

If the above budget looks unrealistically low to you, don't be boondoggled! It's probably because you have been exposed to only traditional methods and budgets. Many worthwhile pictures have been done for much less.

When the last roll of *Marley's Revenge* film had been removed from the camera, about $17,000 had been spent! Better organized, it would have cost still less.

Earl Owensby, a prolific producer born and raised in the South, was interviewed by Morley Safer on CBS's *60 Minutes*. "If someone gave you, say, $10,000,000, how would you use it?"

"I'd put it in the bank," he answered without hesitation, "and make a movie a year for the rest of my life on the interest."

E.O. made pictures with notably greater budgets than what is discussed in this book but he learned the money-saving tricks early in the game and uses them judiciously. All his pictures are assumed to be worthwhile projects, since he doesn't lose money on them.

He lives in the South. But even the South has labor laws, withholdings and S.E.C. regulations. He, like any other good, successful businessman, simply knows how to use the rules to his advantage.

In August 1986 on the analytical TV show, *Adam Smith's Money World*, Mr. Menahem Golan (who doesn't live in the South but in Hollywood) stated how his company, Cannon Films, does it—or doesn't. He said that you don't eat outside your premises or go to heavy restaurants. You don't fly everybody first class or give a limo to every second technician. And you work in countries where the dollar has a greater value. (The South could be interpreted to be one of those "countries" where the dollar value is higher.) He also said, in effect, that if you don't overspend you are bound to make money off your product.

There are two possible approaches to the *Scarecrow* budget as it appears here. One is to get the entire $40,400 from your backer(s) retaining a reasonable and rational portion of ownership for the producer (as noted above). That way everybody gets paid—in money—for his services, even though he is being paid substantially less than a professional rate.

The other approach is to get the $18,005 from the primary investor(s), and pay for services with shares of the profits in lieu of cash.

But take this word of warning: Soliciting funds can easily fall into the parameters of an illegal operation, regardless of how honest you are or how good your intentions. To do the above, you may need to form either a corporation, an S corporation, or a limited partnership in which either the producer or the backer is the general partner. There is no legal advice here, because it would be too easy to give you illegal advice. It'll probably cost you about $250 to $500 to get the advice or opinion of a corporate lawyer. Unquestionably this will be money well spent, if you are fortunate enough to find one whose education is based on law and his ethics on honesty. You don't want to get into trouble with the Securities Exchange Commission, because when you battle with the government, even if you win, you lose.

If all the money you use for the project is your own, you won't have an SEC problem. If your lawyer incorporates your company for you, it will probably cost somewhere between $300 and $1,500. Doing only a little research, you can do it yourself for about $100. It is the safer bet to do it through an attorney or CPA.

You'll notice in the Budget Summary that the far left column is cost, the next to last column is expected cash expenditure, and the last is percentage of ownership. It would be difficult to lower the far left column since a budget of this kind is already cut to the quick. The same is true with cash expenditures. But if you can get people to work for you for free (in spite of the forewarning), perhaps on the premise that it'll be a learning experience, then you can cancel most of the cash cost for personnel, if not all of it. But it is your obligation to provide that it really be a learning experience for those contributors. Better yet, pay them minimum wages for their services and charge them twice or three times that amount for the learning experience. Even by withholding taxes and matching social security, you'll come out ahead.

Like the camera which you were advised not to buy solely on the grounds that it was cheap, you don't want to hire people on the grounds that they work cheaper or for free. When you are engaged in a project which represents a lot of money and a lot of people, you can't afford to hire people—at any price—whom you believe will call in to say, "We're having company from out of town Saturday, so I can't be there." Or "My baby was throwing up all night so I'll have to stay with him."

Paid or not, you absolutely must have people upon whom you can depend to make the commitment to be available when necessary regardless of how they have to shift their lifestyles to do so. Staying home next Saturday very well may put the entire project out of business for the day, costing you a day's rent on everything rented or regressing the schedule by one day after everyone had expected to be finished. The schedule must be aligned so that everybody has the same days off, except on those occasions when a particular crew member is not needed anyway.

The people you know can easily be culled. You've heard them tell tales about how they got away with something, how they managed to pass the buck, or their attitude about why they strove diligently to make a particular accomplishment.

When the snow is up to here, the executive is the guy who answers the phone when the other employees call in stranded. Which of these do you want working with you?

There are at least two types of people available who are likely to carry their own weight at minor expense but at the same time offering only a minor problem. One is young aficionados. Kids are a little difficult to work with because they tend to believe their idea is better than anyone ever had. These kids frequently have to be reminded that somebody out there has been doing it *this* way for a hundred years. But it's ok. Learn to live with having to remind them because one of these kids will turn out to be tomorrow's George Lucas. The greatest problem you're likely to have with them is conforming to their bedtime or dealing with their parents' concern about what kind of movie you are making. The best bet in this case is to be sure that both mom and dad know exactly what you are doing with their kid along with when and where. (Look into the child labor laws in your state.)

Equally dependable are retired people. You can find a wealth of talent out there in such categories as carpentry, seamstress/tailor, tool shop (metal), mechanics, art, banking, and business. These people have a permanent income whether they work or not, but they are allowed to make a certain amount above that and many of these folks are eager to have something to do. Just be careful. They are quite independent, so if you offend them or overwork them they are in a perfect position to tell you to stuff it.

You don't need anyone who can pull the rug out from under you. It is very important that you have the advantage over everybody possible, just like the power company and phone company do. It is equally important that as few as possible have an advantage over you. That's not a matter of honor, having the advantage is simply good business. How you handle the advantage is a matter of honor.

Having the wrong crew can stop you cold. If you can't sell the end product, you won't have to pay out on the last column anyway. Having the right people, though they be woefully inexperienced or dollarwise more costly, can help you make a winner and save you money in the long run. If you do sell the fruits of your labors, don't the people who shared in so much work really deserve some of the action and a proper screen credit?

By the way, those who have earned a screen credit are still entitled to it even though their work has fallen to the cutting room floor or, for whatever reason, was not used.

Do not overlook the possibility of buying with screen credits; they have strong buying power. At the same time, don't be deluded into believing that simply anything or everything can be bought that way. Screen credits are a valuable commodity and should be treated as such.

Many locations, props, and services can be bought for nothing more than a screen credit. You should guard them jealously knowing that they cost nearly nothing but have great buying power. But the thinner you spread them, the more they are devalued—that's inflation.

Depending upon the caliber of your picture, you might get new cars to wreck, free food for the entire shoot, beer or soft drinks in truckloads, an entire cast's wardrobe, furniture, set dressing, greenery, and a multitude of other items you would otherwise have to buy or rent to the tune of many thousands of dollars. Your only obligations will be those laid out in a simple written agreement.

If you are given a "Gulp Soda" or "Pasquali's Beer" you will be expected to use it judiciously—in a positive manner where the label can be seen, and probably in several places. Then you must give the donor a prominent and easily read screen credit at the end of the picture. Generally, that is a small price to pay for a great deal.

Once they realize you are serious about what you are doing, many people will offer their time, property, or facilities for free. A first time picture can literally be racked with freebies—and that is o.k., depending upon how you handle them—but you won't likely succeed if you seek out freebies on a second picture. Those who took you seriously the first time will cease to do so if you still can't pay now that you are "somebody."

Conversely, one of your most serious constraints will be that many do not take you seriously. Having succeeded the first time will help you to overcome that pitfall.

At this stage, you'd want to go over the budget and make rational summary reductions based upon those things which you believe you can get less expensively, and make increases where you think they are necessary.

All this resolved, it's time to take a look at other options which will have a direct effect on expenditures.

Film and mag stock, lab bills, and transfer services must be paid. Sometimes in advance. But not all of this is etched in stone.

Film, for example, can sometimes be bought on a deal. Here are some of the options.

1. Reserve a single emulsion number from Kodak—which will insure matching image quality and nonrepeated edge numbers—and pay the full price for the stock as you order it. Call (800) 242-2424 and get information on the right representative and number to call for ordering from your part of the country.

Kodak, of course, isn't the only supplier. Here are two others who make motion picture stock: Fuji Photo Film, call (800) 241-7695 after noon eastern time; Agfa/Gaveart, call (201) 440-2500 x4370 after 9:00 eastern.

2. Buy ends (aka short ends) from a company who buys rolls. This film is guaranteed (only by replacement and sometimes not at all) and often fills the bill. Just be sure not to buy either dissimilar emulsions or an emulsion type for which the process is discontinued. Mixing Kodachrome and Eastman Color Negative just ain't the way to do it, no matter how good the deal. But buying ends wisely can save you half to two thirds the cost of fresh film from the factory. Fresh film from the factory is still the safer dollar bet.

3. A more direct approach would be to buy directly from an overstocked local commercials producer whom you know and whose film you can trust. You'll want to buy and test a roll before you commit yourself to a bulk purchase. Even so, you'll eventually have to go to the manufacturer to get enough of the same stock.

There's a good chance you can get once-used full coat rolls from a local producer at a pretty good price too. Avoid edited (much spliced) rolls while accepting ones which were used for a pre-mix or final mix. It is advisable to bulk erase it before you reuse it. Even then you'll want to use it only for sound effects while using fresh full coat for dialogue, music, and masters.

New full cost is not particularly expensive although you may not need very much of it. Twelve hundred feet costs about $25. Call 3M Atlanta Sales Center; 2860 Bankers Industrial Drive; Atlanta, GA 30360-2764; (404) 447-7130. (They sell bulk videotape as well.)

Finding lab services on a special deal is not likely. Their profit margin vs. mishap conditions are so close as not to allow business out of the ordinary. They also get lots of stock offers, mostly losers, for their services. Labs willing to do that have become extinct.

Not having lots of money, you may not want to rent your camera and recorder from a rental house. While such cameras are quite dependable, they are rented on a daily or weekly basis. Your best bet is to find a camera user or owner who will rent you a complete set of gear for a fixed price. The next best bet will be to buy one. But whatever you do, remember your camera and recorder are mechanical devices and are the most likely pieces of equipment to fail. An equipment failure will put you out of business until repairs or replacement can be effected.

Let's take this approach. A well used Eclair NPR or Arriflex BL will cost about $5,000 to buy. They are state of the art cameras. Such equipment will save you a lot of money if you have a big budget. It can cost you more than your budget on a low budget picture. You can pick up a good, albeit obsolete, camera for a lot less, but there are

Location, Personnel, Financial and More 97

This Auricon Pro 600 was bought for $750. The price included a 12–120mm zoom, two 400 foot magazines, a 120v battery pack, magnetic head and audio amplifier.

criteria to be met. Naturally, you can't afford just any camera on the grounds that it's cheap.

Silly though it seems, an Auricon Pro-600 or Cinevoice with a zoom lens and zero finder (that is, one built into the lens) can be compared to an Arriflex BL. Because of the zero finder, they both qualify as reflex cameras. In good condition, they both have movements smooth enough to superimpose steady titles. That's good enough in any case. Features are shot on tripods or dollies negating the importance of camera weight. Both will use 400 foot magazines. The Arri will work easily on battery power in the field. The Auricon may or may not, but in the making of features, there's an abundance of 110v or 60 Hertz power anyway. The Arri can be threaded faster than the Auricon, but for a difference of three to five thousand bucks, you can do a lot of slow threading.

Many TV stations have an Auricon Pro-1200 which you could talk them out of for, perhaps $1,000 to $1,800 if it has three prime lenses, or $1,500 to $2,200 with a good Angenieux 12–120 zoom. Or they could have a Pro-600 which, under the above conditions, might bring $1,000 to $1,600 respectively.

The most likely camera in the corner gathering dust would be an Auricon Cinevoice converted to a 400 foot magazine capacity. With prime lenses, it's worth about $150, or $600 with the Angenieux zoom. They could also have a Scoopic 16 with a 200 foot film capacity for $150 to $600 or a CP-16 which, depending upon the lens, would bring $1,600 to $2,500. All the above may or may not come with magnetic sound heads and amplifiers, but they all run at sound speed, and more or less quietly. If they do have sound gear, make the seller understand you won't pay an additional nickel for it because nobody shoots single system anymore. But be sure to get the amplifier and sound head anyway if they're available. The station has no use for them, but you will. You'll learn why later on page 99.

Meanwhile, you'll want to test the lens for sharpness, color, and contrast. Contrary to popular belief, they can wear out from physical use or abuse, or can lose their optical qualities over a period of time because of atmospheric conditions.

A proper but quick test is to look at the image the lens makes through a reflex finder or prism. (A zero finder built into the lens doesn't count; the image must be projected onto a ground glass.) If the image is too soft or too flat, the lens may not be any good. Also look into the lens from the front to see if there is any fungus or separation of the elements. A minimal amount of either, especially around the periphery, probably won't be perceptible on the finished film, but finding it may help you get the price down a little. A film test is best to confirm the quality of everything in the system. Using Type A Kodachrome, shoot 15 seconds or so in the sunshine with an 85 or 85B filter at the proper exposure. This will test the lens for contrast and the camera for light leaks. Then go inside. Adjust a light on a card so that you get a proper exposure with the lens wide open. Shoot another test at five feet, focused at five feet but zooming to full wide and back. Back off another five feet and repeat all this while focused on the card at ten feet, repeat at 15, then at 20, and at 25 if you can. A hallway and a single reflector with a 200w lamp at about two feet will do quite well. Only the card need be illuminated. Shooting a digital electronic stopwatch or an electric clock with a sweep hand for 20 seconds (480 frames) will help you determine loosely whether you're running at sound speed.

Be careful when bargaining for a lens which has obvious problems. Repairing any zoom lens can cost as much as simply buying one in A-1 condition.

This CP-16 is not the reflex model but with the 12:1 zoom lens and zero finder the result is the same. With the lens, two magazines, two batteries, and a 110v power supply, it cost $1,500 in 1987.

98 Location, Personnel, Financing and More

This Bolex H was bought for $20 without a lens. The lens, an extra on another deal, was therefore free.

Send the film to the drugstore lab. Any drugstore can send your Kodachrome to a quick turn-around photofinisher. Kodachrome is the most precise film process and one of the fastest to get back. "Precise" is the key here, though.

You'll want to test the camera for movement steadiness. If it runs properly and is not noisy, chances are it runs as accurate a speed as it ever did. Having a technician check it out (if one is available) ought not hurt the seller's feelings.

The way to test the camera is to photograph white cross hairs on a black field for 30 seconds. (White adhesive tape top to bottom in the center of a two foot by three foot black show card, and another strip across the center, left to right.) The camera must be mounted rock steady and set to the widest angle of your zoom lens. Or use a wide angle lens. After you shoot, back crank the film in the camera if you can. If you can't, remove it and rewind it in total darkness. Rethread it into the camera. Reposition the camera just slightly and shoot a second time. When the film is developed, if you see no movement between the sets of cross hairs, or movement so slight as to be acceptable to you, you have a steady movement.

With careful planning, both the lens test and the camera test can be done as a unit.

Every TV station in the country has or had a Bell & Howell camera. If you can get it for a bargain, go ahead and take it. You'll need it for grab shots and cutaways. If you can't get one so easily, there are plenty of Bolex H's and Kodak Model K's and Cine Specials around that are available for a song. Or if you sing a little louder, you could pick up a good Bolex Rx or Pathe. Whatever camera you get, be sure to test it at all speeds before principle photography begins.

The Kodak Model K is not versatile except for having several transport speeds and a three lens turret. Used for possible throw-aways, a pair of these was bought for $130.

The Kodak Cine Special was a standard for Disney's nature series. It is one of the most versatile 16mm cameras. Two hundred dollars bought this one with a case, a magazine, two lenses, and the mattes that divide the image into several parts for special effects. Like the Bolex, it is noisy.

A Nagra recorder with a crystal sync pulse generator is the state of the art system for double system film recording. A good used one can be obtained for perhaps $1,500 up to about $6,000 for a new one. Using a recorder with a sync pulse is the proper way to record. Resolving the pulse on playback is the proper way to transfer to full coat. Doing that insures synchronization. If your budget won't allow such a machine, you could spring for a substitute for $50 to $300.

While you're at the station, you might also try to talk them out of their edit viewer and a two or three gang sync block if the price is right. You're going to need them too. Don't pay too much though. Since video is taking over the market, there are plenty of good film equipment deals around.

Location, Personnel, Financing and More   99

If you are not electronically oriented, find a friend and have him help you find a one quarter inch reel-to-reel machine. It must accept a five inch reel and have professional frequency response. You must speed test it. That is, test the running speed by recording a beep or clap, running exactly ten minutes by a stop watch, then a second cue. Play back the tape on a different machine, one which you can trust. If the beeps are within two seconds accuracy (that's no more than one second in five minutes), you're o.k. (Not good, but o.k.) If not, play it back on another machine you trust. If you're still more than two seconds off, find a different machine. Most nonprofessional one quarter inch recorders are multitrack machines. If you can't find a full track machine you may settle for half track. Four track is not recommended, especially if you have someone else transferring your sound. In no case are you allowed to use more than one direction of recording on a tape, although you may use two tracks if you use them simultaneously, or if you are recording in stereo, mixing two mikes into the recorder, or if their comparative levels are already balanced during original recording.

A VCR—any format—will run precisely at speed. Using one will insure proper sync in playback. Although you are recording sound-only on videotape, depending upon your machine, it may be necessary to record video also (even though there is no picture) in order to insure the recording of a sync pulse.

Using a VCR will require that you do your own transfer to full coat and probably require the sound man to mike through a mixer to maintain proper audio levels during original recording.

If the lab you've chosen offers to transfer the sound to full coat for the price of the stock, take them up on the offer and send along the one quarter inch tape with the film to be processed. If they don't, here's your chance to use the magnetic recording head you demanded when you bought your camera.

Break down your 1200 foot rolls of full coat into 400 foot rolls and load one into the camera. Feed the output of your one quarter inch recorder into the appropriate input of the camera amplifier through a mixer. Your camera is now a full coat dubber. Dub the circled takes onto the full coat and you're ready to interlock the full coat with the work print. Since you've determined that your recorder runs at proper speed and the camera will run at the same speed at which the film was shot, you will have correctable, if not correct, synchronization.

If you can't afford a Nagra, the one above probably will do. The one below probably won't.

If you have use of a good magnetic sound projector, you might be able to use it to dub your sound to full coat. The sound camera runs at sound speed helping to insure that the synchronization stays reasonably accurate. The mag projector is not likely to run quite so accurately unless it is an interlock projector which, by the way, will solve your next problem. It is worth a try even if it isn't. If you're within a frame or two of accuracy at the end of long takes, that's easily correctable in editing. If sync is too far out, find another way to do your recording.

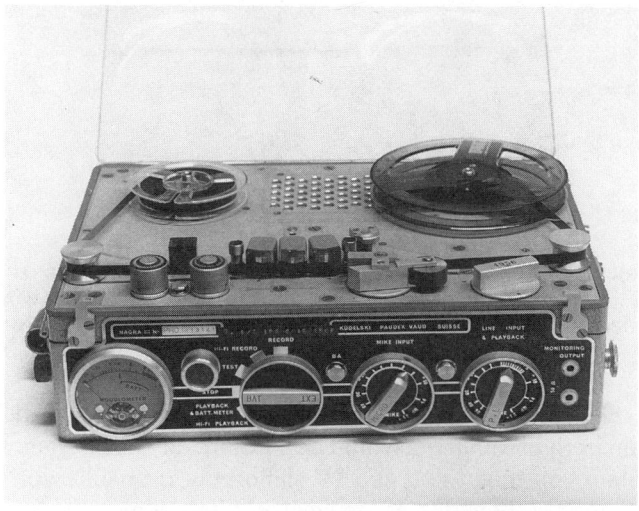

Nagra is the state of the art film recorder.

100 Location, Personnel, Financing and More

This and the facing page illustrate a way to make an interlock projector using a Bell & Howell 302. *Opposite page, left:* The threading diagram for the projector above. *Opposite page, right:* An alternate method using a nonmagnetic projector together with a sound reader. The worst drawback with these two methods is the need for an extra pair of projector arms, two for picture, two for sound and a motor to drive the additional take-up.

Chances are that when you bought all this junk from the TV station you got a sync block that had sound heads on it with the viewer. In a worst case scenario, you can watch your interlock this way. It's better than nothing, but only barely.

The film can be edited on the "worst case" viewer but an upright Movieola would be substantially better. It is an item you might find at a TV station but probably won't. Good used Movieolas are available from film equipment dealers anyway.

Location, Personnel, Financing and More 101

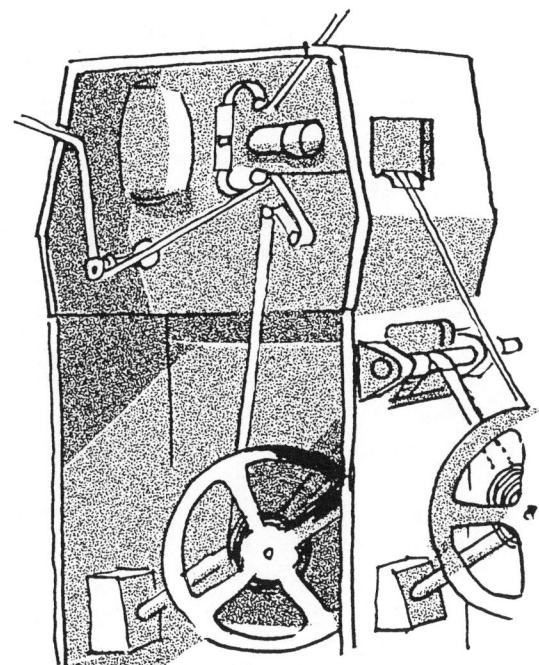

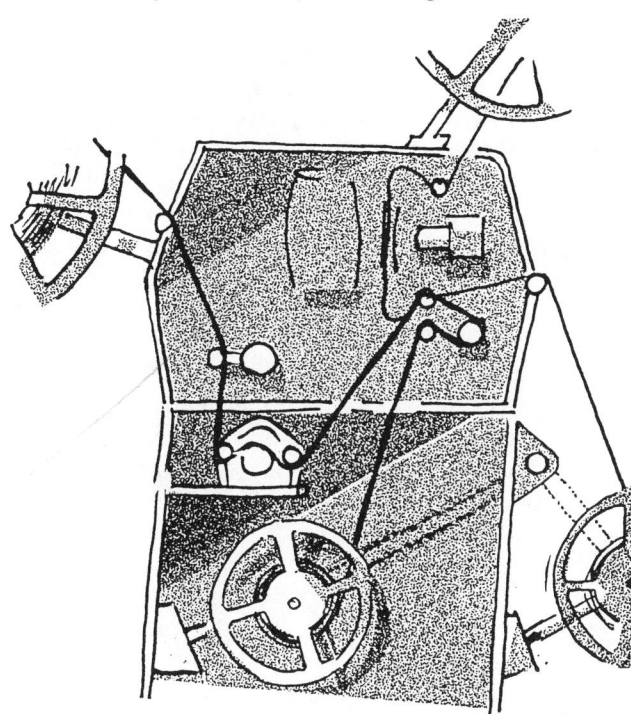

Having one with a picture and two or more mag sound heads would do the trick for $1,200 to $2,500, an amount you would pay for four to six hours editing in a videotape studio. Such an instrument is not hard to find.

In the process of editing the picture, you're going to discover that the sound may begin to drift somewhat on the longer takes. Having made the original recording without benefit of a sync pulse to resolve, several dubbing steps later, you're a little out of sync. So you drop in a frame or two of blank here and pull a frame or two between sentences there. You can do a whole film full of it and nobody will ever know. It'll take a little longer to edit, but you'll have saved $1,000 to $3,000 if you are doing your own editing or if you have a package deal with an editor. If you are paying him by the hour, it could cost you more than you've saved.

If recording a proper sound track was not possible during the filming of your picture, a poor one can be used as a scratch track (that is, simply a guide to the making of a good one). But the nuisance can take its toll with the editor's creativity.

Using your interlock system, even though it be nothing more than the Movieola, transfer the picture and sound to videotape using your consumer video camera, if that's all you have. Quality at this stage is not important, but sync speed is! Playing back that picture on a video monitor and the audio on earphones for the talent to watch and mimic in order to redo their lines will give you an extraordinary opportunity to enhance the sound quality.

You can, by this means, use somebody else's voice if you choose or when you have a character who is no longer available or whose voice needs to be changed. This is called looping, and is done a scene at a time, over and over, until it's perfect. Each looping tape is recorded on your audio recorder until you are satisfied. A log sheet is kept numbering the takes. When a satisfactory one is made, the next relevant scene is brought to the video screen for the talent to preview. This technique is continued until all voice takes *by that character* in the entire film are done.

They are then transferred to full coat and cut to match the picture. Dialogue between two characters need not be looped at the same time. In fact, it may be easier for each of them if they do their dialogue alone and allow the editor to keep them on separate rolls for later mixing.

While looping is an industry standard technique, this peculiar little method is not.

Actually, none of the above techniques is recommended! The use of a recorder with a sync pulse system and a camera whose speed is controlled accordingly will eliminate having "to fix" sync in editing. But if you have more time than money, the above stuff really works. More time, less money—always a trade off!

Remember that you didn't read here that using this used TV stuff was a good way to make a movie. It is a *cheap* way to make a movie while upholding the quality at least enough to be commercially viable. But uncontrolled, *cheap* can weigh quite heavily upon efficiency, quality, and ultimately upon salability. As your stock of money decreases, the value of efficiency increases. But when your money is depleted, efficiency has no value at all.

Sound mixes are done in one of two ways today. One or two inch audio machines with all the tracks on one tape are state of the art and an expensive proposition, but using an interlocked gang of full coat dubbers is still the most popular method.

If you prefer to do your own mixing, you can probably

make do with as few as two dubbers and one recorder. Mix rolls A and B to X, rolls C and D to Y; then mix rolls X and Y to Z. Then Z is your master sound track roll. On a serious budget picture you may have as many as 30 rolls to mix, whereas on an extremely low budget picture, it's unlikely you'll have more than four or five but you could have as few as two. If you do have additional rolls, continue mixing pairs until you have them all down to one. Of course, if you have more dubbers, play back on as many as you can effectively mix in a single pass to minimize degeneration of audio quality.

There are plenty of labs and sound companies who can mix your sound for you. If you don't do so on a regular basis, chances are, that even unsupervised, they can do a better job than an inexperienced film maker. On a simple project where only three to five rolls are mixed, buying the service could well be less costly than mixing sound yourself, especially in terms of frustration.

Such mixing can be done from a cluster of one quarter inch machines dubbed over to a single recorder, but you are at the mercy of having false starts and of frequently drifting out of sync. A final mix is impossible to correct. It simply requires starting over and redubbing.

If your project uses a lot of music or background sound such as traffic or babbling brooks, and very little sync sound, a one quarter inch mix can be both effective and economical. Simply put beep tones at the beginning and end of each eight or ten minute segment of one quarter inch roll. Mix it and if all the beeps come up together, you know you have held sync.

Since *Scarecrow* was a 16mm project for videotape release, the only sensible method of transferring to video was to do so from a low contrast positive. Depending upon a number of factors, this print would cost anywhere from $2,500 to $5,000 including the answer print. (Transferring from the original unedited negative would be the first choice except that all the editing would have to be done on tape at several hundred dollars an hour. Second choice would be to conform the negative and transfer that to tape. There is some disagreement by the video houses regarding doing that. (Some claim 16mm splices jump going through the printer gate while 35mm ones don't.) Transferring from a lo-con pos also will cost about $450 per hour for about six to eight hours work while doing so from the original negative will take, probably, three to five times that long—at the same $450 an hour.

Before printing the lo-con master, scene to scene color and density correction is done in the lab. This is called "timing" and you may supervise it or not. Usually, you are charged more per hour if you supervise and it will take two to four times as long. But as long as the timer understands what you expect from each shot, such as "Scene 42 beginning at 470 feet is day-for-night," you'll probably get a better result leaving him alone than if you help him. He does it every day because he's good at it.

You'd just be a thorn in his side. The lo-con is made, without a sound track, and transferred to videotape, again with scene to scene enhancement. Once more, you can interfere if you wish, but the rules above apply. Once the picture is completed, the master sound mix is then simply dubbed over to the master videotape.

A benefit afforded by the making of an I.P. rather than a lo-con positive print is the option to make a 35mm blow-up negative for printing in the event you sell rights for theatrical release. While this won't necessarily help the producer financially, it could provide a little leverage to help sell either a domestic or a foreign distributor on the project. (Keeping in mind the potential for selling the product to a foreign distributor, you'll want to preserve the unmixed full coat rolls so he can replace the English dialogue rolls with a foreign language and mix it together with your original rolls of other sound effects and music.) Having the interpos is also a safety measure protecting against negative loss or damage.

Instead of making a lo-con positive, you can make a conventional print with optical soundtrack and have it transferred to videotape. The timing for such a print is identical to that mentioned for the interpos or the lo-con.

If you elect to do this, add $1,200 to the budget for sound-track negative and $.03 per foot for one more printing pass, $200 for transferring, and subtract the preexisting video transfer rate.

Many video rental stores will willingly do a transfer for you, but will definitely require a conventional 16mm print with an optical sound track (or a Super/8 with a magnetic track). They're o.k. and they are cheap but you can't use the result as a dubbing master. This is an obvious savings, but will you be able to sell this reduced quality image to a distributor? Maybe.

The TV business is in a constant state of flux. While a few TV stations are jealously maintaining their film equipment, a greater number are scrapping all film gear. Some may be able to help you while others cannot.

Doing this is not necessarily a bad idea. If you are short on funds during the post production stage, you may save money by doing it this way and still have something worthwhile to show a potential client or distributor who may be willing, after a deal is made, to pay for the lo-con and first class transfer. In fact, you could simply send him the 16mm print to view without making a video at all.

The woods are full of thieves, and if you are as suspicious as most producers, you may elect to make a dupe of the transfer with the title keyed in across the bottom of the frame through the picture from beginning to end. That's the same as portrait photographer's stamping "proof" across the face of his prints—to preclude unauthorized use.

Since all this "transfer" business is so confusing, here is a summarizing rundown.

Timing costs are absorbed by the regular answer print which will reduce the cost of the lo-con (if the lo-con price already includes the cost of timing). Note: Never put a lo-con on a projector! A single pass through the gate will scratch it. If you need to run it through the projector, get a print!

Video production houses can transfer from any medium. They're all good but expensive.

Blowing up from 16 to 35 before transferring will offer no increase in transfer quality.

10
Equipment Choices

VHS, Beta, and 8mm Video

For several reasons making a feature on videotape is not likely to be worthwhile. Invariably, if you do a good job, some buyer—or buyers—will want to distribute the product in film as a medium. If all you have is tape, forget it. In the unlikely event you can make a sale big enough to cover your hopes, you'll need to know some of the following information.

Conventional consumer equipment of this ilk is not recommended, not even for student projects. While many such cameras make a pretty picture under the right conditions, even those pretty pictures are sadly lacking when compared to professional grade video images.

VHS, Beta or 8mm video editing equipment which is worth having for commercial or industrial purposes is a rare find. Because editing is done by the duplication process, and since the duplication of VHS, Beta, or 8mm degrades the image so badly, your result from such equipment may be good for fun, perhaps even for corporate safety films or student projects, but is *not marketable* at all.

To make matters worse, to step up to three quarter inch, BetaCam or one inch in order to edit may leave you at a transfer speed at which you cannot sync a sound track other than the original one.

Beta (not to be confused with BetaCam) is essentially dead in the United States. VHS and 8mm video equipment rent from video stores for about $35 per day, but you'll get a little break if you rent by the month. You can often find used examples of both types in pawn shops and camera stores. If you really need one, you're better off taking the best retail deal you can find.

Super VHS and High-Band 8

S/VHS lives in a world unto itself. It is good to watch on a S/VHS monitor, but seen on a standard TV set looks like any other VHS. It has at least two advantages over standard VHS; it will hold sync to FCC standards when stepped up to an editing format and it does not lose image quality quite so badly from one step to the next. A fourth generation copy can be quite good.

The same argument can be made for the High-Band 8 (also known as Hi/8). In fact, Hi/8 looks better on a conventional screen than does S/VHS and typically loses less image quality in the duplication process.

There are a number of renegade producers using one of the two formats quite successfully. If you were to interview them all you would probably find that those who use S/VHS are doing a low budget, early morning show in its entirety with that camera or are doing it live in the studio with taped inserts done with the S/VHS camera. Most of those who are using the High/Band 8 are shooting footage in which they are intercutting with footage shot with a high-dollar camera. A classic example would be to shoot the "safe" footage of a documentary with a $70,000 Ikigami camera and the white water rapids or parachute jump with a High/Band 8.

You'll find both S/VHS and High/Band 8 cameras available at around $2,200 to buy and, perhaps, can be rented at $50 to $75 per day. It's difficult to find either of them used but, if you do, simply apply your best judgment.

The TV show *Shag News Network*, a show targeted at people interested in dancing to beach music, was distributed in many parts of the United States. Evidently no one perceived that it was done entirely—including the commercials—on Hi/8.

Industrial Cameras and Recorders

Typically the industrial grade camera will do a good broadcast quality job for you; that is, not only will the electronic signal hold up but so will the visual quality.

All the high dollar manufacturers—those who make the $70,000 cameras—also make the $5,000 to $7,500 industrial variety. The $5,000 and the $7,500 units may well be the same camera, but the higher priced camera will sport a higher quality lens, one which producers invariably claim is worth the difference. A rank amateur may not be able to differentiate visually between the two.

Ordinarily, together with one of these cameras (which have no internal recorder), the user will elect to use a portable three quarter inch recorder which will cost about $3,500 to $4,500 depending upon the model. (Similar machines can be had for only a few hundred but the resulting image is no better—if as good—as standard VHS.)

Even at the estimated $11,000 price a fluid head tripod, spreader, and a number of expensive electrical connectors and batteries will be required at an additional price. Renting a system like this will run about $750 per day but typically you'll be charged for four days if you rent by the week.

The bad news is that if all you've ever used is a camcorder you'll need to rent a technician to go with the camera. Just as you would not hire a pilot for your airplane on the grounds that he's successfully flown a model airplane, you cannot operate a sophisticated video camera without substantial experience. Professional equipment, whether video or film cameras, accomplish almost nothing without direction, while amateur equipment do automatically a number of things without your knowledge, input, or permission.

Furthermore, doing a proper job with one of these cameras requires a separate video engineer with an oscilloscope to monitor the video signal. He can handle the job of sound recordist at the same time. Having the help of such an engineer, however, might allow a good film cameraman to use a video camera as skillfully as he would a film camera.

The Top of the Line

The $70,000 camera is the camera which delivers the highest quality image and electronic editorial capability. Like the industrial equipment, it requires experienced technicians to operate it. This is the equipment used to shoot the best of the networks' video programming and the advantage lies in its superlative visual quality.

Some models are designed in a modular fashion so that a BetaCam recorder is dockable to the camera unit resulting in a camcorder configuration. Those same models can feed into a three quarter inch or one inch machine but are not dockable with them.

There is such a variation in the attributes of each brand or model that some machines will not play back in the field, some will play back only monochrome while others will play back in full color. Nearly all have black & white monitors but several color monitors—eye pieces—are already out there in videoland.

When you're ready for a high-tech camera, something like the cameras in these two photos are what you will get. (Photos by John Autrey.)

Editing with a BetaCam from one-inch will cost the $450 an hour which we've discussed, although you can still use the time code window for your primary edit on a VHS dupe. The three quarter inch can be edited at most postproduction facilities for under $100 per hour.

Interestingly enough, these cameras rent for the same rate (more or less) as the industrial cameras. The advantage in these, as already stated, is the image quality. The disadvantage is found in the editing rate.

11
Less Common Equipment Options

What About Super/16!

Super/16 is a format designed to offer the advantges of both 16 and 35mm while displacing the disadvantages of either. The advantage of 35mm is its image size. Because it exhibits four times the frame area of 16mm, it is bigger therefore better. It is also the preferred format for optical work.

The advantages of 16mm are that the equipment is smaller, lighter, cheaper, and gives more running time on a single load. Also equipment is quite abundant.

Let's explore reasons to use—or not to use—Super 16.

First, take into account why it wasn't considered on *Scarecrow*. The picture was intended for video release only, while keeping an option open for theatrical release an an ancillary market if someone *else* wanted to do so.

If we change our primary goal to putting the picture into a theater, we can consider Super/16 or 35mm. If video were the primary goal while *we* proposed to put it in theaters, Super/16 would have been a good choice. Do not be duped into believing that Super/16 is superior to 35mm because it is not. It simply can be a less expensive tool with which to arrive at a 35mm (theatrical) format. With rare exception, theaters use 35mm and 70mm and that's that.

In California, more specifically the San Francisco Bay area, many filmmakers are shooting Super/16 projects. Some labs and optical houses are following suit to provide services specifically oriented for their requirements. The reasons are econo-qualitative ones—to coin a word. The producers are getting the 35mm look at a production cost only slightly greater than 16mm.

The difference between the two is a matter of the image size. Super/16 cameras take advantage of existing standards (that is, ordinary 16mm single perforated film), allowing them to use not only the normal picture area but the portion of the film set aside for the sound track, a space on a negative stock reserved but never used. The result is a frame 45 percent larger than the standard 16mm frame and exhibiting an aspect ratio of 1.66:1, the same as 35mm wide screen—but only 15 percent smaller.

You'll notice that the advantage of Super/16 is drawn partially from the additional image area but more so from using all of the regular 16mm image rather than cropping it at the top and bottom. In other words, it is necessary to crop regular 16 in order to get a wide screen format, whereas Super/16 blows up—full frame plus about one third—a standard 1.66:1 aspect ratio.

Cameras have to be modified for Super/16 by widening the aperture, recentering the lens mount, and redefining the picture area in the finder. This is impractical for some cameras, quite practical for others.

When entering into the realm of Super/16, it is necessary to develop a cognizance of things which do not necessarily apply to conventional 16.

In converting a camera, tests must be made to insure that the available lenses cover the wider image area. If you're using a zoom lens, it must be tested through its full range of focal lengths.

The only difference in film stock is that it must be single perforated stock without a mag stripe, and may be either reversal or negative.

Plan for the fact that color negative film (especially Eastman color) basks in overexposure, particularly when shooting in a dark environment (such as woods at night) or dark subjects (such as a black car in the shade). Some additional exposure helps to achieve a less grainy negative enlargement. Since Super/16 is not used for purposes other than blow up, sacrificing as much as one f/stop of exposure to minimize graininess may be necessary.

It is said to be critically important to focus and roll-focus with more attention to precision than with media not blown up, because every little problem is magnified and accentuated. The rational argument exists that all film images are blown up for the theater screen anyway, therefore any reasonable cinematographer will focus as accurately as possible without further motivation.

Trying to compose correctly for both TV safety and wide screen will be the source of constant nightmares. Check with the lab who will transfer your film to video to find out whether they can shift the image so as to print from the center of the Super/16 frame. If they can, you may compose for both with a greater degree or ease.

You'll quickly discover that not all labs deal in Super/16, but in the earlier stages of your endeavors it may not be necessary to switch labs for that purpose.

Standard film processing machines and contact printers (for work prints) will not likely scratch the edge, but color analyzers might. It is advisable to shoot a foot or two of subject matter ahead of each slate or at action's end, identify it, and file it so that when the time comes to color correct your film, it can be done from these in lieu of scratching the printing negative.

For your own edification or private screening of the work print, you can widen the image aperture of practically any 16mm projector by removing the aperture plate from the film gate and putting a small file to it. Naturally, you won't want to do this with your best machine, but there are plenty of good projectors out there, available for a song, that will do the job quite well. Remember, this is not for exhibition, but simply to check your dailies.

When editing time comes, you will already have rejected any takes which are bad because of what does or doesn't appear in the extra area. Not being able to see it on your viewer while editing will not likely cause you a problem; you will edit as if you were editing regular 16. If you prefer, of course, you can rent or buy a Super 16 editor or have your own converted.

Because making an optical blow up, in this case, is preferable to making a contact printed intermediate, conforming the negative for zero cuts is favored to keep the splices from jumping in the printer gate.

A contact interpos, on the other hand, will save you a few bucks if your lab does not have a flat rate for the combination of interpos/dupe neg, but for a contact interpos you wouldn't conform the negative for zero cuts. The choice must be made before negative cutting begins.

Zero cutting is a method whereby the scene beginning and end is indicated by the negative cutter but is accomplished mechanically in the optical printer. The scene on the A roll may extend any length past the cut while the following scene may begin at any point before the cut. To the negative cutter, the only important issue is that the picture be in the proper cutting orientation at the point where the zero cut occurs.

Zero cuts can be made from single rolls as well. The negative cutter simply puts three frames of black leader between the takes and indicates to the timer where each cut is made using a communication they both understand. However it's done, single roll zero cutting has to be a nightmare of confusion and a hotbed for errors.

Ultimately, you will want to make a video master for TV or video release, as well as video prints as "screeners" by potential distributors. With zero cuts, you have a double option for the transfer to video. First, and probably preferable, you can make a video directly from the 35mm interpositive, saving transfer time and therefore money. Or you could transfer directly from the zero cut original negative which may look the tiniest bit better but cost notably more—about three to seven dollars more per splice in addition to an increased number of hours in the making of the transfer. The quality difference will be less noticeable than the cash difference.

The only serious advantage in the zero cutting technique is the preservation of the original negative integrity for later film editing with different cuts.

You'll find it prudent to get a quote from your video lab before postproduction begins in order to know the most cost effective route to take.

Since there are labs all over the country doing regular 16mm, there's little point in recommending one or to list who's who in the lab business. There are fewer Super/16 labs. The two listed here not only would like to have your business but surely can answer any number of questions if you're serious about using Super/16.

They are: Interformat (an optical house), 1000 Brannon Street, San Francisco, CA 94103, (415) 626-1100; and, Monaco Labs (a wet lab), 234 9th Street, San Francisco, CA 94103, (415) 864-5350.

Monaco Labs also offers the unusual service of transferring Super/16 to videotape while extracting the video image from the center of the Super/16 format.

The expense of shooting Super/16 is not identical to regular 16. That extra foot or two shot for timing must be accounted for although the price of an equal number of feet of single perf raw stock is the same.

The cost of converting or of renting a camera must also be considered along with the slight increase of processing and printing if you choose a lab specializing in Super/16 (which, by the way, is recommended).

If you are interested in renting a Super/16 camera, try Adolph Gosser at (415) 495-3852, or Lee Utterback at (415) 974-1982.

The most expensive single item is the combination interpositive and dupe negative to 35mm, a price you'll have to get from the lab or optical house you deal with. (Be reminded that when shooting in Super/16, or other formats requiring an optical step, that not only do you need an interpositive but also a dupe negative made from it.) If you shoot in standard 35mm, and if you plan to make a limited number of prints, you won't need an IP and a dupe negative. But not having an intermediate is risky—having one is insurance against loss or damage.

Some labs or optical houses make CRI's (color reversal intermediates). If they do, they can made a duplicate 35mm negative from a 16mm original negative in one step. This saves one generation but is a more expensive process. Get a quote for both and see how the numbers work best for you.

All these things once considered and resolved will dictate whether shooting 35mm or Super/16 will be the cheaper and at what shooting ratio. For example, if you plan to shoot at the unlikely ratio of 3:1, it would be cheaper to shoot in 35mm and save the blow up expense. But 3:1, although not out of the question, is an improbable ratio for most shoots—even especially cheap ones. Shooting 4:1 probably will still be cheaper than

108 Less Common Equipment Options

Regular 16 blows up like this.

Super/16 and a blow up, but doing your calculations around 5:1 and 6:1 surely will reveal just where the break-even point is.

A general overview will indicate that the above appraisals alone will dictate which of those two formats will best serve your budget, but it is important not to forget that no matter what format is used, almost all other elements of expense remain fixed. Your talent will charge a given amount regardless of the format. So will the sound man. You'll need the same lights and light stands for 16mm as you would for 35. If you were to raise the budget enough to shoot in Super Panavision, it wouldn't be a low budget picture and the crew you would need is not likely to settle for eating at the golden arches every day.

Techniscope

Now would be a good time to consider Techniscope. Unfortunately, Techniscope is no longer an economical option. When Techniscope came on the scene, it really was a good idea. It was a come-on instituted by Technicolor to get business into their labs.

Techniscope was simply a two perforation pull down format. Standard cameras were converted as were *some* editing benches and interlock projectors. Only half the negative stock was consumed, half the processing and, *in some cases*, two perforation work printing was used, saving substantial money. Technicolor made optical work prints, anamorphic IP's, and dupe negatives at contact printing rates thereby bringing in lots of new business.

According to the folks at Technicolor, Techniscope is still alive and living in California, but is not exactly thriving. Due to the low demand for this format in new projects, it is used today for only the upgrade of work done in the past which is being reused or reissued for a modern production. So that knocks Techniscope out of the running as an economical format.

It is a valid format only for special purposes. Because it is historically significant, a brief explanation follows.

Shooting underwater, Techniscope allows twice the shooting time before having to surface and reload, saving valuable diving time. In the tail section of a sailplane, where a camera can't be reloaded, a 200 foot magazine of film would get as much running time as 400 feet of academy footage. So Techniscope can still be efficient and economical on a wide screen 35mm production (especially if you have a Techniscope editing table), but it's simply out of the question for "cheap."

The following are quoted passages from a letter Technicolor, Inc., wrote to me in June of 1972.

> "The Techniscope system was designed by Technicolor to provide a 2.35 to 1 aspect ratio anamorphic theatrical presentation in color at a production cost substantially below that required for conventional anamorphic or wide screen photography. The difference in cost is one-half the negative and negative developing and one-half the protective master positives. A further savings is effected in that there is less than one-half the waste in short-ends.
>
> A picture photographed in one of the standard wide screen formats, for instance 1.85 to 1 or 2.0 to 1 aspect ratio, wastes more than one-third of the negative area available and a like amount of projection light in the theater. By arranging the camera so that the film travels through it at one-half the conventional rate, making each negative frame one-half the conventional area, and then enlarging in a vertical direction only in print manufacture, these losses are recovered and the resulting screen image remains as good as the conventional 1.85 or 2.0 to 1 aspect ratio wide screen with greater screen brilliance. Theatrical release prints are compatible with other anamorphic projection systems.
>
> Prints may also be made in wide screen format for theaters not equipped for anamorphic projection. In this form, the aspect ratio is 1.85 to 1. 16mm prints may be in 1.85 to 1 wide screen or 2.66 to 1 anamorphic. [They go on to discuss prints made by the extraordinary but now defunct Technicolor dye transfer process which is also historically significant but has no relationship with cheap.]
>
> The only special equipment required is the camera; all editing and projection is done in standard form. Standard camera lenses of all focal lengths may be used, including zoom lenses if desired. As with any photography, care should

S/16 blows up like this.

be used in selecting and calibrating quality lenses. [In the original letter they continue by naming several companies who can supply the cameras most of whom, in the intervening twenty years, have fallen by the wayside.]

There are still companies who can modify your 35mm camera for you if you feel safe doing so. You can get more information from Technicolor, Inc. (818) 769-8500.

Anamorphic

Since anamorphic has been brought up in the discussion of Techniscope, and because it has historical significance, it does deserve at least a brief discussion. The white mouse illustrated example in this section of an anamorphic print done from Techniscope depicts what such a print looks like. Shooting a picture in anamorphic simply means that the camera is set up to make the original negative that will achieve this print.

The Robe, a religious extravaganza from the early 1950s, was the first CinemaScope production. And what a dynamic format it was! It was a superwide—an almost wraparound image—with a four-track, four-position stereo sound that boggled the senses.

It required special equipment installed in the theater and on the projection equipment. Not all theaters subscribed to these expensive changes (which still allowed the exhibition of conventional prints), but those who did profited handsomely.

CinemaScope lenses were made specifically for CinemaScope productions. Because of its popularity, other companies came out with assorted lenses or lens attachments allowing varying degrees of squeeze both in shooting and projection, depending upon the aspect ratio. As popularity waned, the paraphernalia in most theaters were removed and replaced with 35/70 projection equipment.

The diminishing popularity was actually brought on intentionally by the producers who found production to be heavily encumbered by the use of anamorphic lenses. Zooming wasn't possible. Follow-focus shots were more difficult than normal requiring talent to hit the mark and hold the mark. Cameras with special apertures and sprockets were required, and in some cases, narrow pull-down claws were needed. Lenses were slow, requiring more light than otherwise. Anything that was out of focus had a distracting appearance and prints required special four-track magnetic sound. The whole system was cumbersome.

It turned out to be simpler to shoot in 65mm and make anamorphic prints, since production techniques and the projected image would then be back to standard.

After the popularity of CinemaScope declined, theaters set up for "scope" could exhibit those squeezed prints made from the new 70mm productions without further mechanical encumbrance until such time they installed their new 35/70 systems. The look was even better and since then has become today's standard.

As a practical matter, it's out of the question to shoot a picture in a "squeezed" format today because it will be tough, although not impossible, to find someone to exhibit it. Since we've discussed a cheaper-than-normal way to do almost everything, why stop the discussion at anamorphic?

Back in the 1970s a friend had written a script which we wanted to shoot as absolutely cheap as we could and still have a viable theatrical release. (Remember, there were no video releases back then.) Here's what we concocted.

Using a 16mm Arriflex with a 17-75mm zoom lens, we would shoot Anscochrome film and blow it up to a 35mm negative. In order to preclude cropping top and bottom during blow up, we would film with a 16mm anamorphic projection lens supplement attached to the zoom lens giving us a squeezed original image. Blowing up the entire 16mm frame in a standard optical printer would result in an anamorphic 35mm negative.

But the test of the pudding is in the eating! We shot some trial footage on the prescribed inexpensive Anscochrome film (which is long since out of manufacture).

110 Less Common Equipment Options

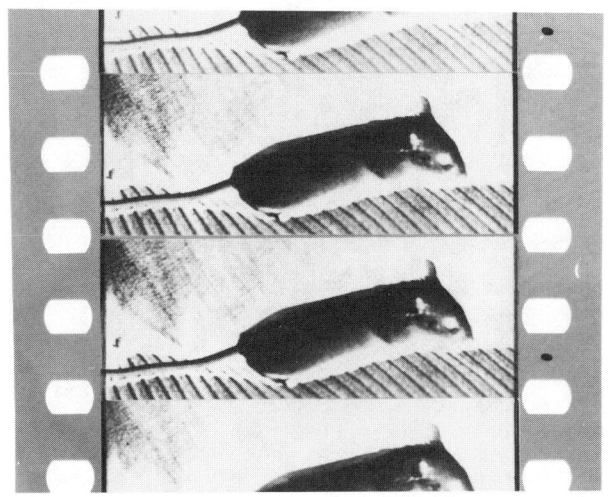
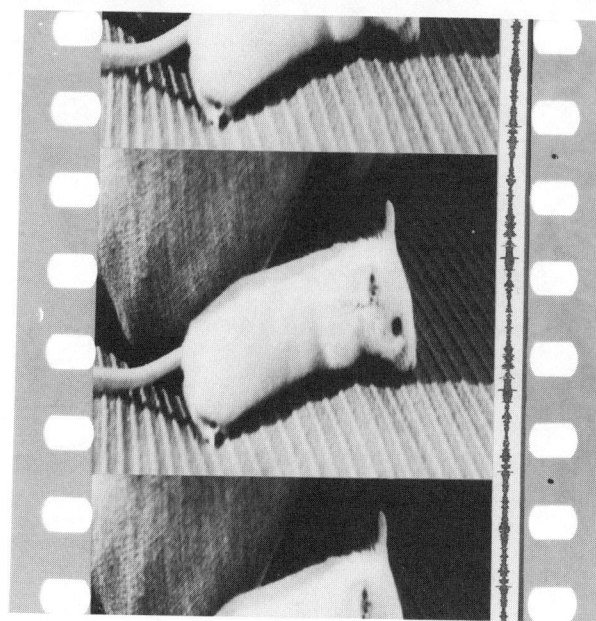

Top left: A Techniscope negative; *top right:* an anamorphic print; *bottom:* a flat release.

By projection, we compared it with a 35mm print of *The Russians Are Coming, the Russians Are Coming!* (which, at that time, was in current release). We were stunned to note that acuity, focus and color saturation were as good on our test as they were on the 35mm print.

The test had broken all the rules of anamorphic. Out of focus elements did not look unusual, the lens lost no light level owing to the supplementary element, follow focus wasn't tricky, the equipment was not appreciably more bulky, and so on.

It is fair to note, of course, that the 35mm print was at least third generation (as release prints are) while ours was the camera original, but still, that is a stunning comparison.

Alas, not liking his own script, my friend withdrew it and the project was dropped. A shame! I'd like to have done it if for no other reason than to prove that I can be a tighter tightwad than the next guy in line and still get the job done right.

Three-Perf

Three-Perf, a trade mark belonging to Clairmont Camera (not to be confused with 3-Perf, a trade mark belonging to Panavision Corporation), also bears a similar definition but its goal is somewhat different.

By pulling down three perforations per frame, it also exhibits a slightly wider aspect ratio than academy, all of which can be printed as standard 4-perf print for theatrical release. At the same time, by cropping only slightly on both the right and left, most of the 35mm frame can be transferred to video with the 35mm look.

(It is interesting to note that while doing research for this book I found no one who uses Three-Perf for theatrical release, or even makes a film print. So the theatrical attributes don't really apply.)

The goal of Three-Perf primarily is the savings of some technical application dollars while upholding high-dollar quality. Its cropping theory is a little different from that of Techniscope. All of Techniscope's image was projected in the theater but cropped heavily in video transfer, leaving roughly a portion for TV equal to a 16mm frame.

The Elwood Dolly System. (Illustration provided by Tony Elwood.)

Three-Perf crops only slightly in video retaining the quality of 35mm in both cases.

Most of the Three-Perf cameras have a 30 fps frame rate which translates perfectly and directly to video, that is, one film frame for one video frame rather than the 24:30 ratio which is typical. For all practical purposes, the 30 fps frame rate cannot be printed as a 24 fps for theatrical projection. But then who cares if they aren't going to use it for that purpose.

According to Technicolor, nearly everybody who shoots Three-Perf transfers directly from the negative to tape via a Rank Cintel or a Bosch machine, circumnavigating the need for a Three-Perf editing table or optical printer.

Three-Perf is not something to look down your nose at. *Hunter, Thirtysomething,* and *Jake and the Fat Man* were filmed in the format because it saves 25 percent of the negative stock and processing, and thus adds 25 percent to a magazine load. On projects that require shooting day after day, year after year, the savings add up. For what it's worth, the system makes it easier to compose for the combination of theatrical and video release. For additional information contact Clairmont Camera, 4040 Vineland, Studio City, CA 91604, (818) 761-4440, or customer service at Technicolor, Inc.

The Dolly

The use of a dolly will substantially enhance the look of an otherwise bland picture. *Body Shop* had only one dolly shot. *Marley's Revenge* had only one. In both cases a three-wheel transport dolly was used. Such dollies are not recommended because they are not especially smooth, except on a very smooth floor, and because they tend to veer off to one side unprovoked and unexpectedly. Even so, they are better than nothing since any picture deserves more than a single dolly shot.

Nearly all worthwhile pictures have dolly shots from

112 Less Common Equipment Options

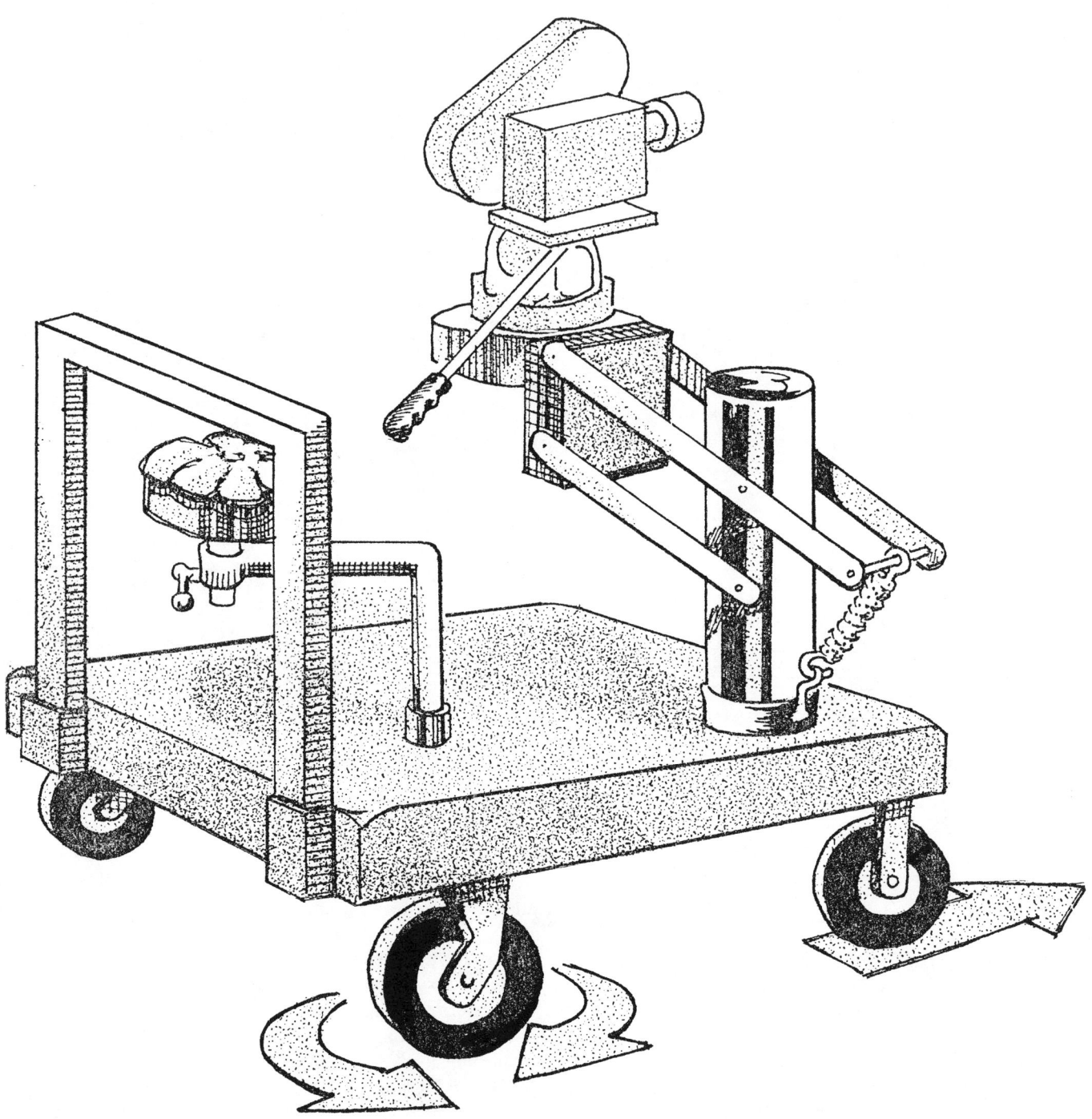

This is the design for a dolly which requires no track but is quite efficient on a hard floor or outdoors on sheets of one inch or three quarter inch plywood. (Given the choice, I'd use Tony's outdoors and this one indoors.)

Neither dolly will crab, but since this one has swivel wheels on the rear, moving carefully, it can be slowly pivoted while the camera operator pans in the opposite direction offering the illusion of crabbing.

beginning to end. If you were on the set of almost any Hollywood picture, you'd see the camera resting on a dolly, not on a tripod.

Dollies are expensive to rent and a great deal more expensive to buy, so if you don't want to use a wheel chair (an excellent temporary substitute) or a pair of roller skates (a less-than-excellent substitute), you might consider building one of the following.

Tony Elwood was kind enough to give you the plans and information for the first one which he built and used on *Killer*.

Here's what he says:

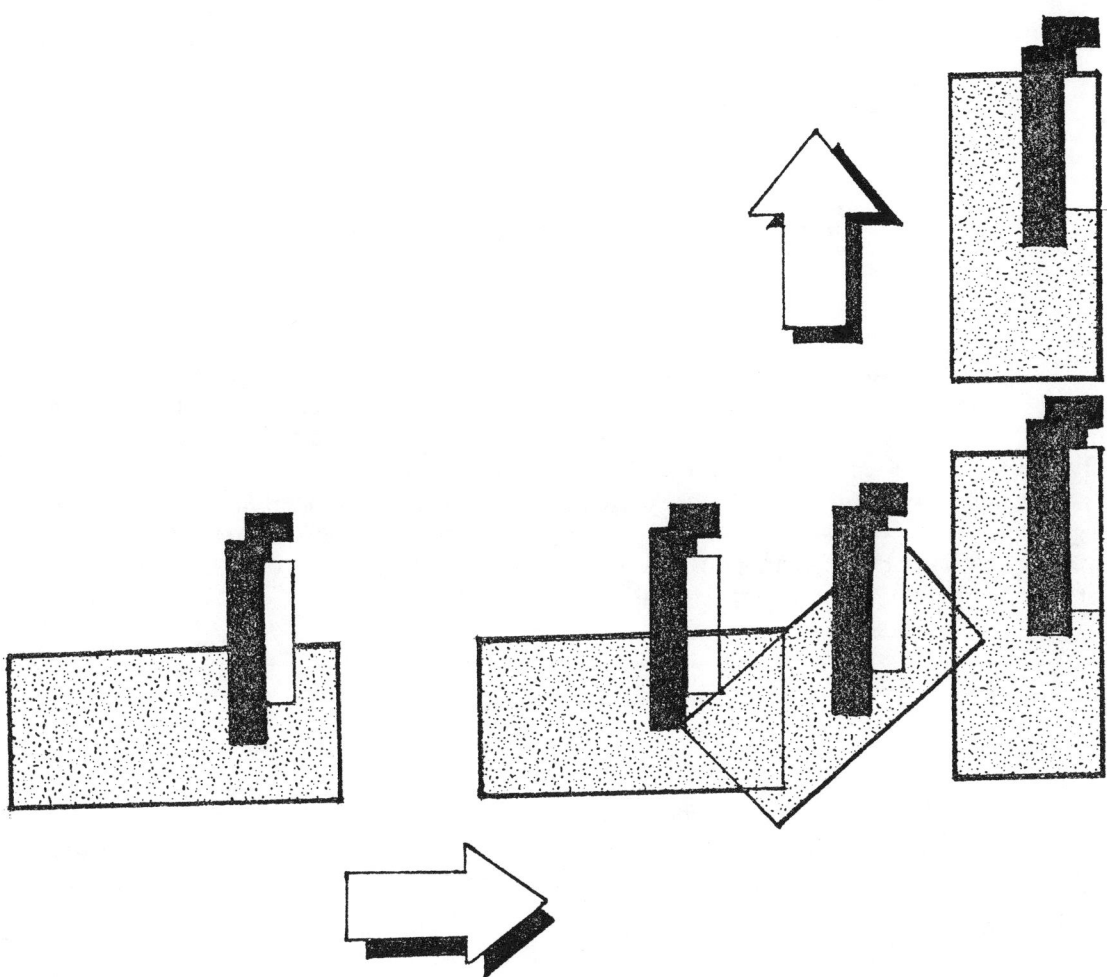

The move of the dolly in the previous drawing must be made according to this diagram. The spring-loaded parallel arm arrangement allows the camera to move vertically.

Developing a cost effective dolly system was very important in the making of *Killer*. The film required dozens of tracking shots, which would have been impossible to keep steady with the light weight of most Super/8 cameras. So I developed an inexpensive tracking system using commonly found materials.

The key to the simplicity of the Elwood Dolly System is the wheels. I used large theatrical pulleys—wheels with grooves cut inside—for the passage of large ropes. The groove makes a perfect passageway for PVC pipe.

I attached all the wheels to the outside corners of a large 2 inch × 4 inch × 2 inch base plate. For extra support I placed two 2 × 6's under each side of the plywood then attached the wheels to the boards. Using 5 inch screws, I attached the wheels to the platform.

To fashion the handle, iron plumbing fixtures and pipe turned out to be the best combination of cheap and good. (I suggest you experiment with this and develop your own style for what suits you best.) I then drilled three 1 inch holes into the wooden platform for the legs of the tripod to nuzzle into. Once the tripod was in place, I taped the legs into the holes for extra security.

I measured the distance between the grooves in the wheels. It is very important that you make sure your wheels are spaced properly to keep the pipe from dragging against the wheels.

Once I got my measurements I proceeded to take two 2 × 4's and lay them out on the ground. I began with an 8 inch section and cut my PVC pipe 8 feet 2 inches to allow one inch of pipe to extend from the 2 inch × 4 inch. If you need to add another section of track, simply insert an inner-connector which slips into the PVC and onto the adjoining section.

To attach the track to the 2 inch × 4 inch I drilled six holes in the top of the pipe (large enough for a small screwdriver) and, directly below them, six smaller holes for the screws. This keeps the screwheads below the surface of the pipe, keeping it smooth. After mounting the pipe, I cut several 2 inch × 4 inch pieces into 2 feet 5 inch sections. These were used as cross ties to the 8 foot sections, and were attached precisely according to the distance measured from the grooves on the wheels.

Used together with 2 inch × 4 inch × 6 inch wedges this railroad-like device offers a track that my dolly can ride smoothly upon. These are the basics on how I created my dolly. While it was a life saver, it still can't take the place of a Pee Wee or Chapman.

Being rigged for track operation limits it to just that, but affords it the ability to be used both indoors and out.

12
Strange Equipment

Why Not Standard 35?

While 35mm is the most expensive of the standard formats, it is not altogether out of the question for relatively inexpensive production. Very few feature films are done in any other gauge.

Based upon the very important assumption that the result is theatrical distribution, it can be less expensive than 16mm or Super/16. Earlier comments regarding blow up negatives alluded to the cause of the difference.

With total disregard to other ramifications of production, look at compared rates for 35mm, 16mm and Super/16. (Rates are average for 1993. They are valid only for comparison and general overview. It is imperative you not use them for any other purpose.)

For Theatrical Release

SHOOTING RATIO, 4:1	12,000' 16mm or Super/16		40,000' 35mm using 16mm sound & wp
Film stock	2,258		13,040
Film processing	1,440		4,800
Work print (all ftg.)	2,730		
16mm reduction work print		(circled takes)	5,860
16mm interpositive	3,100		
35mm dupe negative	19,000		
16mm full coat	1,600		1,600
TOTAL	30,128		25,300
SHOOTING RATIO, 10:1	30,000'		100,000' using 16mm sound & wp
Film stock	5,656		32,600
Film processing	3,600		12,000
Work print (all ftg.)	6,825		
16mm reduction work print		(circled takes)	13,024
16mm interpositive	3,100		
Dupe negative	19,000		
16m full coat	1,600		1,600
TOTAL	39,781		59,224

Shooting in a 4:1 ratio, you'll notice that 35mm is less expensive and vice versa in a 10:1.

There is a conspicuous absence of three things—35mm dupe negatives from 35mm originals, 35mm work prints, and 35mm full coat.

Many labs don't have reduction printers. Those who do

don't like to use them for work prints. It truly is not a moneymaker for them and, they claim, it puts a little extra stress on the original negative. But the making of a 16mm work print and full coat recording is your choice and an option worth considering because it will save approximately 45 percent on the cost of those items. Since the work print is not the finished product, there's little reason to use the bulkier, more expensive 35mm work print. You will discover, when looking at price lists from the various labs, that reduction work prints from 35mm negatives are the same rate or only slightly more costly per foot than contact work prints from 16. Working in 16mm requires only about one third the total footage with the added advantage that you will print only the circled takes from the 35mm negative. So you save twice.

The same is true with full coat. There's little point in working with 35mm full coat when you're editing a 16mm work print. There is no doubt that a transfer from the faster transporting 35mm full coat yields a higher fidelity result. But reasonable savings is our goal here, not increased quality. The audio deficiency in this case is not likely to be perceptible to any but the well trained ear of a technician.

By editing in 16mm, you have yet another advantage of providing yourself with some 16mm equipment at prices you would not be able to duplicate in 35mm equipment. Just for comparison, let's take a look at the 4:1 ratio again but this time all 16mm in its own column, plus blow up. Likewise the 35mm which uses 35mm sound and work print. To see the dollar difference, we are making 35mm work prints and 35mm full coat recordings.

For Theatrical Release

SHOOTING RATIO, 4:1

	12,000' 16mm or Super/16		40,000' 35mm using 35mm sound & wp
Film stock	2,258		13,040
Film processing	1,440		4,800
Work print (all ftg.)	2,730		
35mm work print		(circled takes)	17,580
16mm interpositive	3,100		
35mm dupe negative	19,000		
full coat	1,600		7,200
TOTAL	30,128		42,620

While there is an abundance of 35mm equipment available as used items, you'll find a smaller variety than in 16mm.

Starting at the top you could find an Arri 35BL for $20,000 to $25,000 with a 25–250 zoom lens. Certainly no less a camera is the Mitchell BNCR for about $12,000 with a complement of Super Baltar lenses, or a BNC may do the job for you at about $8,000 or $9,000. There is the smaller Arriflex such as the II series which you would have to put into a blimp to use, but there's nothing wrong with that if you get a good enough deal.

Regardless of which of the above cameras you get, you will need a handheld camera for grab shots, or MOS shots where there simply isn't enough room for a large camera, or a problem angle such as shooting from high in a tree. If you don't have the Arri as mentioned above, you'll need an Eyemo for that with an 18mm and a 25mm lens. Expect to pay $300 to $500.

From time to time isolated or singular deals pop up in which you may find a Wall 35 or a Mitchell NC or such for a third of the above rates. Unlike the 16mm gear you may haul out of a TV station, such a deal is less likely to fall into the lap of a user than that of a dealer.

There are only a handful of dealers in the entire United States of which few offer an unusually good deal. For a package deal or a bargain buy, on everything from lighting to lab equipment to camera gear, give this outfit a call: Martin Hill, 10100 Sam Black Road, Midland, NC 28107, (704) 455-9345.

70mm—On a Cheap Movie!?

Actually, 70mm is only the projection format. Many such films are shot on 65mm film. The additional 5mm's are added to the print stock to accommodate the multiple sound tracks. (It's only fair to note that many 70mm films are shot on 35mm and blown up in order to take advantage of much brighter projection and substantially better sound. *Dick Tracy* is a classic example.)

The 5mm discrepancy from 65mm won't save you a

Martin's 35mm Mitchell NC served well on *Body Shop*.

dime. The argument exists that money can be saved on the rental of less popular equipment on the grounds that it doesn't get rented very often. To make the deal economical, the savings must be enough to pay for the difference in the cost of the 65mm negative, negative processing, optically reduced work prints, and a few other compensatory expenses. This idea may seem farfetched but might work in your favor if the character of your production is such that you will spend a very long time shooting little bits and pieces every day. It may pay you to get prices anyway if you intend to do some 65mm background plates for traveling mattes. (And don't forget that all the peripheral equipment—lights, recorders, dollies—cost the same in all formats.)

This argument applies only if your market is theatrical and if you would have otherwise filmed in 35mm. Because a 65mm negative must be reduced for 35mm release printing, only the *difference* in the price of optical reduction must be accounted for as a separate matter since a somewhat less costly contact dupe negative would be made from a 35mm original anyway.

Super/8!—For Feature Filming?

What about taking a look at Super/8 as a possibility? The worst thing it has going against it is reputation; a properly bad one based on two premises. First, Super/8 cameras are so automated as to keep them just out of control no matter how you shoot, and second, the film is so tiny as not to be able to contain a particularly well detailed image. Both points offer a good argument.

Super/8, though many hate to admit it, is a medium to shoot a really commercially viable, super-cheap feature (if not a really super, cheap feature) for video release.

Several successful Super/8 films have been released in video stores. Don Swan's *Gourmet Zombies from Hell*, Tony Elwood's *Killer,* and Mark Pirro's *A Polish Vampire in Burbank*. These three were done with varying degrees of expertise, each used a similar budget (an unconfirmed guess is "less than $15,000 each" while one is known to be $12,000), and exhibit different quality levels.

They were all worth doing. *Killer* got Mr. Elwood a backer for a 35mm theatrical—that's a giant step, and that alone would have made it worthwhile from his point of view.

All the above titles (as well as *Body Shop*—also known

as *Dr. Gore*—and *Marley's Revenge*) are available on VHS tape through Multi-Video, Inc., 1424 E. Independence Blvd., Charlotte, NC 28205, (704) 377-1269, (704) 334-0531, (800) 289-0111 or FAX (704) 334-1058. (Multi-Video also sells *Amazing Special Effects You Can Do with Your Camcorder.*)

Super/8 is not expected to hold the image quality of 16mm or any larger format, but in film stock and lab costs may well save $3,000 to $5,000 over the price of 16. You'll save an additional $1,500 to $2,000 by not having to buy a 16mm editing machine because work printing it, editing it, and conforming it is folly for a serious Super/8 project. If you don't already own video editing equipment or have some available to you at an affordable price, most or all of the money you will have saved shooting Super/8 will be spent editing the tape transferred from it. It's a little like shooting in 16mm and spending the money you saved blowing up to 35mm. You must diligently search for mathematical answers before making the final decision.

If you intend to engage in Super/8 production, consider that you'll need the most precision of everything you can get your hands on. Film-Video Supply Co., P.O. Box 704, Orange, NJ 07050, (201) 672-2223, is reputed to have the Super/8 splicer to end all splicers, the WURKER S/8 which gives you pop free sound and doesn't cover up your balance stripe. They say it is a "must" for S/8 filmmakers.

Transferring from Super/8, by the way, will not cost any more or less per hour than doing so from 16mm. However, 16mm probably will be transferred from edited footage so you will transfer on a 1:1 ratio. The Super/8, on the other hand, will be a "transfer all good takes" affair for later editing on tape. Be careful not to do your calculations on a footage basis. Convert your footage to transfer time and then calculate the rate, because one hour of 16mm involves about 80 percent more footage than one hour of Super/8.

The name of this company tells you a little of what they do. If you need to do title designs, composites, Super/8 to 16mm or 35mm, optical effects ranging from the simple freeze frames and optical pans to bi-packing for mattes, or video transfers you can give a call to Interformat, 1000 Brannan Street, San Francisco, CA 94103, (415) 626-1100.

You'll also want to check Rupert Taylor's Film Studio, 500 Middle Road, Belmont, CA 94402, (415) 592-5824.

Rupert Taylor's Film Studio could well be the most cost effective outfit for Super/8 transfers. Be prepared to give him detailed notes on how you think each scene ought to look. Discuss sending him a short roll to test.

Super 8 Sound, 2805 West Magnolia Blvd., Burbank, CA 91505, (818) 848-5522, has the capabilities of transferring your film on a Rank-Cintel machine.

Rank-Cintel will give you the best image possible and will provide you with limitless techniques on improving your film. In fact, if you don't have your film transferred on a Rank-Cintel—or equal equipment—it may never be of a good enough image quality to sell! Call them well in advance of your required transfer date because their machine stays busy. They are reputed to have anything you need for single or double system shooting and editing.

Because they're good, Brodsky & Teadway, 10R Oxford St., Sommerville, MA 02143, (617) 666-3372, stays booked. You'd be wise to call them ahead of time too.

Since Super/8 represents the least quality of the film media, having a good transfer is going to be paramount. While video stores all across the country will transfer 8mm and Super/8 to video for $25 to $50 per hour, even the best of these is inadequate. If you plan to spend the $10,000 to $30,000 to make a feature, you need to pay the price to have the transfer professionally done on a scanner. It ain't cheap. But if you can get it into the video stores, your tape will rent for the same price as *Gone with the Wind, Exterminator II,* and *Attack of the Killer Tomatoes.*

The proper way to recalculate the budget would be to subtract all the 16mm raw stock, processing, work printing, negative cutter, 16mm video transfer, camera and recorder; then add back Super/8 raw stock, processing, Super/8 video transfer, and single system camera or double system camera with recorder. (Just be sure to use a 24 fps camera.)

As mentioned earlier, one of the most serious drawbacks of Super/8 is the automatic camera. Like camcorders, nearly all Super/8 cameras adjust exposure to suit themselves regardless of the cameraman's choice. Using them can make it nearly impossible to do a day-for-night shot, an intentionally over or underexposed shot, or gain proper exposure of an extremely contrasty or strangely composed shot. A sure cure for the problem would be to use one of several cameras which allow the operator to override the automation.

Such cameras as the Bolex Rx and Pathe have manual models of their cameras which use double Super/8 film on spools. They use interchangeable lenses allowing you to choose the optical system you prefer. While these cameras are as good as—in fact, identical to—their 16mm counterparts, readily available, and sell for quite a reasonable price, you can't get the film you would need for them through ordinary channels.

If you'll call Chambless Productions, 2488 Jewel St., Atlanta, GA 30344, (404) 767-5210, you will find that they can provide you with Double Super/8 Kodachrome film, as well as the cameras in good or new condition. (Be aware, however, that if you plan to use FUJI that their films do not come in the Double Super/8 format.)

Bi-Rite Photo & Electronics, 15 East 30th St., New York, NY 10016-7080, (800)223-1970, also can provide you with Super/8 film and processing combination at a good price.

If the film you buy doesn't include processing you'll want to contact Multi-Media, Inc., 7154 E. Nevada, Detroit

Michigan, (313) 366-5200. They process original, make prints, and are dealers representing Super/8 companies. Multi-Media does transfers using Aerial Image and Telecine on VHS, the dying Beta, and three quarter inch.

Doing acceptable matte work and most other effects in Super/8 is out of the question. They can be done in a larger format and reduced to Super/8 before transfer, preserving the bulk of production as Super/8 or done on tape after transferring from any film format.

While it's been implied that it's folly to edit a Super/8 work print, it's not impossible. (It wouldn't be possible to edit the original, either, but it would be destroyed by the time you were ready to use it.) The folly comes into play on the premise that the stuff is so tiny it is difficult to work with and could easily be scratched or mishandled in the process of conforming.

So if your intention is to shoot Super/8, transfer it to tape and edit the tape, you can get an excellent result. You'll still get the film look at little more than the materials cost of shooting videotape.

In contrast to the statement above, watch out for a flood of "high resolution" or "high definition" video soon to come on the market. There is speculation that it will be wide screen and in consumers' homes. There is equal speculation that it will not. There is the possibility that it will be used only for production to supplant film, then converted to film for theatrical release. Those of us who love film hate the prospect, but eventually, it'll happen. The "new" video will have a look better than that of today's film. I've seen it! When will it be available? Nobody knows.

Super/8, of course, is an excellent first medium for students since it costs so little. It limits the student forcing him to use his imagination in production rather than depending on the lab's ability to bail him out—an inconvenience but an advantage.

A student should be led rather quicky to 16 or 35mm. Once he's past phase one, he needs to take advantage of the capabilities, services, and advantages that larger formats offer of which he is deprived in Super/8 or videotape.

Since We're on the Subject of Videotape...

If the goal is to release the product in any medium other than video, shooting in video is pointless. Making a transfer from video to film stinks and is very expensive. Besides, seldom would anyone buy the product.

Video does indeed have a superb array of attributes that invite a producer to shoot in that medium. He will be restricted to distribution in that medium, but in the age of electronics that's not so bad. The only place he can't exhibit is the American theater. Other than TV, what's left?

Well, several things. Consider this. TV is not simply TV. TV means one thing; the local TV station. But, there's also network, movie channels, and cassettes for video stores, in-flight movies, oil rigs at sea, ships at sea, American construction companies and government bases in foreign countries, and so on. These media are increased each time you can sell your product to a foreign distributor.

Probably the greatest advantage of shooting video is in being able to see the result *right now*. Depending upon your budget and the equipment you have, you may not be able to control the "look" of the result you see *right now*. Using a consumer camera is out of the question, if you intend to sell the product on any basis other than prurient interests.

Video being your choice of media, you have few cameras from which to choose.

The Ikigami camera is the top of the line at around $50,000 followed by several Sony models at around one third of that price. Both require an expensive separate recorder.

The BetaCam is the Ikigami of the camcorders. It is disputable whether the Super/VHS or the High-Band 8 is the better. They are for different purposes. SVHS looks like regular VHS on a standard TV. Hi/8 and 8mm look much better than VHS on a TV. They are different enough to cause difficulty in the establishment of a good argument but cost about the same. Depending upon your choice or availability of editing equipment, you may be able to exit from the original tape in all cases. Confirm *everything* before making your choice.

These cameras are broadcast quality while consumer cameras are not. (Be sure to note the definition of *broadcast quality* in the glossary.)

Other Uses for Video

On the sets and locations of *Marley's Revenge*—as on many others—a video documentary was being made with a consumer camcorder. The typical interiors and exteriors on tape looked just like the film. The night exteriors, on the other hand, were brightened up by the camera's automatic exposure system and looked more like daylight than night. O.k. for a documentary, but intolerable for feature work.

If you have the opportunity to use one of the state of the art broadcast cameras, controlling it properly can put you ahead of the game because in the process of shooting you will have the advantage—and obligation—of doing color, contrast and density corrections as you go. You'll find that doing such corrections from video to video is more limited than from film to video, but usually, less necessary.

Shooting special effects with video can be a boon. The result of using ChromaKey is essentially the same for video that traveling matte is for film but the effort required is practically nil.

Traveling mattes will cost hundreds of dollars per minute—if not thousands—in the 35mm format, but "keying" is essentially *free* in video. In conjunction with a character generator, so are "matted" titles.

Other Uses for Video 119

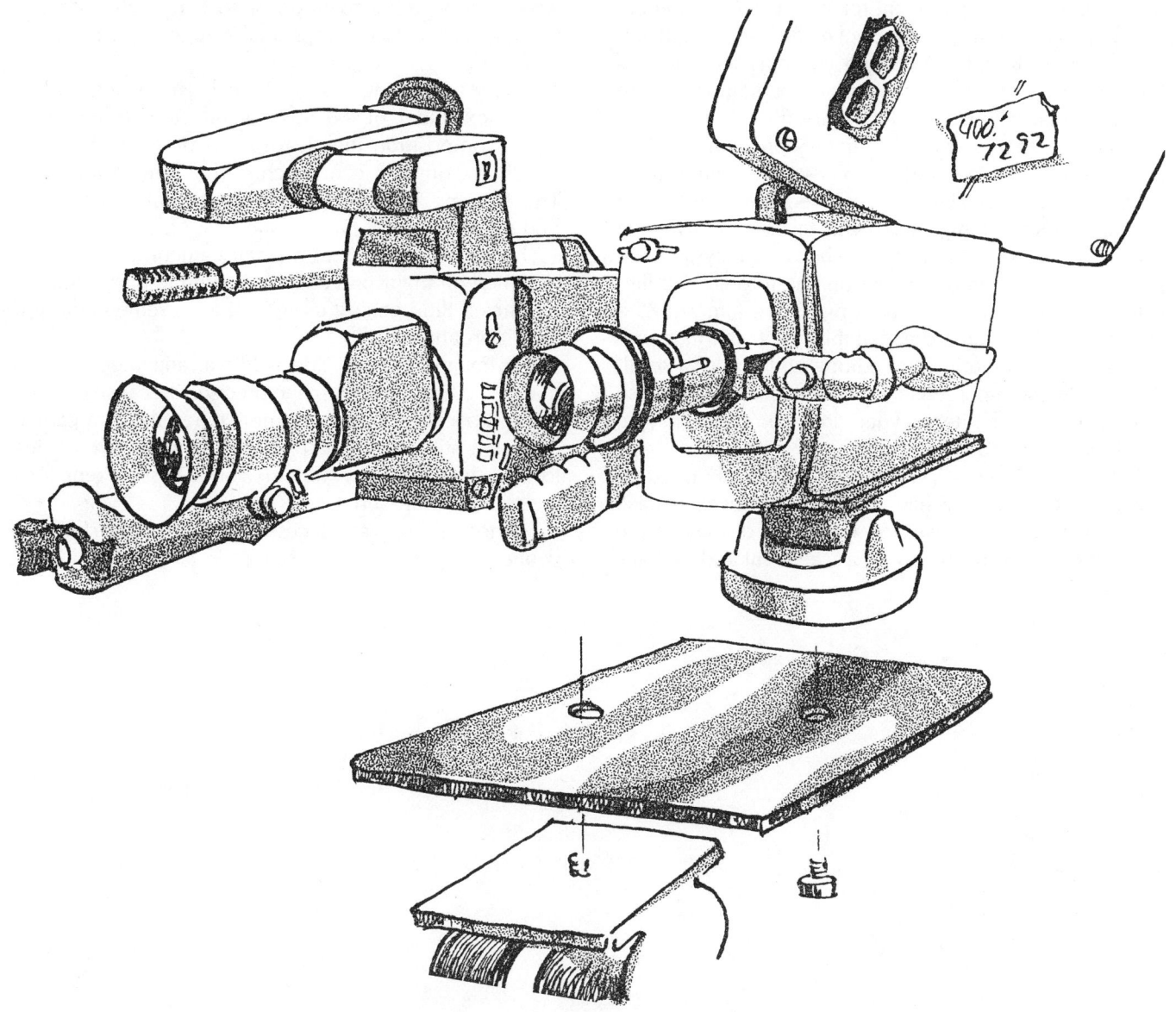

Here's how the video assisting device was set up in *Marley's Revenge*.

If an inordinate number of effects may be required in your production, perhaps for background replacement or an invisible man, the ability to do them cheaply on video, as well as where and how the product will be released, should influence your decision of what format to shoot.

Remember the title "BOOM!" In video that could be done using a character generator and an effects generator. In a few minutes a really sharp technician could complete the effect without the mess of making show cards or litho negatives.

Chances are that when you get it back it will have been done right on the first pass because the technician is constantly monitoring it and tweaking it up as he goes.

On film, the operator has to begin again almost from scratch each time he makes even a subtle change.

Depending upon whom you know or what arrangements you can make, you might have to supervise the editorial process for $450 an hour or, with some luck, arrange to do a hands-on project by yourself for $25 to $50 an hour.

The former will take substantially less time because it's automated, but even so it wouldn't take many hours to overshadow the "hands-on" arrangement at such a rate. In both cases, having a time code window will allow you to take home a VHS tape so you can do your pre-editing between two consumer machines or with a pencil and paper.

This time code displayed on the screen can be done whether your original is on tape or film. So if it will help you, take advantage of it.

In the use of a video system rather than a film camera system, about the only production differences you'll find

120 Strange Equipment

will be that your requirement for light will be lessened. The quality of lighting is a product of the kind of light you use, not how bright it is. While you may need less illumination, you'll need the same kind of lighting units in the same places you'd need them for film.

By far, the greatest difference in the appearance of film production and video production lies in the technique of shooting and editing. Directors of videotape features tend to shoot tape in long, drawn out takes—usually wide shots, then zooming in and out—because they lack the subconscious vision of money running through the film gate that they have when shooting 35mm film at $75 a minute. Thinking film instead of thinking tape in the processes of both shooting and editing will render a result with an almost imperceptible difference. (And if you use an appropriate fog filter on your video camera, it may be totally imperceptible.)

The use of video as VideoAssist for filmmaking ought not be overlooked. While it can't serve as a release medium, it can serve well on the set to display to the director or talent just how well a take went and perhaps what can be done to improve it. It can also serve to display continuity of props, make-up, angles, positions, and so on.

VideoAssist in the most technical sense is tied in with the reflex finder of the film camera, thereby getting a video composition identical to that of the film camera which the director can watch during filming and later. The systems are expensive enough that a super low budget simply can't handle one.

Ther is no reason that a small camcorder cannot be mounted on the tripod coaxially with the film camera. It requires a little getting used to, that is, remembering to turn it on and off.

The image from this side-saddle arrangement will not match the film camera image precisely because of parallax and because it's not zooming when the film camera does. It is still equally helpful as explained yet costs less to buy than a proper system would cost to rent for a reasonably short shoot.

The technique was successfully used on *Marley's Revenge.*

13
Cheaper Lighting Possibilities

We'll need some lights, won't we?

The lighting industry has made strides in improvement of lighting systems, not the least of which is the latest HMIs. Their cost instantly implies to you that they have no place on a cheapie set, but they may.

From a qualitative point of view, you really ought to shoot with proper and appropriate film-type lighting units for either film or tape. Motion picture lighting units are expensive, and buying them takes a serious investment. When depreciated over a reasonable period, this investment is an efficient way to do business.

If this is your first film, there is no clear indication that it will not be your last. You can strengthen the efficiency of buying your lighting units by buying good used ones, but at the same time choosing each unit on the basis of potential resalability of you don't manage to stay in the film business.

You could buy new ones on the same basis, but the layout of cash will be greater while the resale price will be stable. The newly designed units also take newly designed lamps, the prices of which soar above those of older models. Finding a good package price on all the lights you'll need either as a purchase or a rental is a good idea.

Don't be deluded by the "rental price only" when you hear it since you'll probably have to buy your own bulbs or, at least, replace those which blow while in your possession. And bulbs are expensive! Ascertain the price of the lamps and their estimated burning time before you make a commitment for the units. It is assumed you know how bright the individual units are and how each type is used. Wattage is only a vague guide to the brightness of lamps and no guide at all regarding the qualities it exhibits. When you buy or rent lamps, it is important you understand what you are getting. If you don't, get help from someone who does.

While you may be able to make a wooden tripod, build your own sets, or drive the stunt car yourself, you probably won't be able to make your own light bulbs. But then, maybe you can!

Marley's Revenge got a good deal on two lighting units, one a 2K scoop, the other a 2K Fresnel. The price of the BVY lamp in late 1988 was $58.11 wholesale and almost triple that retail. The proper lamp in the unit gave up the ghost. We had one of our special effects men gently remove the glass envelope from the base, solder an appropriate length of 12 ga. copper wire to the wires inside the ceramic insulator, and fill the cavity with plaster. When the plaster was set, the copper wire was bent to accommodate any one of a 350, 500, 650, 1000, 1,500, or 2,000 watt quartz bulbs. These vary in price from as little as $4.50 to perhaps $30. The BVY ceramic unit became part of the permanent equipment and quartz lamps were installed as needed.

Alas, it had a minor problem. The copper wire having no spring action would allow the bulb to drop out from time to time. Ultimately, the copper wire was replaced with appropriate piano wire. Since it offered spring tension, it did the job.

The moral is that, since your situation is unique, just use a little imagination and you can save a buck or two.

The 2K scoop was handled a little differently. It originally used an EGK lamp which carried the same inflated price tag. Since the frong of the scoop was not covered by a Fresnel lens in this unit, the Pre-Focus base was removed and replaced with a mogul base which would accept a #4 photoflood lamp (1,000w). An adapter was purchased at the hardware store for under two dollars which would adapt that socket for household base, allowing also the use of #1, #2 photofloods, or any other bulb with a standard base.

While any good lighting man will tell you there is no good substitute for a focusable Fresnel lamp, he'll also tell you there are other types of lamps he needs. Many a film has been made without Fresnels, but if you can provide several of them, it will make the lighting man's job a little easier, more quickly executed, and decidedly better.

A trip to the hardware store will yield two units that can become indispensable. Clamp-on reflectors (scoops) will handle #1 and #2 photofloods and can be bought for between $2.95 and $7.95. Outdoor 350w quartz units (which are parking lot lights) can be bought for around $10. The former can be clamped onto a door, window sill, putty knife, pole, and numerous other available doodads and gadgets. The quartz unit is made to be mounted into a junction box. A single unit junction box with a standard

122 Cheaper Lighting Possibilities

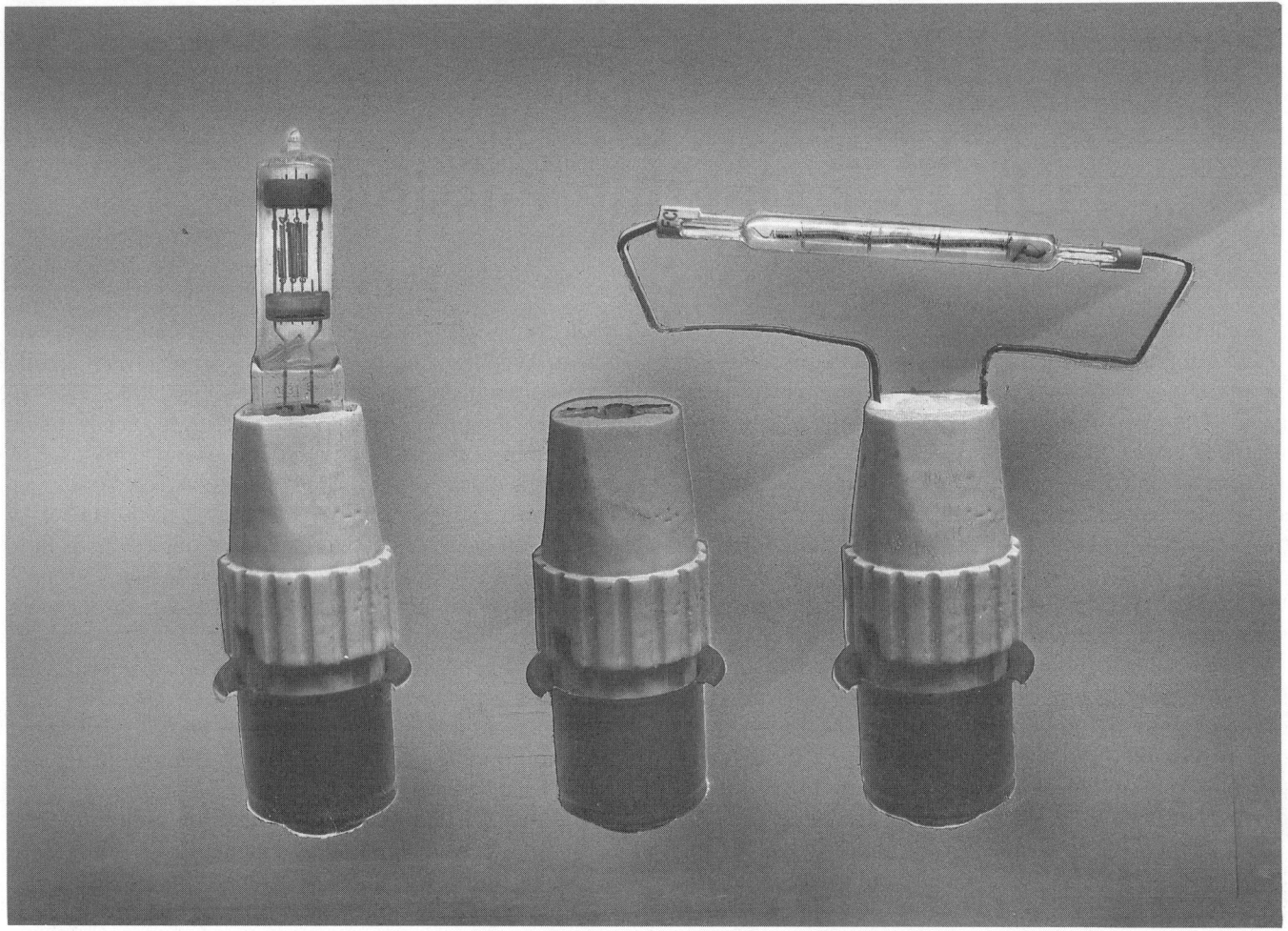

This photo shows how the homemade replacement bulb was made. Objects, left to right, are the original BVY, the ceramic portion with the burnt bulb removed, and the new unit.

toggle switch will hold the lamp nicely and can, itself, be mounted on a light stand by whatever clamping method you choose. Both units will tilt. The photofloods will be 3,200 degrees Kelvin while these particular quartz lamps are around 3,050. Too little difference in color to be concerned with for the difference in price since it is invisible to even the most sensitive viewer's eye.

Outdoor sealbeam spot and floodlights come in several wattages and fit into standard household sockets. Even the bright ones are dim in photographic terms but they can be a boon to the lighting man with an empty wallet who is shooting indoors or needs to put some subtle light outdoors in the shrubbery or under some cars, or to highlight a watered down street. And, since they are low wattage, a standard extension cord will support several of them.

When wandering around a hardware store considering the purchase of such lamps, it's important to remember that wattage alone is not a true description of the brightness of a lamp. While it is a reasonable guide, it is footcandles or lumens (one lumen equals one international footcandle) that count, and they are seldom listed on a bulb package. (At night, your kitchen would be about 40–60 footcandles while typical daylight is 1600.)

Perhaps the best way to effect a proper experiment would be to buy one of each type of bulb you think may do the job and meter them, preferably outdoors at night, comparing each to a standard such as a #2 photoflood at 15 feet. Chart them in a way you can understand. If you have a good relationship with the boss at the hardware store, he may let you do this on the premises, so you can do your calculations and buy the bulbs you need.

If you elect to procure your lighting in this fashion—which from a professional motion picture point of view is purely oddball—you are going to be left at your own discretion with regard to how you are going to come up with barn doors, cookies, flags, screens, nets, cutters and a host of other devices typically set in the path of light. For that matter, you will need to come up with some light stands of some sort, professional, amateur, or homemade.

Once on the set, you'll quickly discover that rather than having a couple of 5K's and 2K's, you're going to have a

Cheaper Lighting Possibilities 123

Standing back, one will notice only a pair of lights on a stand. One or two others are just out of sight.

ton of smaller units. More likely than not, when combined to generate enough light, these smaller units will cast multiple shadows. The same hardware store will sell you a couple of plastic fluorescent lamp lenses to smooth out the problem. Those lenses are made to do just the opposite of Fresnel lenses, to average the light from several sources and spread them over a general area. These seldom make good key lights, but they are dynamite for fill.

While you are there, you may want to pick up a couple of cheap mirrors. Glue something to the back of them (using epoxy or silicone rubber caulk) to allow you to mount them to a light stand or C-stand. Proper placement of such mirrors can augment the amount of light in a small room without increasing the temperature or can cast light from a place where a unit won't fit.

All these different types of light sources deliver different colors of light which can be a nightmare to the cinematographer who is meticulous about his color balance. Making little or no effort to correct them often appears to be a natural, intentional imbalance when used indoors. Outdoors, correcting them is a simple matter of using appropriate blue gel.

If you need some gel samples, write Rosco, 36 Bush Avenue, Port Chester, NY 10573-9978, and ask for a Cinegel sample. They'll send you a fantastic variety of samples made specifically for film work.

In *The Country House*, almost all of the lighting was done by replacing conventional light bulbs with #1 and #2 photofloods throughout the house, augmented by a number of clamp-on reflectors. Those lights, increased by an occasional light stand with the same bulbs bounced off the ceiling, were sufficient to shoot 5254 (the predecessor of 5247 rated at ASA 100) at f5.6 on every interior shot. No professional cinematic type lighting was used.

Even night-for-day interiors were filmed by using several blue SunGuns on the front porch or yard and aimed through the windows. No one seemed to notice it was dark outside the same windows through which "sunshine" cascaded over the furniture and onto the carpet.

For another project, the cinematographer built his light stands just like the professional models by buying aluminum tubing, flats, and other standard pieces from a well stocked hardware store. Using large aluminum wok-like reflectors, he installed discarded mogul bases on some to receive 1,500w stadium lamps which he got on a deal and were relatively inexpensive. This set-up made some pretty neat broads for fill.

On the others, he installed two Edison ceramic bases to accept #2 photofloods for the same purpose. The total investment for each was around $18. A commercially made model would have cost between $150 and $200, used.

The reason that Hollywood sound stages are so large is

124 Cheaper Lighting Possibilities

Even on a sound stage, you'll see small lights on stands and a No. 2 photoflood in the fixture above. (Photo by Chris Allen.)

to take advantage of the characteristics of light. Let's set up a simple situation. Assume you have a couple sitting side by side on a piano bench. Their heads are one foot apart and the only light source is one foot to the side.

If you meter both subjects individually, you'll find that the person nearest the light is exactly four times as brightly lit as the other. That's two f/stops. (According to the inverse square law of light, as you double the distance, the light decreases by a factor of four.) Two f/stops is too great a difference for the film's latitude to offer a good picture on the same frame.

Now back away the light, say 15 feet, and meter the two subjects again. Rather than a ratio of 4:1 as you had before, you now have a ratio of 100:93, a difference that is effectively nil, offering both subjects an equal, though much reduced, light level.

In order to get this same even illumination on a set 12 feet wide, it would be necessary to back off the key light to about 50 feet giving a ratio of 19:16, still within the latitude of any film. But it takes a large studio to back off 50 feet or more. (A ratio of 19:16 is a difference of less than 1/6 of a stop, too little to be visually noticeable.) Even so, it's typical to light a set sectionally. In all but a few sets, the characters frequently move from light to shadow to light to shadow, and so on. The technique is certainly more realistic and more interesting than an overall field of flat light.

Many outdoor scenes are filmed indoors on a sound stage. Disregarding cloud shadows, an actual outdoor scene is always evenly lit by the sun from close to horizon.

When a wide exterior scene is simulated indoors, it is important that the lighting be even. Sufficient space to back off the lighting equipment is required to combat the problems of fall off described by the inverse square law. A number of carefully placed smaller units with appropriate flags, fingers, and diffusers can achieve a flawless simulation of even lighting too.

You doubtlessly noticed a rather modern approach to TV lighting in the mid 1960's and early 1970's. A single light source perpendicular to the axis of the camera usually leaves the far side of the subject in darkness for the lack of a fill light but is pleasing to the eye.

This pseudo-Rembrandt style evolved as television developed popularity. The explosive expansion of color programming of that era demanded more and more color filming, requiring much greater volume of lighting than black & white did. Fast black & white needed comparatively little light and frequently could be done with available light alone. Color, being a slower emulsion, required more light of a specific color temperature. For the vast number of producers invading the industry, large, expansive studios were not available. Consequently, the new lighting approach took effect.

The large light source, not the bright one, is the only weapon to combat the fall off effects of the inverse square law of light. As long as the subject was no further from this bounce-light wall than the diagonal dimension of the (roughly square) wall itself, the light on him wherever he moved would be of constant brightness.

Such a light source could be set up in a relatively small area, had little or no fall off, was pleasing to the eye and, for electronically primitive TV, suited the video camera's eye to a T. (Note that in the earlier days of TV, and still today to some extent, the TV system was incapable of reproducing good detail in a high contrast lighting situation. The large light source offered either of two things which solved the electronic problem: first, the overall light was flat, eliminating the contrast problem, or second, the light source was well to one side which was contrasty, but offered a few middle tones to deal with.)

It's also noteworthy that this technique cannot be used to simulate outdoor conditions because it has all the earmarks of window light. It is an excellent approach to simulate outdoor light entering through a window or skylight.

In those sound stage situations which offer little latitude for lighting, many generalized sequences can be executed with little or no changes in lighting. That can help economically on the basis that progress can continue without having to wait for lighting changes and fewer light fixtures will need to be bought or rented.

This technique is simulated even today in TV news sets. The large bounce-light area is just that except the light is directed from scoops and broads instead of bounced. There are so many such units which are quite close together—clusters—that combined they constitute a single giant source.

Being individual, they do offer the ability to insert a Fresnel here and there for lighting control or turning off every third lamp to reduce either heat or light level. But then, TV stations today have little need for belt-tightening to the extent we are discussing here.

If you can shoot on a sound stage, day in and day out,

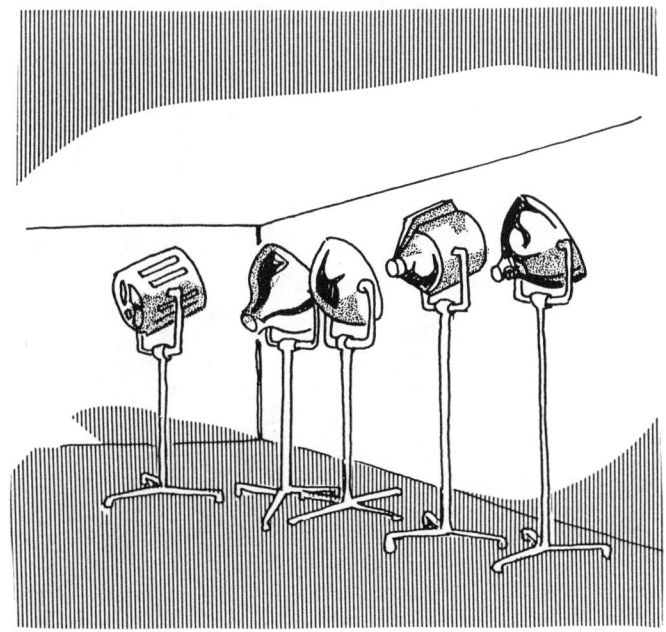

A bounce light set.

with minimal changes (like a soap opera) either on film or on tape, the old TV studio approach of having several soft lights and a spot or two may be the answer.

Whether you intend to use direct lighting or bounce, the creative electrical gadgeteer can cook up some unusual lighting fixtures using household electrical supplies and, even better, industrial electrical fixtures which the "man on the street" won't even be aware of.

Don't forget about the homemade lighting fixtures used on *Body Shop*. They had Edison bases, but the reflectors were made of aluminum roof flashing from the hardware store. While they weren't used for the main lighting, they worked quite well for fill and the supplementary work they did.

There is no limit to the systems you can invent and use to satisfy a specific purpose. Think of the used car lots that have strings of 60w naked bulbs to light the area. The result—if you don't look up at the sky—looks like daylight.

Knight of the Demons was a picture planned to be shot in the woods at night (but was never produced). The intention was to light all of the night footage that way so it could be left intact until finished.

126 Cheaper Lighting Possibilities

Units like these have little dignity, but they can do miracles.

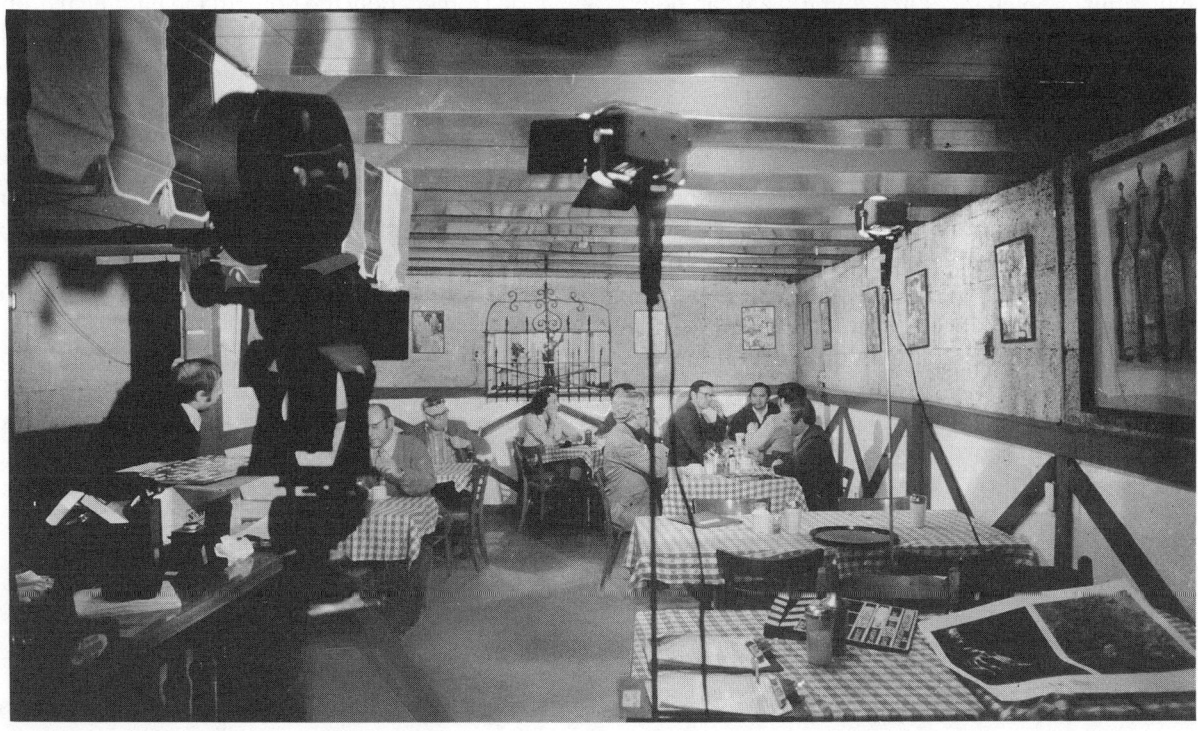

Only two SunGuns light the Open Kitchen Restaurant set of *Body Shop*. (This scene was ultimately edited out before the movie was released.) Although bright, the set has a natural look. (Photo by Chris Allen.)

Cheaper Lighting Possibilities 127

In the living room of *Body Shop,* a much closer set, only two SunGuns are lit (one blocked by the camera) while the third stands by. Bouncing most of their output off the ceiling causes their illumination to be that of natural light. (Photo by Chris Allen.)

While a few other lamps of different types and wattages undoubtedly would have improved the look of this interior *Body Shop* shot, it does not have an unnatural appearance. (Photo by Chris Allen.) This photograph of Pat and his leading lady is the result of the lighting set-up shown in the previous photograph.

128 Cheaper Lighting Possibilities

The indoor "beach" in *Body Shop* was lit by three SunGuns and a naked #2 photoflood for fill. Fifty pounds of sand topped off the illusion. (Photo by Chris Allen.)

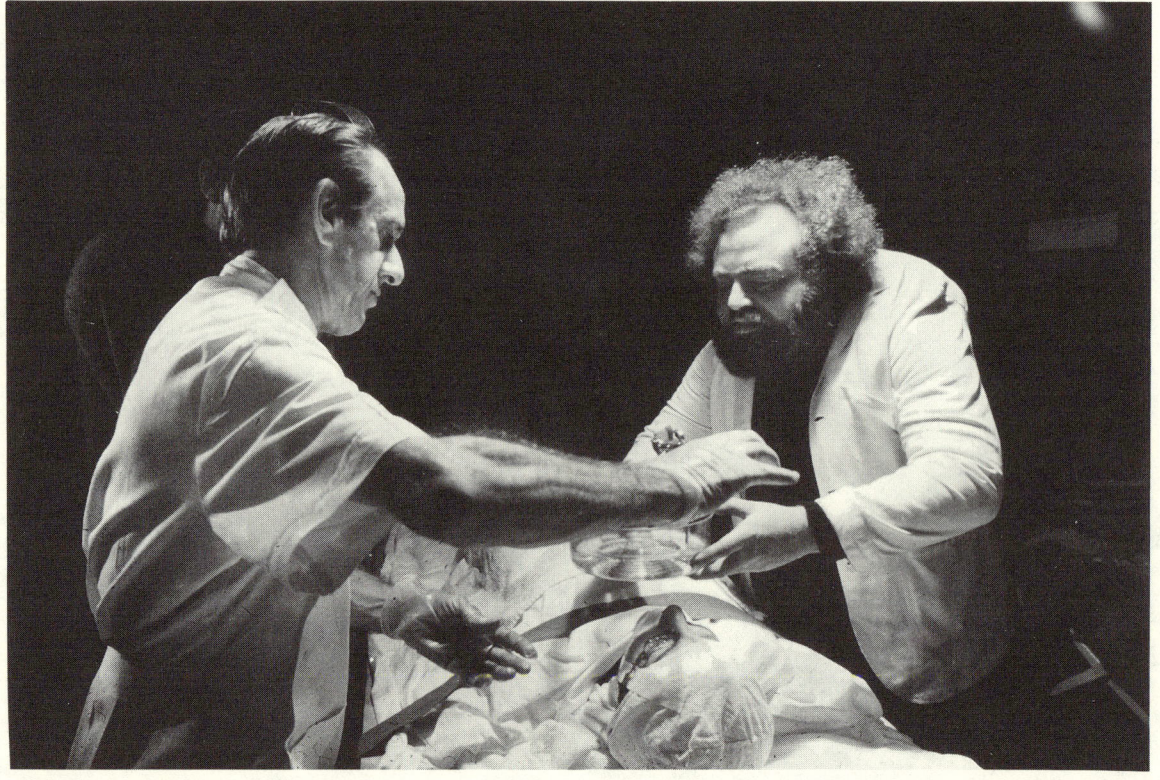

Vicky O'Neal keeps an eye out for mad doctor, Don Brandon, and the mute Greg. This surgical scene in *Body Shop* was lit with a single #2 photoflood through a diffuser but no reflector. It is dramatic and more pleasingly soft in the film than in black & white. (Photo by Chris Allen.)

Cheaper Lighting Possibilities 129

Having only a single 20-amp circuit, the *Body Shop* castle living room was photographed using available electrical light together with natural light. Since the windows were quite large, maintaining a sufficient light level was no problem. (Photo by Chris Allen.)

14
Music

There's not a great deal to say about music without discussing its creative ramifications. Simply said, the cheapest way to get music integrated into a film is have an individual compose and perform it; someone who (an amateur, perhaps) can perform it on his own instrument or synthesizer.

As mentioned earlier, on *Marley's Revenge* a camcorder was set up and a video was taped off the editor screen so the voice dubbers would have something to go by. That same tape was given to the music composer. He would watch it, try an idea on his keyboard which he would record, then play it back for the director's approval. If the director liked it, it would be developed further.

The great advantage of a synthesizer lies in its ability not only to simulate all other instruments, but to do so with many at the same time so as to sound like a band or orchestra, or to sample and replicate sounds other than musical ones as a base.

Doing so gives you the creative opportunity, if you choose, to use tire screeches, water splashes, burps, or any other sound performed as music, once you have given a sample to the synthesizer's computer.

If you find your music is somewhat too long or too short, one can easily have the synthesizer play back the same music a little faster or slower without changing the pitch at the touch of a button.

Of course, not having access to such a device ought not alter your opportunity to have good music. A good musician who has only a guitar or a flute very well may be able to do a creative job for you with that single instrument.

The music for *Harley's Gadget* is based upon the premise of having Harley represented by a bassoon, his wife by an oboe, and his daughter by a flute (in precisely the same way as Laurel and Hardy were represented by a slide whistle).

Such ideas as these can greatly simplify the creation of music, generate a strong emotional effect and, at the same time, save money.

The musician who did the music on *Body Shop* simply played an electric organ, improvising as he watched the film just like the organists in the old silent theaters. I understand he did it in a single pass.

The option of buying prerecorded or "canned" music should not be overlooked. Many recording studios and film labs with a sound department offer the service of sorting out possible selections from their library—sometimes at no charge—making a nominal charge for dubbing it over to ¼ inch tape and a one-time mechanical charge and royalty for the selections you actually use in your production.

There are records available with themes and bridge music which include in their purchase price the royalties for their use. They typically offer limited use however, so be sure to understand the contract printed on the cover before publishing such music.

If there are specific popular selections you would like to use, it's not impossible. If done by a well known performer or group it could become expensive, but expensive is relative. Get in touch with ASCAP, BMI, or SESAC in New York City. They deal with newcomers every day. While the process is not a simple one, they can helpfully lead you through the problems of organizing and licensing commercial music for your project. It can take several days or even weeks to clear a piece of music for which the composer, lyricist, performers, musicians, agents and goodness-only-knows who else must be compensated. Even then, you may be denied the right to use a specific piece of music. So start early.

Making assumptions can also get you in trouble. Arthur Smith's "Dueling Banjos" was thought to be an old mountain tune in public domain. Not checking it out cost the producer of *Deliverance* more bucks than he otherwise might have paid. Believing that Johannes Strauss' "Also Spracht Zarathustra" was in public domain caused a similar problem. Strauss' grandson, as it turns out, had the rights to it. The point is to be sure to research what you think might be available so that you will know that it is available, because even "Happy Birthday" is copyrighted!

A few features have used the psychology of no music at all. One or two have used a single bass note from a pipe organ or a cello as bridge music throughout the film; perhaps a C minor chord followed by a D flat diminished chord and repeated as often as necessary.

The opening music from *Jaws* wasn't especially melodic, but it certainly had impact. This technique was especially popular in the 1950's and 1960's for quickly done TV episodes. It was also popular before movies were invented. Bach's "Tocatta and Fugue in D Minor" is the pipe organ opening (tocatta without the fugue) that always blows your socks off and announces that this is a horror movie that takes place in a huge castle that has a pipe organ.

Lynn Dunn who did the titles for *West Side Story* asked the late, great Leonard Bernstein how long the final music would be so he could adjust the closing credits. "I don't know," Bernstein answered, "How long will the credits be?" "I was going to make them as long as the music," Dunn came back.

Finally, Dunn did the credits each to run as long as looked good. Bernstein repeated the last bar of music, over and over, as many times as was necessary, each with a different instrument until the finish. Teamwork counts in any category.

A final note would be the prospect of having no music at all, just for effect. Sure would be a money saver, wouldn't it? Of course, it could be a bit hard to sell.

15
It's a Wrap!

While we're on the subject of final notes, copyrighting your work is certainly in order.

It is advisable to copyright your script with the Copyright Office, a division of the Library of Congress, as soon as it is in a form as advanced as you expect to get it.

You will need the form PA which is for works of the performing arts. Class PA includes published and unpublished works prepared for the purpose of being "performed" directly before an audience or indirectly by means of any device or process. Some examples of works in this category are musical works, including any accompanying words; dramatic works, including any accompanying music; pantomimes and choreographic works; motion pictures and other audiovisual works.

If you continue to make corrections, deletions, and additions, it will not impinge upon the validity your copyright since the form CA for supplementary registration will support those efforts. You will use this form to re-apply after an initial registration has been made—to correct any error or changes in the information given on the original application form.

You will also want to copyright the finished film. In both cases the Copyright Office will want two copies plus a small fee. For more specific information you can call 202-287-8700 weekdays between 8:30 and 5:00. If you need application forms, you may call 202-287-9100 at any time of day or night to leave your request as a recorded message on the Forms Hotline of the Copyright Office. Such requests are filled and mailed promptly.

Both sides of the Form TX are found in the Appendix. You may duplicate them and save yourself a phone call.

Understand that the Copyright Office is only a registry; they will not do battle for you in a court of law. They will simply state that you registered a certain work on a certain date. They do no research to ascertain that the work is actually yours.

The Writers Guild, found both in New York City and in Los Angeles will also register your script for a nominal fee. If a confrontation occurs regarding a possible infringement, they could well do you more good than having only a copyright. Calling them from anywhere in the United States shouldn't cost more than a single dollar. So, give it a shot.

You'll discover as your preproduction progresses that your lists of things to change, repair, negotiate, buy, find, borrow, paint, replace, return, pay out, apologize for, eat, throw away, resolve, lie about, get, and simply do will evidently never end.

If you got nothing else from this book but this one edict it will have been a priceless reminder; use your head. *Just use your head!*

Whether you make movies or bicycles, bridges or buttons, that which ought to have been obvious will become so. You won't need to guess, you'll discover how to find out for sure. Don't slow down; if you do, you'll stop. Once you're on a roll, sustain your momentum. You can.

Then, when you do, you ought to write a book about it, and I'd like to have a copy. Turn about is fair play. Seek me out. That's one way to get your money back for having bought mine.

Persevere. Good luck!

Appendix A: Official Checklists

This checklist is comprised of a number of things that are fruitlessly searched for during every shoot because they don't appear on an official list. You need to add to the list every time you think of something that applies. When the time comes to use it, make a Xerox copy, scratch out everything you can't possibly use, then procure everything left on the list.

General

1 set Allen wrenches
6 ea. 3-way adapters (cube taps)
1 carton garbage or leaf bags
canned air (Dust-Off)
2 brooms, 1 standard, 1 whisk broom
single edge blades or box knife

lens brush
1" paintbrush to clean magazines
6 ea. 20" bungie cords
1 ea. 4' × 4' or 3' × 3' carpet
1 ea. 18" × 18" carpet
chalk and pencils
stop watch

2 doz. metal paper clamps
2' square black cloth
2 doz. clothes pins
6 ea. 18 ga. ext. cords 6' w/3 outputs (zip cords)

electric drill (cordless if poss.) & bits
can of dulling spray
standard flash light
clear fingernail polish
step ladder (if practical)

oil lantern & fuel (if practical)
bubble level
magnifying glass or lupe
matches or lighter
black magic markers

1 dental mirror
box of rubber bands
can of black spray paint
Polaroid camera, film & flash
Q-Tips
30' rope or clothesline

5–10 10# sandbags, 5–10 20# sandbags
saber saw (cordless if poss.)
jeweler's screwdrivers
scissors
ball of string
1" black masking tape or cloth camera tape
gaffer tape
1" white masking tape
roll of paper towels

1 dozen medium, 1 dozen small safety pins
6 ea. turf screws (like cork screws)
black, brown and silver Tips & Streaks
hand truck (if practical)
tool box (see below)
can of WD-40
12 ea. 2" × 4" × 6" wooden wedges

6 medium cardboard boxes (to cut up for flags, etc.)
5 cleaning rags
4 ea. 6", 12", and 24" 2 × 4 boards
3 small mirrors
2 ea. light bulbs, 25w, 75w, 100w, 150w
   or 40w, 60w, 100w, 150w

Tool Box Must Include:

1 set of Allen wrenches
3 most needed screwdrivers with standard shank
3 most needed screwdrivers with long shank

1 doz. ea. 1", 1½", and 2½" wood screws
1 doz. 1" × ¼" #20 stove bolts, 1 doz. 2" stove bolts,
   1 doz. 4" stove bolts; each with 2 washers and 1 nut

134 Appendix A: Checklists

#1, #2 Phillips screwdrivers
standard pliers
standard crescent wrench
standard Vice-Grip pliers

12 or 16 oz. claw hammer
¼ lb. ea. of 1½", 2½", 3" finishing nails
soldering iron and solder
cable ties or bag ties
super-fast drying glue (such as Zap w/Zip Kicker)
1 pint or quart contact cement

CAMERA AND SUPPORT SYSTEM

This list can be complete only after you have determined precisely what you'll need to do the job you have in mind. Most of the gear is listed here. Much of it you won't need. There are special items that you will require which only you can determine.

Camera

camera(s) (sometimes more than one type are needed)
extra camera battery, if applicable
battery charger
110v. power supply
prime lenses, zoom lens

filters, 85 and ND's, UV (and/or gels)
lens brush and blow bulb and/or canned air
lens cleaning fluid
color patch and/or gray card
camera barney and heater, if appropriate
exposure meter

color meter
small flashlight
gray & black gaffer tape
black felt tip marker
dolly, tracks or plywood (if applicable)
pan heads(s)

stix (tripod legs, standard)
baby legs
spreader
hi hat
obie light & mount
camera reports
French flag

changing bag
film cores, cans, & black bag
slate w/clap stick, chalk, rubout cloth, tab numbers
the script
your glasses
this checklist
3 ea. 24" bungie cords
and film for the camera

Sound

tape recorder
battery charger
110v power supply
extra recorder batteries, if applicable
extra tape reels & boxes (empty)
microphones

appropriate complement of cables and adapters
stopwatch
mixer (if applicable)
FM receiver if wireless mikes are used
fishing pole

1 doz. moving van blankets
silver & black gaffer tape
white marking tape
black felt tip marker
electrical tape
alligator clips
sound log
bull horn if needed
Claxon horn & bell

Lighting

lighting units as appropriate: broads, scoops, softs, soft
    boxes, spots (w/snoots), strips, clusters, brutes, nook
    lights, inkies, inkie-dinkies
exposure meter
color meter
light stands (to suit units on hand)

tie-in box
4 knife blade hangers
1 junior offset
1 baby offset
2 butt plugs

2 junior pipe risers 3'
1 ea. baby pipe riser 6", 12", 18", 24"
4 chain clamps
trombones
polecats

stepladder
lo-step ladder
Gatorclips, wall plates, wall sled
trapeze, t-bone or floor spreader, targets
cluster hangers

goose neck w/clamp
extra bulbs
dichroic filters
extension cables as needed
2 math gags

1 baby sidearm
1 junior sidearm
6 mafer clamps

4 Celotex hangers
2 ea. baby clamps 4", 6", 8"

2 ea. junior C-clamps 6", 8", 10"
1 ea. baby junior triple header
stage plug and other connectors as needed
dimmers
3 ea. 1' × 4' (dime store) vanity mirror
sandbags, 10# & 20#, one for ea. stand + 2
gels & other Roscoe type colorizers as appropriate
gray, black & white gaffer tape
electrical tape
scrims
reflectors

barn doors, snoots
work gloves
100' 12 ga. electric wire
electrical fixtures for temporary measures

Grip Equipment

targets, fingers, dots, cookaloris
flags, cloth cutters, diffusers and nets
3 ea. 4 × 8 sheets Foam-Core and/or art card
C stands one for each light stand + 25%
hi risers

6 ea. 4 × 8 × ¼ Luan
¾ inch plywood, several 4×8 sheets
2 dozen 10' white pine 2 × 4 boards
100 ft. rope, nylon or sash cord
dozen 4" C-clamps, dozen 3" C-clamps
color coded tape; red, yellow, blue, green, etc.

gray and black gaffer tape
10 ea. 10# sandbags, 10 ea. 20# sandbags
transport dolly
stepladder
hand truck
black, white, gray, silver spray paint
dulling spray, several cans

axle grease, lubricating oil
skill saw
saber saw, extra blades
electric drill, bits
C-clamps, 4 ea. 2", 2 ea. 3", 2 ea. 4", 2 ea. 6"

100' bailing wire
fog machine & juice
bee smokers
1 dozen step blocks (a.k.a. 2-4-6 blocks)
2 dozen 2 × 4 × 6" wedges

1 dozen 2 × 4 × 24" blocks
4 heavy duty flashlights w/fresh batteries
appropriate work lights for after dark work
   (preferably 300w outdoor quartz)
glue gun and glue or Zap and Zap Kicker
with 110v generator (of apprpriate amperage)
   if needed
oil lantern, fuel and matches or lighter

appropriate complement of apple boxes, half apples,
   quarter apples and pancakes
furniture polish
cleaning rags
4 × 8 sheet of Plexiglas or Lexan
directors' chairs

2 or more motorcycle (ratchet) tie down straps
carpet tape (double sided)
vehicle(s) to haul all the above

Obviously not everything on the above lists will be needed on every shoot. Furthermore, there is much overlap. Each department needs its own gaffer tape, for example. If one or two people are running all those departments, fewer rolls will do. The main issue is making the list work for you, allowing you to continue shooting by having a seventy cent 3-way adapter on hand instead of having twenty people standing around playing switch while someone goes to the hardware store or snatches one from elsewhere in the building. Likewise, it would be fruitless to have everything on the list only to haul it around and never use it. The use for some things on the list may seem elusive, but a little imagination will express their need.

On a movie location, trash bags are used less for trash than any other practical purpose. They serve quite well as rain and dust covers for equipment—and for people.

A sixty cent paintbrush from the hardware store does as efficient a job as the ten-dollar camel's hair ones the dealers sell you for camera and magazine interiors. Just don't use a junk brush on a lens.

"It was a dark and stormy night..." when I got down on my belly to look through the finder for a low angle shot. Without the piece of carpet (which I'd kept dry) I would have gotten wet. That same piece of carpet served as a tripod spreader indoors when I broke the real thing. On another shoot, it turned out to be the only thing available for the leading lady to sit on when an unexpected shower came up and wet everything else.

A good telescoping fishing pole for a mike cost about $120 in a sound shop. The same brand—identical—cost $8.50 at the paint store where you buy paint roller extensions.

The Zap mentioned in the list is an extremely strong liquid glue which, when sprayed with Zip Kicker, sets in the short period of one to three seconds, permanently. Be careful not to glue your fingers together. Found in hobby shops, it's a little expensive but well worth the cost when people are waiting for you to get something done.

Appendix B: Forms

Many centuries ago man sought out a method to consign his memory to a more reliable system simply because he did whatever was the cave man's counterpart to forgetting to stop at the corner store and buy some milk and bread.

Regardless of how clear your mind is you cannot keep track of all important records. Even if you could, having records where money is concerned, is vital if only for the IRS or the other guy you're dealing with.

Pilots invariably refer to a checklist before starting the engine. You must do so before starting a production. The pilots continue by referring to another list before take-off no matter how good their memories, all in the name of safety. It simply is too easy to forget something important or even vital—whether you are flying a plane or producing a film.

For that reason the following pages of forms have been prepared for you to use in the preproduction, production, and postproduction of your picture. You will find some of them to be most important while others, for your purposes, will be useless. These and others found in the text can be a guide for you to make up your own for your specific requirements.

Rarely is such a form copyrighted. These are not. Copy them, alter them to suit yourself, and make multiple copies.

Not every line item need be addressed. Owing to the fact that many items can appear in separate places, many need to be avoided on one page but filled out on another. It may be wise to thoroughly examine each block of forms and eliminate line items depending upon how you prefer to run your own business.

Because forms are intended to be simplistic, they are quite uncreative.

Appendix B: Forms

Summary Production Costs

	DATE	PRODUCER
...UCER	DIRECTOR	WRITER
...ER	START DATE	SCHED. TERM. DATE

acct #/classification	budget cost to date	est comp date	over/under budget
01 Story			
02 Supervisors			
03 Cast			
04 Direction			
Total Above the Line Costs			
05 Director's Staff			
06 Camera			
07 Set Operations			
08 Set Const. Costs			
09 Set Design			
10 Set Dressings			
11 Special Effects			
12 Process Effects			
13 Miniatures			
14 Draperies			
15 Props			
16 Live Stock, Handlers, Equip.			
17 Locations			
18 Transportation			
19 Lighting			
20 Wardrobe			
21 Makeup			
22 Film & Laboratory			
23 Sound Recording			
24 Sound Royalties			
25 Sound Dubbing & Scoring			
26 Editing			
27 Titles & Inserts			
28 Music			
29 Studio Rentals			
30 Tests & Preproduction			
31 Studio General			
Total Below the Line Costs			
Total Direct Cost			
40 Contingency			
50 General Studio Overhead			
TOTAL COST			

Remarks:

prepared by _____ date _____ prepared for _____

Production Cost Statement

TITLE _____ date _____

		BUDGET	COST TO DATE
01-000	STORY		
01-001	Rights Purchased		
01-002	Rights Developed by Buyer		
01-003	Stenograph & Reprint		
01-004	Rewrite		
01-005	Screen Play		
01-300	Miscellaneous		
		TOTAL	
02-000	SUPERVISION		
02-001	Producer & Assts.		
02-002	Production Mgr.		
		TOTAL	
03-000	CAST		
03-001	Stars & Lead		
03-002	Supporting Cast		
03-003	Day Players		
03-004	Extras, Stand-ins, Doubles		
03-005	Silent Musicians		
03-006	Commissions		
03-300	Miscellaneous		
		TOTAL	
04-000	DIRECTION		
04-001	Director		
04-002	Dialogue, Techn'l, Choreographers		
04-003	Miscellaneous		
		TOTAL	
05-000	DIRECTOR'S STAFF		
05-001	Assistant Director		
05-002	Script Supervisors		
05-300	Miscellaneous		
		TOTAL	
06-000	CAMERA		
06-001	Cameraman, Stills, Assistant, Loader		
06-002	Rentals		
06-003	Miscellaneous		
		TOTAL	

Production Cost Statement, *Continued*

	BUDGET	COST TO DATE
03-000 CAST		
03-001 Stars & Leads	_____	_____

Character   Player

_____
_____
_____
_____
_____
_____
_____
_____
_____
_____
_____
_____
_____

Sub-Total _____

03-002 Supporting Cast _____

Character   Player

_____
_____
_____
_____
_____
_____
_____
_____
_____
_____
_____
_____
_____
_____
_____
_____
_____
_____
_____
_____
_____
_____
_____
_____

Sub-Total _____

03-003 Day Players _____
03-004 Extras, Stand-ins, Doubles _____
03-005 Silent Musicians _____
03-006 Commissions _____
03-300 Miscellaneous _____

TOTAL _____

Production Cost Statement, *Continued*

Code	Item	BUDGET	COST TO DATE
07-000	SET OPERATIONS		
07-001	Company Grips		
07-002	Company Prop Men		
07-003	Set Operations (Stand-by)		
07-004	Set Maintenance		
07-005	Green Work-Maintenance		
07-100	Materials/Supplies		
07-200	Rentals		
07-300	Miscellaneous		
	TOTAL		
08-000	SET CONST. COSTS		
08-001	Construction Labor		
08-002	Set Striking		
08-003	Scaffolds		
08-004	Backing		
08-005	Green Work		
08-100	Material/Supplies		
08-200	Rentals		
08-300	Miscellaneous		
	TOTAL		
09-000	SET DESIGN		
09-001	Unit Art Directors		
09-002	Assistant Art Directors		
09-003	Sketch Artists		
09-004	Model Makers		
09-005	Draftsmen		
09-006	Set Supervisor		
09-100	Material/Supplies		
09-300	Miscellaneous		
	TOTAL		
10-000	SET DRESSINGS		
10-001	Set Dressers and Swing Gang		
10-005	Loss and Damage		
10-006	Set Dressings Constructed		
10-010	Set Dressings Purchased		
10-110	Set Dressings Rental Contract		
10-200	Rentals-Outside		
10-300	Miscellaneous		
	TOTAL		
	TOTAL		

Production Cost Statement, *Continued*

		BUDGET	COST TO DATE
11-000	SPECIAL EFFECTS		
11-001	Labor		
11-100	Materials		
11-200	Rentals		
11-300	Miscellaneous		
	TOTAL		
12-000	PROCESS		
12-001	Backgrounds made		
12-011	Labor operating		
12-016	Plates		
12-200	Rentals		
12-300	Miscellaneous		
	TOTAL		
13-000	MINIATURE		
13-001	Labor		
13-013	Matte Shots		
13-015	Contract		
13-100	Material		
13-200	Rentals		
13-300	Miscellaneous		
	TOTAL		
14-000	DRAPERIES		
14-001	Drapery—Labor		
14-100	Material		
14-200	Rentals		
14-300	Miscellaneous		
	TOTAL		
15-000	PROPS		
15-001	Labor-Swing Gang		
15-005	Loss and Damage		
15-006	Props Constructed		
15-010	Props Purchased		
15-011	Props—Inserts Made		
15-200	Rentals		
15-300	Miscellaneous		
	TOTAL		
	TOTAL		

Production Cost Statement, *Continued*

		BUDGET	COST TO DATE
16-000	LIVESTOCK—HANDLERS & EQUIP.		
16-003	Operators & Animal Handlers		
16-006	Equipment Constructed		
16-010	Animals & Wagons		
16-200	Rentals		
16-300	Miscellaneous		
	TOTAL		
17-000	LOCATIONS		
17-001	Sundry Employees		
17-002	Hotel & Meals		
17-012	Traveling		
17-200	Rentals		
17-300	Miscellaneous		
	TOTAL		
18-000	TRANSPORTATION		
18-001	Labor		
18-100	Material/Supplies		
18-200	Rentals		
18-300	Miscellaneous		
	TOTAL		
19-000	LIGHTING		
19-001	Rigging & Striking		
19-002	Operating		
19-100	Material/Supplies		
19-110	Globe Insurance		
19-150	Electric Current		
19-200	Rentals		
19-300	Miscellaneous		
	TOTAL		
20-000	WARDROBE		
20-001	Designer		
20-003	Wardrobe Men		
20-005	Wardrobe Women		
20-100	Wardrobe Purchased		
20-200	Rentals		
20-300	Miscellaneous		
	TOTAL		
	TOTAL		

Production Cost Statement, *Continued*

		BUDGET	COST TO DATE
21-000	MAKE-UP & HAIR DRESSING		
21-001	Make-up Persons		
21-002	Hairdressers		
21-100	Materials/Supplies		
21-200	Rentals		
21-300	Miscellaneous		
	TOTAL		
22-000	FILM & LABORATORY		
22-010	Negative Raw Stock		
22-012	Videotape & Transfers		
22-160	Laboratory Charges		
22-170	Stills Lab Charges		
22-300	Miscellaneous		
	TOTAL		
23-000	SOUND RECORDING		
23-001	Recording Crew		
23-100	Materials/Supplies		
23-200	Rentals		
23-300	Miscellaneous		
	TOTAL		
24-000	SOUND ROYALTIES		
24-001	Domestic		
24-002	Foreign		
	TOTAL		
25-000	SOUND DUBBING & SCORING		
25-011	Labor—Operating		
25-110	Rent—Dubbing & Scoring Room		
25-200	Rentals		
25-300	Miscellaneous		
	TOTAL		
26-000	FILM/VIDEOTAPE EDITING		
26-001	Editors & Assistants		
26-110	Rental of Cutting Room		
26-200	Rental of Equipment		
26-300	Miscellaneous		
	TOTAL		
	TOTAL		

Production Cost Statement, *Continued*

		BUDGET	COST TO DATE
27-000	TITLES & INSERTS		
27-016	Main Title		
27-020	Fades & Dissolves		
27-100	Stock Shots		
27-150	Montages		
27-160	Inserts		
27-300	Miscellaneous		
	TOTAL		
28-000	MUSIC		
28-001	Music Director		
28-002	Music Rights		
28-003	Composers/Arrangers		
28-005	Singers		
28-006	Musicians		
28-150	Royalties		
28-300	Miscellaneous		
	TOTAL		
29-000	STUDIO RENTAL		
29-001	Stage Rental		
29-002	Street and Set Rental		
29-245	Wood/Metal Shop Facility		
29-246	Paint Shop		
29-300	Miscellaneous		
	TOTAL		
30-000	TESTS and Preprod. Shooting		
	TOTAL		
31-000	STUDIO GENERAL		
31-001	Contrib. to Vacations, Holidays, Health & Welfare		
31-010	Social Security Taxes		
31-011	Compensation & Public Liability Ins.		
31-015	Cast Insurance		
31-016	Negative Insurance		
31-031	MPPA Fee		
31-300	Miscellaneous		
31-340	Secretaries & Clerical		
31-350	Office Rent		
31-370	Reserve for Retroactive		
	TOTAL		
40-000	CONTINGENCY		
	TOTAL		
	TOTAL		

146 Appendix B: Forms

The preceding pages, when filled out, will give you the information to fill out the general page 1 which is a summary.
The following pages were originally designed for commercial or documentary filmmaking but have been reoriented for feature production. You'll find them to offer somewhat greater detail.
A model release form should be signed for every person appearing in a scene. You may forego the release if he is not recognizable, but for safety sake, it would pay you to get one anyway. If he is not otherwise paid, you should pay him $1 to make the deal legal.

Motion Picture Cost Estimate Sheet

Prepared by _____   Prepared for _____

TITLE _____   date _____

Category	Budget	Cost to date
Research		
Writing		
Prod. Planning		
Casting		
Location Scout		
Set Const.		
Set Dressing		
Stills Photog.		
Title Photog.		
Sound Recording		
Sound Mix		
Editing		
Rushes Preview		
Rewrite		
Neg Cutter		
Stand-by		
Strike Set		
Miscellaneous		
Office		
Contingency		

Category	Budget	Cost to date
Raw Stock		
Mag Tape		
Full Coat		
Props Rent		
Props Buy		
Equipment Rent		
Travel & Meals		
Actors		
Narrators		
Sound X-fer		
Producers		
Writers		
Cinematog.		
Music License		
Opticals		
Sound Track Neg		
Answer Print		
Release Prints		
Contingency		

Sub Total _____   Sub Total _____

TOTAL _____

Remarks:

Motion Picture Cost Estimate Sheet, *Continued*

Prepared by _____   Prepared for _____

TITLE _____   date _____

CATEGORY	BUDGET	SPENT TO DATE	OVER/UNDER BUDGET
001 Script			
A Story Purchase			
B Screenplay			
C Storyboard			
002 Continuity & Treatment			
A Writers			
B Secretary			
C Printing			
D Research			
003 Producer			
A Producer			
B Asst. Producer			
C Secretaries			
004 Director			
A Director			
B Asst. Dir.			
C Secretaries			
005 Talent			
A Principal Actors			
B Supporting Roles			
C Stand-ins			
D Crowds			
006 Extras			
A Overtime			
B Service Fees			
C Stunt People			
D Stunt Adjustments			

PAGE TOTAL _____

Motion Picture Cost Estimate Sheet, *Continued*

CATEGORY	BUDGET	SPENT TO DATE	OVER/UNDER BUDGET

007 Production Staff Salaries
- A Production Mgr.
- B Unit Mgr.
- C 1st Asst. Dir.
- D 2nd Asst. Dir.
- E Dialogue Clerk
- F Script Clerk
- G Dance Director
- H Casting Director & Staff
- I Technical Advisors
- J Comptroller
- L Location Secret.

008 Production Operating Staff
- A Camera Operator
- B Camera Assistant
- C Focus Puller
- D Magazine Loader
- E Dolly Pusher
- F Stills Photog.
- G Sound Recordist
- H Mixer
- I Boom Operator
- J PA System Operator
- K Sound Effects Person
- L Equipment Maint. Personnel

009 Wardrobe Department
- A Wardrobe Designer
- B Wardrobe Buyer
- C 1st Wardrobe Girl
- D 2nd Wardrobe Girl
- E Wardrobe Man
- F Tailor
- G Seamstress
- H Assistants

010 Makeup & Hairdressing
- A Head Makeup Person
- B 2nd Makeup Person
- C Head Hairdresser
- D 2nd Hairdresser
- E Body Makeup Girl
- F Assistants

PAGE TOTAL _____

Motion Picture Cost Estimate Sheet, *Continued*

CATEGORY	BUDGET	SPENT TO DATE	OVER/UNDER BUDGET

011 Grip Department
- A Key Grip _____
- B Best Boy _____
- C Set Operation Grips _____

012 Property Department
- A Head Prop Person _____
- B 2nd Prop Person _____
- C Assistants _____

013 Set Dressing Department
- A Set Dresser _____
- B Assistant Set Dresser _____
- C Swing Gang _____
- D Drapery Person _____
- E Drapery Assistant _____
- F Extra Assistants _____

014 Electrical Department
- A Gaffer _____
- B Best Boy _____
- C Electrical Operators _____
- D Generator Operator _____
- E Electrical Maintenance _____
- F Wind Machine Operator _____

015 Special Effects
- A Special Effects Man _____
- B Special Effects Assist. _____

016 Set Operators
- A Set Operator _____
- B Carpenter _____

017 Wranglers
- A SPCA Person _____
- B Head Wrangler _____
- C Wranglers _____

PAGE TOTAL _____

Motion Picture Cost Estimate Sheet, *Continued*

CATEGORY	BUDGET	SPENT TO DATE	OVER/UNDER BUDGET
018 Set Construction			
A Art Director			
B Asst. Art Director			
C Sketch Artist			
D Draftsman			
E Set Supervisor			
F Materials/Supplies			
G Construction Supervisor			
H Miscellaneous			
019 Summary Set Operation Expenses			
A Camera Equipment Rentals			
B Camera Equipment Purchases			
C Camera Car Rentals			
D Camera Crane Rentals			
E Wardrobe Purchased			
F Wardrobe Rentals			
G Wardrobe Maintenance			
H Grip Equipment Rented			
I Prop Equipment Rented			
J Props Purchased			
K Props Rented			
L Prop's Petty Cash			
M Props Loss and Damage			
N Set Dressing Rentals			
O Set Dressing Purchased			
P Makeup Purchased			
Q Hairdressing Purchase			
R Hairdressing Equip. Rental			
S Electrical Equipment Rental			
T Electrical Equipment Purchase			
U Electrical Power			
V Vehicles Rental			
W Misc. Rentals & Purchases			
X Special Effects Purc. & Rent			
020 Editing			
A Editor			
B Assistant Editor			
C Music Cutter			
D Negative Cutter			
E Intermediates			
F Opticals			
G Titles			
H Answer Print(s)			
I Cutting Room Rental			
J Coding			
K Editorial Supplies			
PAGE TOTAL			

Motion Picture Cost Estimate Sheet, *Continued*

CATEGORY	BUDGET	SPENT TO DATE	OVER/UNDER BUDGET

021 Music

- A Music Supervisor
- B Director
- C Composer
- D Musicians
- E Singers
- F Librarian
- G Purchases
- H Music Licenses

022 Sound

- A Dubbing Room Rental
- B Foley Studio Rental
- C Dubbing Personnel
- D Dubbing Talent
- E Sound Equip. Rental

023 Transportation

- A Drivers
- B Car Rentals
- C Truck Rentals
- D Bus Rentals
- E Car Allowance
- F Fuel/Oil

024 Location

- A Traveling
- B Hotel
- C Lodging
- D Location Sites Rental
- E Special Equipment
- F Location Office Rental
- G Scouting
- H Permits & Police Assist.
- I Miscellaneous

025 Studio Rental

- A Sound Stage
- B Street Location
- C Portable Dressing Rooms
- D Toilet Facilities
- E Office Facilities

PAGE TOTAL

Motion Picture Cost Estimate Sheet, *Continued*

CATEGORY	BUDGET	SPENT TO DATE	OVER/UNDER BUDGET
026 Preproduction Tests			
A Film & Equipment Tests			
027 Retakes			
A Retakes			
028 Publicity			
A Advertising			
B Publicity Person			
C Trade Paper Subscription			
D Publicity Stills Salary			
E Publicity Stills Supplies & Laboratory Charges			
F Press Preview Expenses			
G Postage & Shipping			
H Miscellaneous			
029 Food			
A Caterer			
B Restaurant			
C Cooking Facility			
D Cook/Assistants			
030 Fees & Taxes			
A Cast Insurance			
B Life Insurance			
C Workmans Comp			
D Public Liability			
E Negative Insurance			
F Miscellaneous Insurance			
G Social Security Taxes			
H Other Taxes			
031 Distribution			
A Prints			
B Literature			
C Postage/Shipping			
D Secretarial			
E Customs			
F Insurance			
G Miscellaneous			

PAGE TOTAL _____

Transportation/Lunch Sheet   Day # _____

Title _____ Date _____ Location _____ Rain or Shine
                                                                    Weather Permitting

for	meals	car	bus	leave time
Staff _____				
Producer _____				
Asst. Producer _____				
Secretary _____				
Director _____				
Asst. Director _____				
2nd Asst. Director _____				
Script Clerk _____				
Production Manager _____				
Asst. Production Mgr. _____				
Unit Manager _____				
Asst. Unit Manager _____				
Location Manager _____				
Dialogue Director _____				
Technical Advisor _____				
Technical Advisor _____				
Other _____				
Other _____				
Other _____				
Other _____				
Art Department				
Art Director _____				
Asst. Art Director _____				
Others _____				
Camera Department				
Cinematographer _____				
Camera Operator _____				
Camera Assistant _____				
2nd Camera Assistant _____				
Stills Photographer _____				
Others _____				
Makeup				
Makeup Man _____				
Makeup Assistant _____				
Body Makeup Woman _____				
Hairdresser _____				
Hairdresser _____				
Players				
Cast _____				
Stand-ins _____				
Extras _____				
Camera Effects				
Process Camera _____				
Operators _____				
Camera Assistants _____				
Prop Department				
Prop Person _____				

Transportation/Lunch Sheet, *Continued*

for	meals	car	bus	leave time
2nd Prop Person				
Set Dresser				
Others				
Electrical Department				
Gaffer				
Best Boy				
Electrician				
Wind Machine Operator				
Other				
Sound Department				
Recordist				
Boom Operator				
Mixer				
Cableman				
Other				
Wardrobe Department				
Wardrobe Person				
2nd Wardrobe Person				
Tailor/Seamstress				
Others				
Miniatures Department				
Special EFX Person				
Special EFX Assistant				
Casting Department				
Casting Director				
Asst. Casting Dir.				
Grip Department				
1st Grip				
2nd Grip				
Additional Grips				
Construction				
Carpenters				
Painters				
Scenic Painters				
Sign Painters				
Publicity Department				
Publicity Person				
Guests				
Miscellaneous				
Plumbers				
First Aid				
Police				
Guard/Watchman				
Transportation				
Bus Drivers				
Truck Drivers				
Car Drivers				

Call Sheet

Title _____ Day # _____ Date _____

Shooting Call _____ Crew Call _____

Report to: _____
_____

Set _____
Location _____

CAST	CHARACTER	WARDROBE	ON SET	CALL TIME

Doubles _____

Extras _____

CREW CALL (by name)

Camera Operator _____
Asst. Camera Oper. _____

Electrical Operators _____
Grips _____

Property _____

Makeup _____

Hairdressers _____

Sound Recordist _____
Sound Mixer _____
Boom Operator _____
Cableman _____
PA Operator _____
Camera EFX _____
Mechanical EFX _____

Painter _____
Set Dresser _____

Laborers _____

Drivers _____

Technical Advisors _____

Stills Photographer _____

Script Breakdown

Title _____ Prepared by _____

Set _____ Sequence _____ Location _____

Period _____ Season _____ Day/Night _____

Number of Script Pages _____

CAST	EXTRAS	PROPS, ANIMALS, etc.	SCENE # & DESCRIPTION

Process/Effects

Notes:

Camera and Accessory List

Title _____   Prepared by _____
for day #'s _____   Scene Nos. _____
Cameraman _____   1st Camera Assist. _____

CAMERAS	35 _____	16 _____
	ARRI BL _____	AURICON PRO _____
	ARRI _____	ARRI BL _____
	BNC _____	ARRI S _____
	BNCR _____	ARRI ___ _____
	EYMO _____	BELL & HOWELL _____
	NC _____	BOLEAU _____
	PANAVISION _____	BOLEX RX _____
	other _____	BOLEX _____
		CINE SPECIAL _____
		CP-16 _____
		ECLAIR NPR _____
		ECLAIR _____
		K-100 _____
		MITCHELL _____
		PATHE _____

MOTORS
- 110 v. variable speed _____
- 110 v. sync _____
- 220 v. sync _____
- high speed _____
- 110 v. power supply _____
- 220 v. power supply _____
- Variac _____
- 12/16 v. variable speed _____
- 12/16 v. constant speed _____
- 12/16 v. crystal _____
- extra fuses _____

MAGAZINES

Arri	200	400	1,000	16mm	35mm
Auricon	400	600	1,200	16mm	
B & H	400		1,000	16mm	35mm
Boleau	200	400		16mm	
Bolex		400		16mm	
Cine Special	200	400		16mm	
CP-16 (Mitchell)		400		16mm	
ECLAIR	200	400		16mm	35mm
MITCHELL		400	1,000	16mm	35mm
PANAVISION		400	1,000		35mm
PATHE	200	400		16mm	

ACCESSORIES
- Barney
- Heated Barney
- Blimp
- Bridge Plate
- Camera Cover
- Camera Tape
- Changing Bag
- Camera Reports
- Matte Box & Mattes
- Sound Slate
- Tie Down
- Tilt Wedge

Lens List

	Arri-16	Arri-35	C-Mount	S-Mount	Eclair	NC	BNC	EYMO
7mm								
8mm								
10mm								
15mm								
18mm								
20mm								
25mm								
28mm								
30mm								
32mm								
40mm								
50mm								
75mm								
90mm								
100mm								
150mm								
other								
other								
other								

ZOOM LENSES (specify)

FILTERS   GELATIN/GLASS   3×3   4×4   6×6
               85   85b   85N3   85N6   .10ND   .30ND
               FLT   FLD

               CIRCULAR (list diameter or series)

HEADS   Geared   Friction   Fluid   Other

TRIPODS   Baby-Legs   Standard   Hi-Hat   Hydraulic
               Pro-Junior   Pro-Junior-Baby   Other

Dollies   (Specify) _____

Film   (Specify) _____

Shipping   No. of Empty Cans   _____   Sealing Tape
               Labels   _____   Black Bags
               Cartons   _____   other

Location Requirements

Title _____ Prepared by _____

For day # _____ Location _____

Scene Nos. _____

Staff	Cast (Character Name)	Wardrobe (Costume No.)
Producer _____		_____
Director _____		_____
Unit Manager _____		_____
Asst. Director _____		_____
2nd Asst. Dir. _____		_____
Art Director _____		_____
Dialogue Director _____		_____
Technical Advisors _____		_____
Script/Clerk _____		_____
Cinematographer _____		_____
Camera Operator _____		_____
Camera Assistant _____		_____
Loader _____		_____
Stills Photographer _____		_____
Recordist _____		_____
Mixer _____		_____
Boom Operator _____		_____
Cable Person _____		_____
Wireless Mike Oper. _____		_____
Makeup Person _____		_____
Makeup Assistant _____		_____
Body Makeup Person _____		_____
Hairdresser _____		_____
Asst. Hairdresser _____		_____
Wardrobe Person _____		_____
Wardrobe Assistant _____		_____
Tailor/Seamstress _____		_____
Location Comptroller _____		_____
Location Liaison _____		_____
Publicity Person _____		_____
Company Police/Guards _____		_____

Location Requirements, (Continued)

Title _____ Prepared by _____
For Day # _____   Location _____
Scene Nos. _____

Extras _____   Prop Person _____
Stand-ins _____   Prop Assistant _____
Doubles _____   Greenskeeper _____
Stunt People _____   Set Dresser _____
Singers _____   Grips _____
Dancers _____   Painters _____
Musicians _____   Carpenters _____
                                        Mechanics _____
Total _____   Gaffer _____
                                        Best Boy _____
                                        Electricians _____
                                        Generator Oper. _____

                                        Total _____

EFX

Glass Shot _____   Director _____
Matte Shot _____   Assist. Dir. _____
Stunt Shot _____   Cinematographer _____
                         Camera Operator _____
                         Camera Assistant _____
                         Camera Loader _____
                         Script Clerk _____
                         Grips _____
                         Electricians _____
                         Prop Persons _____
                         EFX Persons _____

                         Total _____

TRANSPORTATION   PROPS
                                        (specify)
Cars _____   _____
Bus _____   _____
Camera Truck _____   _____
Cinemobile _____   _____
Grip Truck _____   _____
Wardrobe Truck _____ _____
Elect. Truck _____   _____
Prop Truck _____   _____
Generator _____   _____
Boom _____   _____

Total _____

Location Survey

Sequence _____

Projected Shoot Date _____ M/T/W/T/F/Sa/Sn

Sound Days _____ MOS _____ Playback _____

Weather Dates _____ M/T/W/T/F/Sa/Sn

Location Name: _____

    Address: _____

    Phone: _____

    Contact: _____

      (home phone) _____

_____

_____

Season/Weather required _____

    When scouted _____

On projected areas _____

Location Headquarters: Name: _____

(if different)   Address: _____

                              Contact: _____

                              Address: _____

                              Phones: _____

Special Equipment Needed _____

_____

_____

Catering Requirements: _____

_____

_____

Scouted by: Production / Director / DP / Elec / Grip / Prop / Sound / AD / WardR

Dates:

Location Release Secures: _____ Date: _____ Date: _____

Map of area with pertinent travel instructions:

Needed to complete:

164 Appendix B: Forms

Interior and Exterior

Height of ceiling _____ color of walls _____ ceiling _____
Description of obstacles:

Floor or ground surface and condition:

Are dolly shots possible? _____ Tracks? _____ Plywood? _____
Number and size of a window _____
Height from ground and accessibility if need to be covered from outside _____
_____
_____

Availability of ladders _____ size _____
Distance from unloading to shooting area _____
Availability of dollies or skids _____
Elevators _____ size _____ capacity _____
Parking facilities _____
_____
_____

Unusual sound problems and frequency:
    Traffic _____
    Railroad/Subway _____
    Aircraft _____
    Construction _____
    Room acoustics _____
    Other _____

Visual incongruities:

Can they be removed or disguised? _____ List suggestions:

Local Supply

Local wardrobe and costume sources and rates: _____
_____
_____

Local prop sources and rates: _____
_____
_____

Local livestock sources and rates: _____
_____
_____

Availability of local craftsmen (sign painters, carpenters, etc.) and rates: _____
_____
_____

Travel means, directions, and costs:

Shipping means and cost per 100 pounds: _____
_____
_____

Additional remarks: _____
_____
_____

Availability of rest rooms: _____
_____
_____

Cherry picker _____

Crane _____

Helicopter _____

Airplane _____

Boat _____

Other _____

Food Catered to Location

Coffee _____ Cold Meals _____ Hot Meals _____

ACCOMMODATIONS: Include number of rooms, phone in room, availability of early and late meals, etc.
_____
_____
_____
_____
_____
_____
_____

Police Dept. _____

Fire Dept. _____

Other _____

Local film unions (avail. personnel & rates): _____
_____
_____
_____

Local talent source & rates: _____
_____
_____

Electrical

Amps in service at 110 volts _____

Amps available at 110 volts _____

Amps in service at 220 volts _____

Amps available at 220 volts _____

_____ wire _____ phase   AC/DC

Type and size of fuse _____

Type of tie-in necessary _____

Number of flights and/or height below or above shooting area: _____
_____
_____

Generator _____ Amps _____ Transformer _____

Draw a detailed diagram of power source and state all pertinent information:

Filling Out Application Form TX

*Detach and read these instructions before completing this form.
Make sure all applicable spaces have been filled in before you return this form.*

BASIC INFORMATION

When to Use This Form: Use Form TX for registration of published or unpublished non-dramatic literary works, excluding periodicals or serial issues. This class includes a wide variety of works: fiction, nonfiction, poetry, textbooks, reference works, directories, catalogs, advertising copy, compilations of information, and computer programs. For periodicals and serials, use Form SE.

Deposit to Accompany Application: An application for copyright registration must be accompanied by a deposit consisting of copies or phonorecords representing the entire work for which registration is to be made. The following are the general deposit requirements as set forth in the statute:

Unpublished Work: Deposit one complete copy (or phonorecord).

Published Work: Deposit two complete copies (or one phonorecord) of the best edition.

Work First Published Outside the United States: Deposit one complete copy (or phonorecord) of the first foreign edition.

Contribution to a Collective Work: Deposit one complete copy (or phonorecord) of the best edition of the collective work.

The Copyright Notice: For works first published on or after March 1, 1989, the law provides that a copyright notice in a specified form "may be placed on all publicly distributed copies from which the work can be visually perceived." Use of the copyright notice is the responsibility of the copyright owner and does not require advance permission from the Copyright Office. The required form of the notice for copies generally consists of three elements: (1) the symbol "©," or the word "Copyright," or the abbreviation "Copr."; (2) the year of first publication; and (3) the name of the owner of copyright. For example: "© 1993 Jane Cole." The notice is to be affixed to the copies "in such manner and location as to give reasonable notice of the claim of copyright." Works first published prior to March 1, 1989, **must** carry the notice or risk loss of copyright protection.

For information about notice requirements for works published before March 1, 1989, or other copyright information, write: Information Section, LM-401, Copyright Office, Library of Congress, Washington, D.C. 20559.

PRIVACY ACT ADVISORY STATEMENT Required by the Privacy Act of 1974 (Public Law 93-579)

AUTHORITY FOR REQUESTING THIS INFORMATION:
• Title 17, U.S.C., Secs. 409 and 410

FURNISHING THE REQUESTED INFORMATION IS:
• Voluntary

BUT IF THE INFORMATION IS NOT FURNISHED:
• It may be necessary to delay or refuse registration
• You may not be entitled to certain relief, remedies, and benefits provided in chapters 4 and 5 of title 17, U.S.C.

PRINCIPAL USES OF REQUESTED INFORMATION:
• Establishment and maintenance of a public record
• Examination of the application for compliance with legal requirements

OTHER ROUTINE USES:
• Public inspection and copying
• Preparation of public indexes
• Preparation of public catalogs of copyright registrations
• Preparation of search reports upon request

NOTE:
• No other advisory statement will be given you in connection with this application
• Please keep this statement and refer to it if we communicate with you regarding this application

---

LINE-BY-LINE INSTRUCTIONS
Please type or print using black ink.

1 SPACE 1: Title

Title of This Work: Every work submitted for copyright registration must be given a title to identify that particular work. If the copies or phonorecords of the work bear a title or an identifying phrase that could serve as a title, transcribe that wording *completely* and *exactly* on the application. Indexing of the registration and future identification of the work will depend on the information you give here.

Previous or Alternative Titles: Complete this space if there are any additional titles for the work under which someone searching for the registration might be likely to look or under which a document pertaining to the work might be recorded.

Publication as a Contribution: If the work being registered is a contribution to a periodical, serial, or collection, give the title of the contribution in the "Title of this Work" space. Then, in the line headed "Publication as a Contribution," give information about the collective work in which the contribution appeared.

2 SPACE 2: Author(s)

General Instructions: After reading these instructions, decide who are the "authors" of this work for copyright purposes. Then, unless the work is a "collective work," give the requested information about every "author" who contributed any appreciable amount of copyrightable matter to this version of the work. If you need further space, request Continuation sheets. In the case of a collective work such as an anthology, collection of essays, or encyclopedia, give information about the author of the collective work as a whole.

Name of Author: The fullest form of the author's name should be given. Unless the work was "made for hire," the individual who actually created the work is its "author." In the case of a work made for hire, the statute provides that "the employer or other person for whom the work was prepared is considered the author."

What is a "Work Made for Hire"? A "work made for hire" is defined as (1) "a work prepared by an employee within the scope of his or her employment"; or (2) "a work specially ordered or commissioned for use as a contribution to a collective work, as a part of a motion picture or other audiovisual work, as a translation, as a supplementary work, as a compilation, as an instructional text, as a test, as answer material for a test, or as an atlas, if the parties expressly agree in a written instrument signed by them that the works shall be considered a work made for hire." If you have checked "Yes" to indicate that the work was "made for hire," you must give the full legal name of the employer (or other person for whom the work was prepared). You may also include the name of the employee along with the name of the employer (for example: "Elster Publishing Co., employer for hire of John Ferguson").

"Anonymous" or "Pseudonymous" Work: An author's contribution to a work is "anonymous" if that author is not identified on the copies or phonorecords of the work. An author's contribution to a work is "pseudonymous" if that author is identified on the copies or phonorecords under a fictitious name. If the work is "anonymous" you may: (1) leave the line blank; or (2) state "anonymous" on the line; or (3) reveal the author's identity. If the work is "pseudonymous" you may: (1) leave the line blank; or (2) give the pseudonym and identify it as such (for example: "Huntley Haverstock, pseudonym"); or (3) reveal the author's name, making clear which is the real name and which is the pseudonym (for example, "Judith Barton, whose pseudonym is Madeline Elster"). However, the citizenship or domicile of the author **must** be given in all cases.

Dates of Birth and Death: If the author is dead, the statute requires that the year of death be included in the application unless the work is anonymous or pseudonymous. The author's birth date is optional but is useful as a form of identification. Leave this space blank if the author's contribution was a "work made for hire."

Author's Nationality or Domicile: Give the country of which the author is a citizen or the country in which the author is domiciled. Nationality or domicile must be given in all cases.

Nature of Authorship: After the words "Nature of Authorship," give a brief general statement of the nature of this particular author's contribution to the work. Examples: "Entire text"; "Coauthor of entire text"; "Chapters 11-14"; "Editorial revisions"; "Compilation and English translation"; "New text."

3 SPACE 3: Creation and Publication

General Instructions: Do not confuse "creation" with "publication." Every application for copyright registration must state "the year in which creation of the work was completed." Give the date and nation of first publication only if the work has been published.

Creation: Under the statute, a work is "created" when it is fixed in a copy or phonorecord for the first time. Where a work has been prepared over a period of time, the part of the work existing in fixed form on a particular date constitutes the created work on that date. The date you give here should be the year in which the author completed the particular version for which registration is now being sought, even if other versions exist or if further changes or additions are planned.

Publication: The statute defines "publication" as "the distribution of copies or phonorecords of a work to the public by sale or other transfer of ownership, or by rental, lease, or lending"; a work is also "published" if there has been an "offering to distribute copies or phonorecords to a group of persons for purposes of further distribution, public performance, or public display." Give the full date (month, day, year) when, and the country where, publication first occurred. If first publication took place simultaneously in the United States and other countries, it is sufficient to state "U.S.A."

4 SPACE 4: Claimant(s)

Name(s) and Address(es) of Copyright Claimant(s): Give the name(s) and address(es) of the copyright claimant(s) in this work even if the claimant is the same as the author. Copyright in a work belongs initially to the author of the work (including, in the case of a work made for hire, the employer or other person for whom the work was prepared). The copyright claimant is either the author of the work or a person or organization to whom the copyright initially belonging to the author has been transferred.

Transfer: The statute provides that, if the copyright claimant is not the author, the application for registration must contain "a brief statement of how the claimant obtained ownership of the copyright." If any copyright claimant named in space 4 is not an author named in space 2, give a brief statement explaining how the claimant(s) obtained ownership of the copyright. Examples: "By written contract"; "Transfer of all rights by author"; "Assignment"; "By will." Do not attach transfer documents or other attachments or riders.

5 SPACE 5: Previous Registration

General Instructions: The questions in space 5 are intended to show whether an earlier registration has been made for this work and, if so, whether there is any basis for a new registration. As a general rule, only one basic copyright registration can be made for the same version of a particular work.

Same Version: If this version is substantially the same as the work covered by a previous registration, a second registration is not generally possible unless: (1) the work has been registered in unpublished form and a second registration is now being sought to cover this first published edition; or (2) someone other than the author is identified as copyright claimant in the earlier registration, and the author is now seeking registration in his or her own name. If either of these two exceptions apply, check the appropriate box and give the earlier registration number and date. Otherwise, do not submit Form TX; instead, write the Copyright Office for information about supplementary registration or recordation of transfers of copyright ownership.

Changed Version: If the work has been changed and you are now seeking registration to cover the additions or revisions, check the last box in space 5, give the earlier registration number and date, and complete both parts of space 6 in accordance with the instructions below.

Previous Registration Number and Date: If more than one previous registration has been made for the work, give the number and date of the latest registration.

6 SPACE 6: Derivative Work or Compilation

General Instructions: Complete space 6 if this work is a "changed version," "compilation," or "derivative work" and if it incorporates one or more earlier works that have already been published or registered for copyright or that have fallen into the public domain. A "compilation" is defined as "a work formed by the collection and assembling of preexisting materials or of data that are selected, coordinated, or arranged in such a way that the resulting work as a whole constitutes an original work of authorship." A "derivative work" is "a work based on one or more preexisting works." Examples of derivative works include translations, fictionalizations, abridgments, condensations, or "any other form in which a work may be recast, transformed, or adapted." Derivative works also include works "consisting of editorial revisions, annotations, or other modifications" if these changes, as a whole, represent an original work of authorship.

Preexisting Material (space 6a): For derivative works, complete this space **and** space 6b. In space 6a identify the preexisting work that has been recast, transformed, or adapted. An example of preexisting material might be: "Russian version of Goncharov's 'Oblomov'." Do not complete space 6a for compilations.

Material Added to This Work (space 6b): Give a brief, general statement of the new material covered by the copyright claim for which registration is sought. **Derivative work** examples include: "Foreword, editing, critical annotations"; "Translation"; "Chapters 11-17." If the work is a **compilation**, describe both the compilation itself and the material that has been compiled. Example: "Compilation of certain 1917 Speeches by Woodrow Wilson." A work may be both a derivative work and compilation, in which case a sample statement might be: "Compilation and additional new material."

7 SPACE 7: Manufacturing Provisions

Due to the expiration of the Manufacturing Clause of the copyright law on June 30, 1986, this space has been deleted.

8 SPACE 8: Reproduction for Use of Blind or Physically Handicapped Individuals

General Instructions: One of the major programs of the Library of Congress is to provide Braille editions and special recordings of works for the exclusive use of the blind and physically handicapped. In an effort to simplify and speed up the copyright licensing procedures that are a necessary part of this program, section 710 of the copyright statute provides for the establishment of a voluntary licensing system to be tied in with copyright registration. Copyright Office regulations provide that you may grant a license for such reproduction and distribution solely for the use of persons who are certified by competent authority as unable to read normal printed material as a result of physical limitations. The license is entirely voluntary, nonexclusive, and may be terminated upon 90 days notice.

How to Grant the License: If you wish to grant it, check one of the three boxes in space 8. Your check in one of these boxes together with your signature in space 10 will mean that the Library of Congress can proceed to reproduce and distribute under the license without further paperwork. For further information, write for Circular 63.

9, 10, 11 SPACE 9, 10, 11: Fee, Correspondence, Certification, Return Address

Fee: The Copyright Office has the authority to adjust fees at 5-year intervals, based on changes in the Consumer Price Index. The next adjustment is due in 1996. Please contact the Copyright Office after July 1995 to determine the actual fee schedule.

Deposit Account: If you maintain a Deposit Account in the Copyright Office, identify it in space 9. Otherwise leave the space blank and send the fee of $20 with your application and deposit.

Correspondence (space 9) This space should contain the name, address, area code, and telephone number of the person to be consulted if correspondence about this application becomes necessary.

Certification (space 10): The application can not be accepted unless it bears the date and the **handwritten signature** of the author or other copyright claimant, or of the owner of exclusive right(s), or of the duly authorized agent of author, claimant, or owner of exclusive right(s).

Address for Return of Certificate (space 11): The address box must be completed legibly since the certificate will be returned in a window envelope.

Copyright Form 169

FORM TX
For a Literary Work
UNITED STATES COPYRIGHT OFFICE

REGISTRATION NUMBER

_____
TX   TXU
EFFECTIVE DATE OF REGISTRATION

_____
Month   Day   Year

DO NOT WRITE ABOVE THIS LINE. IF YOU NEED MORE SPACE, USE A SEPARATE CONTINUATION SHEET.

1 TITLE OF THIS WORK ▼

PREVIOUS OR ALTERNATIVE TITLES ▼

PUBLICATION AS A CONTRIBUTION If this work was published as a contribution to a periodical, serial, or collection, give information about the collective work in which the contribution appeared.   Title of Collective Work ▼

If published in a periodical or serial give: Volume ▼   Number ▼   Issue Date ▼   On Pages ▼

2 a NAME OF AUTHOR ▼   DATES OF BIRTH AND DEATH
                                                              Year Born ▼   Year Died ▼

Was this contribution to the work a   AUTHOR'S NATIONALITY OR DOMICILE   WAS THIS AUTHOR'S CONTRIBUTION TO
"work made for hire"?   Name of Country   THE WORK   If the answer to either
  ☐ Yes   OR ┌ Citizen of ▶_____   Anonymous?   ☐ Yes ☐ No of these questions is
  ☐ No   └ Domiciled in ▶_____   Pseudonymous? ☐ Yes ☐ No "Yes," see detailed instructions.

NATURE OF AUTHORSHIP Briefly describe nature of material created by this author in which copyright is claimed. ▼

NOTE
Under the law, the "author" of a "work made for hire" is generally the employer, not the employee (see instructions). For any part of this work that was "made for hire" check "Yes" in the space provided, give the employer (or other person for whom the work was prepared) as "Author" of that part, and leave the space for dates of birth and death blank.

b NAME OF AUTHOR ▼   DATES OF BIRTH AND DEATH
                                                              Year Born ▼   Year Died ▼

Was this contribution to the work a   AUTHOR'S NATIONALITY OR DOMICILE   WAS THIS AUTHOR'S CONTRIBUTION TO
"work made for hire"?   Name of Country   THE WORK   If the answer to either
  ☐ Yes   OR ┌ Citizen of ▶_____   Anonymous?   ☐ Yes ☐ No of these questions is
  ☐ No   └ Domiciled in ▶_____   Pseudonymous? ☐ Yes ☐ No "Yes," see detailed instructions.

NATURE OF AUTHORSHIP Briefly describe nature of material created by this author in which copyright is claimed. ▼

c NAME OF AUTHOR ▼   DATES OF BIRTH AND DEATH
                                                              Year Born ▼   Year Died ▼

Was this contribution to the work a   AUTHOR'S NATIONALITY OR DOMICILE   WAS THIS AUTHOR'S CONTRIBUTION TO
"work made for hire"?   Name of Country   THE WORK   If the answer to either
  ☐ Yes   OR ┌ Citizen of ▶_____   Anonymous?   ☐ Yes ☐ No of these questions is
  ☐ No   └ Domiciled in ▶_____   Pseudonymous? ☐ Yes ☐ No "Yes," see detailed instructions.

NATURE OF AUTHORSHIP Briefly describe nature of material created by this author in which copyright is claimed. ▼

3 a YEAR IN WHICH CREATION OF THIS   **b** DATE AND NATION OF FIRST PUBLICATION OF THIS PARTICULAR WORK
         WORK WAS COMPLETED This information   Complete this information Month ▶ _____ Day ▶ _____ Year ▶ _____
         _____ ◀Year must be given   ONLY if this work
                             in all cases.   has been published.   ◀ Nation

4 COPYRIGHT CLAIMANT(S) Name and address must be given even if the claimant is the same as   APPLICATION RECEIVED
       the author given in space 2. ▼   _____
                                                                                                       ONE DEPOSIT RECEIVED
See instructions   _____
before completing
this space.   TWO DEPOSITS RECEIVED
                                                                                                       _____
       TRANSFER If the claimant(s) named here in space 4 is (are) different from the author(s) named in
       space 2, give a brief statement of how the claimant(s) obtained ownership of the copyright. ▼   REMITTANCE NUMBER AND DATE

MORE ON BACK ▶ • Complete all applicable spaces (numbers 5-11) on the reverse side of this page.   DO NOT WRITE HERE
                    • See detailed instructions.   • Sign the form at line 10.   Page 1 of _____ pages

Appendix B: Forms

	EXAMINED BY	FORM TX
	CHECKED BY	
	☐ CORRESPONDENCE Yes	FOR COPYRIGHT OFFICE USE ONLY

DO NOT WRITE ABOVE THIS LINE. IF YOU NEED MORE SPACE, USE A SEPARATE CONTINUATION SHEET.

5 PREVIOUS REGISTRATION Has registration for this work, or for an earlier version of this work, already been made in the Copyright Office?
☐ Yes ☐ No   If your answer is "Yes," why is another registration being sought? (Check appropriate box) ▼
a. ☐ This is the first published edition of a work previously registered in unpublished form.
b. ☐ This is the first application submitted by this author as copyright claimant.
c. ☐ This is a changed version of the work, as shown by space 6 on this application.
If your answer is "Yes," give: **Previous Registration Number** ▼   **Year of Registration** ▼

6 DERIVATIVE WORK OR COMPILATION Complete both space 6a and 6b for a derivative work; complete only 6b for a compilation.
a. **Preexisting Material** Identify any preexisting work or works that this work is based on or incorporates. ▼

b. **Material Added to This Work** Give a brief, general statement of the material that has been added to this work and in which copyright is claimed. ▼

See instructions before completing this space.

7 —space deleted—

8 REPRODUCTION FOR USE OF BLIND OR PHYSICALLY HANDICAPPED INDIVIDUALS A signature on this form at space 10 and a check in one of the boxes here in space 8 constitutes a non-exclusive grant of permission to the Library of Congress to reproduce and distribute solely for the blind and physically handicapped and under the conditions and limitations prescribed by the regulations of the Copyright Office: (1) copies of the work identified in space 1 of this application in Braille (or similar tactile symbols); or (2) phonorecords embodying a fixation of a reading of that work; or (3) both.

a ☐ Copies and Phonorecords   b ☐ Copies Only   c ☐ Phonorecords Only   See instructions.

9 DEPOSIT ACCOUNT If the registration fee is to be charged to a Deposit Account established in the Copyright Office, give name and number of Account.
Name ▼   **Account Number** ▼

CORRESPONDENCE Give name and address to which correspondence about this application should be sent.   Name/Address/Apt/City/State/ZIP ▼

Area Code and Telephone Number ▶

Be sure to give your daytime phone number ◀

10 CERTIFICATION* I, the undersigned, hereby certify that I am the
Check only one ▶
☐ author
☐ other copyright claimant
☐ owner of exclusive right(s)
☐ authorized agent of _____
Name of author or other copyright claimant, or owner of exclusive right(s) ▲

of the work identified in this application and that the statements made by me in this application are correct to the best of my knowledge.

Typed or printed name and date ▼ If this application gives a date of publication in space 3, do not sign and submit it before that date.
_____ date ▶ _____

☞ **Handwritten signature (X)** ▼

11 MAIL CERTIFICATE TO
Name ▼
Number/Street/Apartment Number ▼
City/State/ZIP ▼

Certificate will be mailed in window envelope

YOU MUST:
• Complete all necessary spaces
• Sign your application in space 10
SEND ALL 3 ELEMENTS IN THE SAME PACKAGE:
1. Application form
2. Nonrefundable $20 filing fee in check or money order payable to *Register of Copyrights*
3. Deposit material
MAIL TO:
Register of Copyrights
Library of Congress
Washington, D.C. 20559

The Copyright Office has the authority to adjust fees at 5-year intervals, based on changes in the Consumer Price Index. The next adjustment is due in 1996. Please contact the Copyright Office after July 1995 to determine the actual fee schedule.

*17 U.S.C. § 506(e): Any person who knowingly makes a false representation of a material fact in the application for copyright registration provided for by section 409, or in any written statement filed in connection with the application, shall be fined not more than $2,500.

February 1993—100,000   ☆U.S. GOVERNMENT PRINTING OFFICE: 1993-342-581/60,504

Glossary

Academy The Academy of Motion Picture Arts and Sciences set those standards used in motion picture technology. To say that a camera has an **academy** aperture is to say it has the first standard aperture.

action The activity that takes place for the camera's sake. Also, the command made by the director for the scene's activity to begin.

aluminum flashing Used on roofs under shingles to preclude water leakage. Because it is inexpensive, readily available and easily used, it is often found in the motion picture work shop.

anamorphic Describes a "squeeze" lens, that is one which compresses the optical image laterally more than vertically thereby putting an entire rectangular image in a square frame. In projection the image is unsqueezed by using a similar lens.

ancillary markets Those markets which can add additional profit, or offer a profit margin after primary markets have been accessed.

answer print A first trial print from an edited original. Almost invariably contains errors, but will serve as a release print if it doesn't.

apple boxes Unopenable wooden boxes, typically 14"× 20", used to prop up or elevate people or props. There are ⅛ apples which are 1 inch thick, ¼ apples which are 2 inches thick, ½ apples which are 4 inches, and apples which are 8 inches. They are almost invariably painted green and have handle openings cut in each end.

Arri, Arriflex A manufacturer of 16mm and 35mm film cameras.

ASA/ISO Refers to the relative "speed" or sensitivity of a film emulsion. ASA 125 is half as sensitive as ASA 250. Likewise with ISO. The values of both are identical. The American Standards Association is now defunct therefore the term ASA is obsolete. ISO is used today.

aspect ratio The ratio of the screen or aperature's width to height. A screen 20 feet high by 47 feet wide would be known as a "two thirty five" or a 2.35:1 ratio.

assistant cameraman A person under the directorship of the cameraman or cinematographer whose general responsibility is to be sure the camera is ready to use at the appointed time—the proper lens is in place, the f/stop is set, magazines are loaded, camera is threaded, and other such matters.

assistant director An assistant to the director. He typically does *not* assist in the art of directing.

audio effects Sound effects, whether procured by recording real sounds or manufacturing them artificially.

audio transfer The rerecording of sound from one medium to another.

Auricon A manufacturer of 16mm single system sound film cameras.

available light Ambient light or that light which is present on the set or location without altering or augmenting it.

B&W or **black and white** Monochromatic, colorless. An image comprised of black, white, and gradients of gray.

back crank (1) To rewind film while still in the camera or printer. (2) To film action while running the camera backwards.

back light A subject is said to be back lit when the light source faces the camera and does not regard the direction the subject is facing.

back wind To rewind film while still in the camera or printer.

Bell and Howell A manufacturer of 8mm, 16mm and 35mm film camera equipment.

bi-pack To thread raw stock in a camera or printer together with a camera original or other master for duplication purposes.

black and white see **B&W**

blocking The process of mapping out where actors' positions and camera moves will be made while filming a take.

blow-up (n) An enlarged negative or print from a smaller original. (v) The act of enlarging an image.

Bolex A brand name of 8mm and 16mm film camera equipment.

bracket To make exposures or exposure tests of greater and lesser values in order to determine which is best. This procedure can serve as a safety net in an emergency when proper exposure evaluation is not possible.

broad A lamp whose light is soft and wide-spread.

broadcast quality Defines the quality of electronic control signals in video equipment. There is no relationship between the quality of a video picture and the term "broadcast quality." Consumer equipment is not broadcast quality.

call The time and place at which talent and crew are expected for the purpose of rehearsal or shooting.

call sheet A paper issued once a day during a shoot to indicate to all interested parties whether, what time and where they will be needed.

camcorder A video camera with an internal capacity for video tape.

camera assistant Anyone appointed to aid the cinematographer, cameraman, or assistant cameraman who does *not* have another title. (By interpretation, the lighting people help the cinematographer but are not necessarily assistants.)

camera log A paper kept for the purpose of documenting roll number, scene and take number, f/stop, focal length, and any other relevant data on *every* take.

camera stock Film made for the use of shooting in the camera (as opposed to lab or sound recording stock).

cameraman The camera operator or the person under the direction of the cinematographer who instructs the cameraman.

car mount A device mounted on an automobile to hold a camera for the purpose of shooting a scene from or toward a driver's point of view.

casting The process of discovering the best available actor or actress for a specific part.

Cine Special A documentary type 16mm camera made by Kodak.

cinematographer Literally a cinema photographer. The cinematographer may or may not operate the camera but is responsible for its function and usually for the lighting on a set or location.

circle takes Those takes encircled on the camera log. Those takes which are deemed by the director to be good ones are circled, an indication to the lab that they are to be printed.

clap stick or **clapper** A device (usually simply a pair of hinged wooden sticks) appropriately painted with stripes for visibility. They are held before the camera and smacked together smartly in order to tabulate a scene start mark for both the film and the audio tape. They most frequently are attached to a slate with information readable on the film negative after processing.

close up A shot made as the camera is quite close to the subject. (If the camera is at a greater distance and a lens of longer focal length is used to acquire roughly the same effect, it is called a tight shot.)

color reversal intermediate Also known as CRI. A film stock used by labs to duplicate a negative in a single processing step.

colorist The person who adjusts color balance and brightness. This person is otherwise responsible for the general appearance of a film being transferred to videotape. (See also **timer**.)

ColorTran A manufacturer of photographic lighting units.

conform To conform a negative or camera original is to cut and splice it to match the edited work print.

continuity The responsibility of a person to assure that incorrect changes are not made between scenes or takes. Since scenes are seldom filmed in the order they are used or in the time it takes to watch them, someone must be sure that a candle burns only from tall to short; not from medium to tall to short to medium and back to tall again. Likewise a wet shirt may not be wet and dry and wet again.

continuity person see **script clerk**

CP-16 Either of two models of 16mm single system sound cameras made by Century Precision Optical Company.

crawl Written matter such as end credits are crawled. The words appear to come from below the screen, rise slowly, and disappear off the top of the screen.

CRI see **color reversal intermediate**

crop To compose or recompose an image so as to eliminate something.

cross dissolve see **dissolve**

cross fade see **dissolve**

C-stand Abbreviated term for the trade name Century Stand. A C-stand is used for general purposes but rarely has a lamp mounted on it. More often it holds flags, fingers and other shadow-casting devices.

cue A time or notable element by which a talent or technician knows he is to perform a specific task. Example: When John Doe turns toward the boat, the pyrotechnist pushes the button that blows it up. "Turns" is the pyrotechnist's cue.

cut The command given by the director to stop sound, camera, and action. Is also synonymous with the word edit.

dailies, rushes, work print A daily is a print delivered for Tuesday viewing of Monday's photography. It is a rush if done quickly but not daily. Once it is given to the editor—who cuts it—it becomes a work print.

day-for-night A scene or technique of shooting in the daytime to achieve a visual result appearing to have been shot at night.

depth-of-field A means of describing or measuring the inner and outer boundaries of those elements in a photographic image which are in focus.

dialogue The conversation spoken by on-camera talent.

digital effects Special visual effects done with the aid of a computer.

diopter In optical measurement a diopter is 40 inches. An auxilliary lens to change the focal length of another lens.

director of photography The person who oversees the design of the lighting and the operation of the camera to achieve a specific mood or appearance in the finished film.

dissolve or **cross dissolve** Both expressions denote the same film effect—one scene fades out while another, superimposed over it, fades in. The dissolve denotes a passage of time or a change of venue.

distributor A company or person whose business contacts allow the finished film to be put into the appropriate market place.

dolly (n) The device upon which a camera is mounted in order to move it or to make a shot while the camera is moving. **To dolly** (v) The action of moving the camera while shooting or rehearsing.

dub (n) A duplicate. (v) To duplicate.

dub in To add sound effects after editing.

duplicate negative, dupe neg, dupe negative A negative made from an interpositive.

Eclair A manufacturer of 16mm and 35mm film cameras.

ECN Represents all of the Eastman Color Negative stocks made for motion picture camera use.

Edison A standard (household) lamp base.

effects shots Shots made for the specific purpose of being used for special visual effects.

EFX, FX Abbreviation for effects of any kind.

Ektachrome A reversal film made by Kodak.

ends, short ends Unused film removed from camera magazines which is too short to use for the upcoming take. It can be used for in-lab purposes later or can be sold. Some ends can be almost full rolls.

f/stop The measurement of light passing through a lens. An iris diaphragm is the device used to set a lens at a particular f/stop.

fade in, fade out The bringing up of the light level of a scene from black to normal viewing level, or vice versa. The effect denotes the beginning and end of a sequence.

FAY lamps A 650 watt, daylight balanced, sealed beam lamp.

feature A film or video of about 90 minutes in length which is the primary program in a theatre or television show.

filter A glass or gelatin device put in front of or between lenses to alter the image or qualities of light passing through it.

finder see **viewfinder**

finger A long, slender piece of cardboard or plywood, usually held by a C-stand, to cast a shadow upon something in a scene which the cinematographer does not want lit to the level of those things around it, or to keep a reflection of a lamp off something shiny.

flag Does the same job as a finger but covers more area.

flying wall A wall on a set, usually on wheels, which can be moved for access or space.

focus puller A person whose job is to keep the camera focused on the subject as the subject or the camera changes position during a take.

fog, fogged Film exposed to light, whether accidental or for effect.

fog machine A machine which physically generates fog for foggy scenes.

foley The process of adding footsteps to the sound track. Foley stages have pits in the floor filled with gravel, sand, hard wood, soft wood, stones, dry leaves, and other material, along with a viewing screen and recording equipment.

footcandle A measurement of light, specifically the amount of light a candle emits as measured at the distance of one foot.

format Refers to the size film or videotape used and to the aspect ratio to which it is applied.

frame (1) An individual picture on motion picture film. (2) 1/24th of a second [American]. (3) All of the image within the viewable picture area.

frame rate The speed at which film travels through the camera, printer or projector. Sound speed in the United States is 24 fps.

Fresnel (The s is silent. The word is pronounced Frennell.) A glass lens used mostly on focusable spot lighting units. The design is such that a great portion of the glass bulk is removed leaving the large piece of glass lighter than it otherwise would be.

full coat A film base having the same perforations as picture stock and having a magnetic coating for sound recording. Because of the identical perforations, it can be kept in mechanically synchronous interlock with the picture during intermediate stages.

FX see **EFX**

gels A large variety of colored or frosted pliable plastic devices made for the purpose of altering the quality or quantity of light passing through it.

generation Describes how near the original a duplicate is. Example: A camera negative (first generation) is printed to an interpositive (second generation) from which an internegative is made (third generation) from which a work print is made (fourth generation). A music work print is made from the edited work print (fifth generation), then the interpositive is edited and a dupe negative is struck from it (third generation) and a finished print made from that (fourth generation). You can see from this that generations can but needn't run in a straight line.

generator A device for generating electricity for film production purposes.

glass matte A method of adding image to a shot by painting it or a portion of it on glass and shooting through the unpainted portion.

grip Skilled labor on a film crew.

hanging miniature Miniature models of anything, hung in front of the camera in such position as to appear to be lifesize examples of the real thing.

high key A key or main light put in a high position. The sun at noon is a high key light but is low key at sunset.

high risers Very tall light stands.

HMI Very efficient, very expensive daylight balanced lighting units. They require a quite noisy ballast.

in the can Indicates filming is finished and post-production may begin or has begun.

insert A shot made to bring the viewer's attention to a specific element which might otherwise be missed.

174 Glossary

interlock The mechanical technique of keeping picture and sound, although on separate media, in synchronization with each other.

interpositive or **IP** A low contrast, positive print made as an intermediate step from which a dupe negative is made.

ISO see **ASA**

key light The light which sets the overall look or mood of a picture.

Kodachrome A reversal color film made by Kodak. (It was the first viable color film. Pictures made on it in 1937 look as good today as they did then.) Most color films, negative or reversal, use Kodachrome as the standard or goal for appearance.

lateral reversal To reverse from left to right, a mirror image.

life mask A duplicate made of a live person or live animal's face. It is done in such a way so as not to threaten the safety of the subject.

lip sync To move one's lips to a pre-recorded sound to give the illusion that one is actually saying or singing that audio. Sound which is synchronized with the image of what makes the sound is referred to as lip sync, even though it may be a hammer hitting an anvil.

liquid gate A device used in the process of film printing to minimize the appearance of dust and scratches.

litho film A type of film which renders opaque blacks, clear whites, and no middle tones at all.

lo con see **low contrast positive**

location An exterior place where a film is being made.

loop or **looping** The process of replacing dialogue. It may be done in order to change languages or to replace the actor's voice with a better one. Or an actor may replace his own voice because of poor original recording quality. The act of inserting or replacing other sounds is called dubbing in.

low contrast positive A low contrast print made for the purpose of transferring to videotape. It can be used as a release print.

lumens For practical purposes, one lumen equals one footcandle.

mag stripe Refers to film which has a magnetic stripe for sound recording.

magazine The part of a camera, usually detachable, which contains the film.

Magnasync A manufacturer of audio recording equipment for film.

magnetic camera and **magnetic projector** Equipment capable of sound recording to and playback from a magnetic sound track.

master shot A single shot which includes the entire scene and all its elements, if possible.

master tape A finished tape from which duplicates are made.

mechanical effects Special effects which are done physically in front of the camera. Bullet hits on a wall, for example, are a mechanical effect.

miniature Miniatures are often used (in close-ups) to represent a real thing (in the distance). Miniatures need not be tiny. In *Tora, Tora, Tora*, the miniature ships in Pearl Harbor were 18 to 21 feet long. In faithful detail, they were infinitely cheaper to make than a full size model.

Mitchell George Mitchell invented the Mitchell movement. This movement was used in the series of cameras of the same name which set the industry standard in the 1920's. Even today, the Mitchell movement is used in the finest cameras.

mix To combine two or more sound recordings to get their level correct on the resulting recording.

mixing system A device for playing and recording multiple audio tracks.

model An artificial duplicate of something real. A duplicate may be used for destruction or because the real thing is not available.

model release A legal form releasing purchasers of talent to use pursuant to the contract.

mogul A light bulb base like an Edison but twice as large.

mortar A device used to hold a self-propelled explosive.

MOS A shot made without sound. Typically, sound will be added later.

movement The device in a film camera that transports the film in such a way as to create the illusion of a moving image.

Movieola (1) A manufacturer of film editing equipment. (2) A film editing machine.

music work print A work print made from another edited work print. This can be done in order to have a work print from which the scoring musician can work while the editor continues to do his job. It sometimes is made because the first work print has worn out from editorial use. A music work print is often black & white. Lack of color and its diminished visual quality are unimportant since the intended use is for timing and observation only. This print does not affect the finished version of the film.

Nagra (1) A manufacturer of field recording equipment. (2) A field recorder used primarily for motion picture recording. It uses ¼ inch tape.

napalm An explosive gel made from gasoline.

negative (1) The same image as a positive except all the values from black to white are reversed. (2) The film stock used in film cameras. (3) The camera original film from which the work print and IP's are made. (4) The composite film from which prints are made.

negative cutter The person who, following the edited work print, conforms the negative in order to make intermediates and prints.

negative insurance Insurance bought to financially protect certain elements of production.

negative/reversal Describes the orientation of a particular film thereby denoting its general use. A negative film will render a positive image when printed onto a negative-acting print stock. A reversal film renders a positive image when processed. When printed onto a reversal print stock, it renders another positive image. When printed onto a negative stock, it renders an internegative.

news film Film shot as television news coverage or using such techniques, equipment or materials.

nodal point A point within a lens, or in space behind it, which represents the optical pivot point of the lens.

1-K, 2-K, 5-K, 10-K The K represents 1,000 watts. The expression 5-K means a 5,000 watt lighting unit.

original negative The processed stock used in the camera. Whether the negative has been further used or treated is not relevant to the definition.

overmodulated Sound which has been recorded louder than the equipment or the recording medium can reproduce without distortion.

pan (1) To rotate the camera on its horizontal axis. (2) A shot in which the camera was rotated on its horizontal axis.

Panavision A manufacturer of the industry-accepted finest film camera.

pick-up shots Shots missed, or otherwise not made, during principal photography.

Plexiglas A strong, clear plasticlike glass. It is a trade name.

postproduction All the elements of filmmaking which take place after camera work is finished. Editing is a postproduction element although it can begin as soon as the first foot of work print is available.

pre-mix The re-recording of two or more rolls of edited sound track establishing their relative volume levels as an interim step to re-recording it with other mixed rolls.

preproduction All of the elements of filmmaking which take place before filming begins.

principal photography The photography which includes talent.

print An intermediate or finished duplicate of original photography.

print-thru A technique which allows original footage numbers to be duplicated onto a print.

prints The final films which are exhibited.

production meeting A meeting in which all people concerned are present to discuss problems and solutions regarding the upcoming production.

production value Elements within the scenes which give a picture the appearance of being more expensively done. Example: a car can crash into an abutment of the Golden Gate Bridge. That is a production value. If the impact caused the Golden Gate Bridge to collapse, that is a whale of a production value.

prop A physical item which is used as a visual portion of filming. A lamp on the set is a prop. A light on a light stand is not—unless it is intended to be photographed.

Pyrodex A trade name for a gun powder.

pyrotechnist The person responsible for fires and explosions.

ratio or **shooting ratio** The total amount of film planned to be shot as compared to the amount of film in the finished product. In 16mm, to shoot 3,000 feet for a half-hour show is a 6:1 ratio.

raw stock Material used for a project, usually picture film. It can also refer to audio material such as one-quarter inch tape or full coat.

reaction shot A shot of the person who displays a response to action being filmed. Example: Fred is walking around the room shouting at two female actresses who are not speaking. The master shot would include all three. The close-ups would include Fred. The reaction shots would include either or both of the two women. It is used (a) to show the reactions of the women to what Fred is saying, and (b) to ease the cuts between the master shot and the close-ups of Fred, and (c) to give the editor the option to make a cut to correct an error or remove dialogue.

reduction printer A film printer which will print from 65mm to 35mm, from 35mm to 16mm, or from 16mm to 8mm.

reflectors flat boards upon which gold or silver foil is glued to reflect sunlight into shadow areas.

reflex camera A camera whose image is viewed through the taking lens while in operation.

reflex finder (1) The view finder of a reflex camera. (2) A finder designed to be reflex regardless of the camera.

register or **registration** The holding or placement of a precision position. When the sprocket hole is positioned at the time of pull-down, it must be in the same position as its predecessor within a specified mechanical tolerance. That is, one frame must be in register with another. Image movement in a fixed condition is caused by poor mechanical registration.

rehearsal The practicing of a scene, sequence, or entire production.

release Putting on the market an item.

release print A film print made to use in theaters.

reversal (1) A type of film which renders a positive image from a positive image. (2) The process by which a film is caused to render a positive image from a positive image.

reversal/negative see **negative/reversal**

roman candles A consumer fireworks device that shoots a specified number of bright fireballs about the size of marbles.

rotoscope To project an image using the camera as a projector.

rough cut The first edit of a film or video. A rough cut usually runs two hours or more. It is edited again and again until it is deemed as good as it can be made.

rushes see **dailies**

sand bags Made of canvas, sometimes plastic coated, and have handles. They come in several sizes and are used as weights, usually to keep raised lighting units from tipping over.

Schufftan box or **Schufftan shot** A device and a technique invented for the making of special visual effects and named after its inventor. It is patented although its patent is never enforced.

scoop A deep lamp reflector which uses no lens.

screen credit The acknowledgment of the services of a person or entity.

script The communications device by which all crew and talent know what is to be done and generally what is expected of them.

script clerk or **script girl** or **script & continuity [person]** A person with good observation skills. This person watches the elements of a scene being rehearsed or filmed while being cognizant of those which precede and follow, and at the same time keeps in mind the mandates of the script. Upon the command "Cut," this person immediately reports to the director any discrepancies which may be intolerable.

S.E.C. The Securities Exchange Commission. It is a government agency who can come after you if you sell stock by doing it the wrong way.

second unit The photographing of background plates and secondary imaging which does not include the principal actors.

sequence A series of scenes which has a small climax or which has a resolve within a plot, or which creates more questions or problems.

set An indoor area set aside for acting before a camera for the purpose of filmmaking.

SFX An abbreviation for sound effects.

shadows The darkest portions of a pictorial image regardless of whether they are actually shadows in the general definition.

shooting ratio see **ratio**

short ends see **ends**

shot A length of film or a time depiction. Sequences are comprised of scenes and scenes are comprised of shots.

single perf (perforated) Film which is perforated—has sprocket holes—on one side only.

slate (n) A small board held in front of the camera to record, on film, data relevant to that take, such as roll number and scene number. (v) To identify a take number by either image on a picture or verbally on a sound track.

Sonarex A brand of film projectors.

sound numbers Consecutive numbers beginning at 1 with the first sound take. These numbers have no connection with scene number orientation. It is a faster means to find sound takes for audio transfer than scene and take numbers. Number 29 will invariably follow number 28 (not so with scene numbers).

sound recordist The person who operates a sound recorder.

sound speed 24 frames per second in the U.S., 25 in the U.K.

sound stage An edifice built for the specific purpose of shooting film and sound simultaneously.

"Speed!" The appropriate response, meaning "Ready," when the director calls for camera and sound. This command is the marker's cue to clap the sticks.

split screen Describes two images on a single frame of film. It usually means two separate images which appear to be a single one. The use of a single actor to play himself and his twin usually employs a split screen technique.

spot A spotlight or the light cast by a spotlight. It does not mean "place."

spring wind A motor whose energy is derived from being stored in a clock spring.

squib An explosive device intended to simulate a bullet hit. Legally, its use or purchase requires a pyrotechnical license.

sticks (1) A wooden tripod. (2) Clap sticks.

storyboard A diagram, not unlike a comic book, which gives a visual description of how a scene, an effect, or an entire picture is to be filmed. It is an industry-standard communications device used by the producer, director, cinematographer, cameraman, effects people and lab people.

strike (1) To make, to duplicate, as in "to strike a print." (2) To remove or dissassemble a set when finished.

SunGun A brand name for small, simple photographic quartz lamps.

sweat equity Interest points earned in a project by work performed instead of cash.

sweeten To improve mechanically. To sweeten the sound is to remove both audible and inaudible trash.

sync block A hubbed set of wheels with sprocket teeth to fit film. In the process of conforming, it keeps the work print and negative rolls in perfect frame-to-frame alignment.

sync pulse A 60Hz (50Hz in the U.K.) crystal recording or recording of the main current used to drive the camera motor. The sound lab technician can lock onto the pulse electronically to keep it in synchronization with the picture even though he has no access to the picture.

sync pulse generator An electronic device which puts an appropriate sync pulse (for synchronization purposes) on an audio or videotape.

sync speed 24 frames per second in U.S., 25 in the U.K.

synopsis or **treatment** Basically the script with the dialogue missing. A good synopsis won't exceed one page while a treatment may run around seven to ten pages.

synthesizer (1) A musical instrument which generates a near perfect duplicate of other musical instruments or sounds. (2) An electronics device that duplicates sounds by *first sampling.*

tail slate Gives the same information as slating at the head except that it is done at the end of the shot instead of the beginning. When doing so, the slate is held upside down to indicate its orientation. It usually occurs as an emergency measure to avoid losing the shot because unrepeatable action has started before called for, and filming has begun.

talent Those people who appear or whose voice is used in a movie—whether they have any talent or not.

Techniscope A Technicolor Corporation development. Equipment converted to Techniscope uses a 35mm film frame equal to two perforations rather than the traditional four.

theatrical (n) A film made for exhibition in a theater.

Three-perf, 3-Perf Trade marks. Both have essentially the same attributes as Techniscope for the same reasons but for a different purpose.

tie in An electrical junction box which can be attached to an incoming electrical service. If you are not an electrician, stay away from it.

tight shot (1) A shot made with a longer focal length lens than would be necessary if the camera were closer to the subject. (2) An image which is crowded within the frame, visually cramped.

tilt (1) The pivoting of the camera on its vertical axis. (2) A shot exhibiting a pivot on the camera's vertical axis. See also **pan**.

time code A recording of digital information running together with audio or video on a tape which identifies each individual frame on the entire roll. It can be used to run in synchronization with another tape having a similar or dissimilar time code.

timer A person who decides and establishes the correct exposure and color balance of a film before printing. See also **colorist**.

transfer The re-recording of picture or sound from any medium to an electronic medium.

treatment see **synopsis**

tripod A camera stand with three legs. A light stand or a milking stool with three legs is not a tripod.

tungsten One of two artificial light sources. Flourescent is the other. HMI is a daylight light source—even though it is artificial. Tungsten, flourescent, and daylight describe three discreet color balances.

TV safety The area within a standard frame which will not be cropped out by video recording or transmission.

up crank To operate the camera faster than normal in order to achieve the illusion of slow motion.

VCR A video cassette recorder (and player).

video enhancement An accomplishment made electronically which improves the quality, color, contrast, edging, and other aspects of a video image.

video tape master A finished videotape from which duplicate videotapes can be made.

video transfer The re-recording onto videotape from any medium other than live.

view finder A device on a camera which will allow the operator's eye to see what the film will see.

VNF Kodak's Video News Film. It was made for that purpose but, because it renders a flat (low contrast) image, it is a good original for duplication.

walk-through A rehearsal done shortly before a take.

wet gate see **liquid gate**

wide angle (1) A position from which a broad view can be seen. (2) A lens which will accept and render a broad angle.

work print see **dailies**

Index

Abernathy, Jeneanne 2
The Abyss 69, 71
academy 33, 34
acting, actor 29
Adam Smith's Money World 94
Adolph Gosser (Co.) 107
Agfa 24, 37
Airwolf 24, 37
Alien 14
Allen, Chris 1, 3, 4, 7, 9, 126, 127, 128, 129
"Also Spracht Zarathustra" 130
Amazing Special Effects You Can Do with Your Camcorder 76
American Cinematographer Manual 15
AmVets 91
anamorphic 33, 34, 108, 109
Angenieux 97
Anitra 2, 3, 4, 5, 6, 7, 8, 9, 11; see also *Body Shop*
Anscochrome 109
answer print 24, 25, 44
apple boxes 4
Arriflex 7, 17, 28, 96, 109, 115
art 48, 66, 68
artist, art director 31, 47, 68
ASA 3, 13
ASCAP 130
assistant director, A.D. 22
associate producer 31
Attack of the Killer Tomatoes 117
audio effects 36
audio recorder, recording 10, 26, 38, 41, 101, 116, 117
audio tape 30, 38, 39
audio track 24, 101
Auricon 17, 97
Autry, John 48
Azimov's Probe 77, 78, 82

Bach, J.S. 131
backer *see* investor
background plate 34, 59, 63
BBC 90
Belk, Reggie 5
Bell & Howell 98, 100
Bell Helicopter 41
Ben-Hur 69
Berkebile, Chris 13
Bernstein, Leonard 131
beta, BetaCam 104, 105, 118
Billy 24
bipack 46, 59, 66
Bi-Rite Photo & Electronics 38, 117
bit part 24
black & white 4, 12, 37, 105, 124, 128
Blanchard, Jean-Claud 23

blocking 14, 52, 91
blow up 33, 34, 38, 44, 76, 102, 103, 106, 107, 108, 109, 114, 115, 116, 117
blue screen 63
BMI 130
Body Shop 10, 11, 12, 17, 26, 32, 48, 53, 82, 85, 111, 125, 126, 127, 128, 129, 130
Bolex 15, 18, 98, 117
Bosch 111
breakdown, script 32
Bride of Frankenstein 2
Brideshead Revisited 90
Brodsky & Teadway 117
Broom, Donnie 17, 22
budget 1, 7, 10, 32, 41, 42, 43, 47, 52, 76, 88, 90, 92, 93, 94, 95, 102, 108, 117

C-stand 18, 20, 93, 123
call sheet 20, 82
camcorder 17, 28, 50, 88, 101, 105, 117, 125, 130
camera 2, 14, 15, 18, 22, 23, 29, 33, 34, 36, 38, 41, 42, 37, 47, 50, 52, 54, 55, 56, 57, 59, 63, 64, 66, 67, 68, 69, 70, 71, 74, 76, 87, 91, 93, 95, 96, 97, 98, 99, 104, 107, 108, 109, 110, 112, 113, 115, 119, 120, 124
camera assistant 41, 93
camera log 20
camera operator 40, 57
cameraman 1, 5, 23, 78
Cannon Films 94
car mount 17
Carpenter, John 12
Carpenter, Ralph 12, 13, 15
Carroll, Bob 23
Cassavedes, John 36
cast 32, 76, 85, 90, 96
Castles, Neal 42
caterer 36
CBS 94
Cedar Studios 26
cellophane 42
Cervone, Vincent 25
Chambless Productions 117
checklist 26, 90
Chevrolet 91
ChromaKey 118
Cine Special (Kodak) 15, 18, 98
Cinefex 76
Cinema and Draft House 24
CinemaScope 69, 109
cinematographer 33, 37, 39, 71, 88, 93, 106, 123
Clairmont Camera 110, 111
clapper 23

Clark, Barry 23, 90
Clark, J.B. 23, 90
Cleopatra 69
Clifford, John 17, 24
code, coding 40
The Color Purple 21, 52, 71
Color Reversal Intermediate, CRI 107
Color-Tran 13
communication 18, 31, 77, 78, 82, 87, 88
composite 64
computer 32, 43, 47, 50
conform 43
continuity 53
continuity person *see* script clerk
contract 31
copyright 85, 132
Cosgrove, Harry 20
The Country House 32, 123
CP-16, Century Precision 17, 20, 97
credits 24, 30, 47, 48, 49, 96
crew 13, 19, 20, 21, 22, 31, 32, 34, 41, 42, 52, 53, 77, 85, 88, 92, 93, 94, 95
CRI 59, 64
cut away 36, 86, 98

dailies 3, 107
Davis, Trena 15, 16, 17
daylight 37, 38, 92
Deliverance 130
deMille, C.B. 26
depth of field 50, 64
deStrom, Mike 8
dialogue 10, 11, 22, 42, 53, 55, 57, 58, 86, 87, 96, 101, 102
Dick Tracy 115
director 22, 23, 26, 31, 35, 40, 52, 53, 55, 58, 78, 86, 87, 88, 91, 92, 93, 120, 130
director of photography, DP 2, 3, 5, 40, 41
The Disney Organization 36, 64, 98
distributor, distribution 27, 44, 48, 102, 107, 114
Dr. Gore 10, 117; see also *Body Shop*
documentary 33, 39
documentation 32
Dodge 91
dolly 56, 93, 96, 110, 112, 113, 116
dolly pusher, dolly grip 3, 41, 57
double system 35, 38, 39, 43, 98, 117
Drawbridge Restaurant 8
Driggers, Genny 4, 6, 7, 11
dubber 24, 25
"Dueling Banjos" 130
Dunn, Linn 43, 44, 47
dupe negative 33

180 Index

Eastman Color Negative, ECN 96, 106
Eclair 96
editing 22, 23, 34, 38, 39, 40, 43, 44, 47, 48, 65, 98, 99, 100, 101, 108, 111, 115, 117, 118, 119, 120, 126
editor 26, 40, 52, 53, 55, 58, 78, 93, 94, 130
edge numbers 40
Edison, Thomas A. 7
effects *see* special effects; mechanical effects
8mm 33, 104
Eller, Jet 18, 19, 20, 24, 25, 26, 50
Elwood, Tony 111, 112, 116
ends, short ends 3, 4
E.O. Corporation; E.O. Studios 42, 71
equipment 33, 34
Esco, Hugh 17
Espin, Will 4
Evans, Donnie 13, 15, 16
executive producer 22, 91
extension tube 50
Exterminator II 117
extras, 71, 88, 89
Eyemo 59, 115
Eyes of the Scarecrow 90, 94, 102, 106

Fairbanks, Douglas 28
FCC 104
feature 26, 31, 32, 52, 90, 94, 97, 104, 120, 130, 132
Ferren, Bran 76, 88
film (stock) 25, 28, 38, 39, 52, 63, 64, 66, 68, 76, 91, 93, 96, 97, 98, 99, 106, 107, 108, 114, 115, 117, 118, 124, 125
film industry *see* motion picture industry
Film-Video Supply Co. 117
flag 13
Floyd, Dave 25
focus puller 3, 41
fog, fog machine 13, 15, 77
Foley, 23, 41
format 35
Frazer, John 24
Freeman, Margaret 20
freeze frame 48
front screen projections 76
Fuji Photo 24, 37, 94, 117
full coat 22, 23, 24, 25, 26, 38, 40, 41, 96, 98, 99, 104, 114, 115

Gastonia Gazette 11
glass shot 18, 68–70
Glenn, Defoy 20
Golan, Menahem 94
Goldberg, Whoopie 21
Goldcrest Films and TV, Ltd. 78
Gone with the Wind 30, 117
Goodwill Industries 91
Gourmet Zombies from Hell 116
Granada TV Productions 90
The Great Race 43
The Great Balloon Chase 70
grip 5

Halloween 88
Harley's Gadget 87, 130

"A Heart Dies Every Minute" 8, 11
Heptig, Marie 16
Hill, Martin 1, 2, 3, 4, 7, 8, 9, 15, 17, 19, 22, 115, 116
Hill, Marty 7
Hi/8, high band-8 104, 118
Hi-Riser 13, 19, 20
Hitchcock, Alfred 26, 29
Hix, Bill 8, 11
HMI lights 37, 121
Sherlock Holmes 90
Hostages 32
Hunter 111

I Walk with the Dead 12
Ikigami 104, 118
insurance 42
Interformat 107, 117
interlock 22, 24, 38, 99, 100, 101
intermediate 33, 46, 67, 107
International Brotherhood of Magicians (IBM) 43
interpositive, IP 43, 63, 64, 67, 68, 102, 107, 108, 114
investor 29, 30, 94, 95
IRS 17
ISO 37, 63, 68
Ives, Burl 11

Jake and the Fatman 111
Jaws 88, 130
Jay Howard Studio 25, 26
Jewel in the Crown 90
John Boy 24
Johnson, Alvin 17
Joyner, Kurt 18
Joyner, Robbie 70

K-100, Kodak Model 15
Karo Syrup 9
Keeter, Worth 3
Killer 112, 113, 116
King Kong 64
Knight of the Demons 125
Kodachrome 96, 97, 98, 117
Kodak 13, 15, 24, 37, 96, 98
Kramer, Stanley 26

lab 33, 34, 35, 36, 37, 38, 39, 41, 43, 44, 47, 59, 63, 96, 99, 102, 106, 107, 130
Lamb, Joe 3
Laurel & Hardy 130
Lawrence, Jim 15
Lee Utterback (Co.) 107
lens 50, 52
Lewis, Herschel Gordon 10
Library of Congress 70, 132
light, lighting 3, 29, 55, 58, 63, 64, 66, 67, 75, 88, 91, 92, 93, 94, 108, 115, 116, 118, 121, 122, 123, 124, 125, 127, 128, 129
light box 18
Lindsay, Brooks 23
lip sync 12
liquid gate 25, 36
litho film 46, 47, 48, 64, 67
location 31, 32, 90, 92, 94, 96, 98

loop 23, 101
"The Loving Tree" 8, 11
low contrast positive 24, 44, 102
Luan 70
Lucas, George 26, 95

McClure, Bob 10
Magna-Sync recorder 25
magnetic sound track 38, 39, 43, 44, 102, 109
magnetic stripe, magnetic stock 24, 37, 96
Magnum P.I. 42
Marley's Revenge, the Monster Movie 12, 15, 24, 26, 31, 32, 43, 48, 64, 67, 74, 86, 87, 88, 91, 94, 111, 117, 118, 119, 121, 130
master shot 22
master tape 26, 40, 96, 102
matte (traveling and fixed) 18, 34, 35, 46, 47, 59, 63, 64, 66, 67, 68, 70, 71, 116, 117, 118
mechanical effects 36, 42, 43, 69
Mecklenburg County Courthouse 77
Mehaffey, Roy 6
Metrolina Motion Pictures 11
miniature 11, 36, 42, 43, 70–76, 78
Mr. Ed's Lounge 16, 17
Mitchell camera 1, 7, 28, 115, 116
mix 24, 43, 44, 96, 101, 102
model *see* miniature
Modeler's Hobby Shop 68
Mole-Richardson 20
Monaco Labs 107
motion picture industry 28, 42, 52
movie *see* feature
Movieola 22, 43, 100, 101
Multi-Media, Inc. 117, 118
multi track 26
Multi-Video 26, 27, 76, 117
music 11, 23, 36, 48, 92, 93, 96, 102, 104, 130

Nagra 20, 22, 23, 98, 99
The Natural 74
negative 25, 34, 35, 36, 37, 39, 40, 43, 44, 45, 46, 48, 50, 59, 63, 64, 68, 102, 107, 111, 114, 115, 116
negative cutter 40, 44, 93, 107, 117
news film 24, 33
News Film Laboratory, Inc. 38, 44
Night of the Cat 87
Nightmare (on Elm Street) 88
nodal point 18

one line shooting schedule 82
O'Neal, Vicky 128
The Open Kitchen 8, 26, 126
optical 35, 36, 37, 53, 64, 67, 68, 71, 107, 108, 116, 117
optical house 35, 36, 37, 44, 47, 59, 68, 88, 106
The Optical House 36
optical track 35, 38, 102
Overlook Castle 7, 8, 9
Overton, Mark 7, 18, 24, 26
Owensby, Earl 79, 94

Panavision 2, 29, 110
Paper Doll Lounge 2, 8
Pathé 98, 117
Patterson, J.G. (Pat) 1, 2, 3, 4, 5, 6, 7, 9, 10, 11, 12, 26, 32, 53, 127
photography 10, 13, 14, 22, 29, 38, 47, 66, 67, 68, 98
The Photo-Lab 8, 9, 25
Pickford, Mary 28
Pirro, Mark 116
Plymouth 91
Polaroid 76
A Polish Vampire in Burbank 116
postproduction 36, 107
premier 24, 25
premix 24
preproduction 22
print, print stock 39, 44, 46, 51
Probe 78
producer 31, 74, 76, 87, 88, 92, 93, 95, 102, 109
production, production staff 22, 88, 109
production values 29
projector 76, 99
projector, interlock see interlock projector
prop 31, 32, 74, 77, 86, 90, 91, 93, 94
Psycho 29
"P.T. Barnum" 48
public relations 24, 88
publicity 1, 25
Pyrodex 15

Rank-Cintel 111, 117
ratio 33, 35
reaction shots 22, 57, 58
rear projection 34
recorder see audio recorder
recordist 42
reduction print 34
reflex box 46, 48, 60, 64, 66, 68
rehearsal 14, 55, 58
release 33
release print 44
reversal 37, 63
The Robe 109
Roberts, Lee 13
Roscoe 123
rotoscope 66, 67
Rupert Taylor's Film Studio 117
rushes 3
The Russians Are Coming, the Russians Are Coming 110

Safer, Morley 94
Salvation Army 91
sawdust 18, 19
Scarecrow see *Eyes of the Scarecrow*
scene 32, 54, 86, 87
Schufftan box, Schufftan shot 64, 68
Scoopic-16 97
ScotchLite 76
script 14, 20, 26, 30, 31, 32, 42, 48, 53, 54, 74, 77, 78, 82, 84, 87, 88, 90, 110, 132
script clerk, script girl 22, 53, 78, 92, 93
screenplay 30

S.E.C. (Securities Exchange Commission) 94, 95
sequence 8, 55, 86, 87
SESAC 130
70mm 34, 106
Shag News Network 104
Shaw, Nita 11
Shipman, Harry 23
Siemens projector 24
single system 36, 37, 38, 39, 97
16mm 12, 24, 30, 35, 36, 37, 43, 44, 45, 59, 60, 68, 90, 93, 98, 102, 103, 105, 108, 109, 110, 114, 115, 118
"60 Minutes" 94
65mm 34, 109, 114, 115, 116
slate 3, 22, 23, 35, 42, 47
slow motion 46, 74
Smith, Arthur 130
SMPTE time code 26, 39, 40, 105
Society of American Magicians (SAM) 43
Sonarex projector 22
Sony 118
sound 24, 33, 38, 40, 42, 109
sound effects 23, 41, 42, 91, 96, 102
sound man see sound recordist
sound recording see audio recording
sound recordist 3, 23, 38, 78, 93, 108
sound stage 2, 91, 92, 124, 125
sound track 10, 23, 25, 44
special effects 1, 33, 42, 74, 76, 88, 90, 93, 98, 118
Spielberg, Steven 29, 52, 67
spread sheet 32
Staunten, Eve 11
Steinberg, Jerry 8
Sterling Models 70
story 29, 30
storyboard 31, 36, 76
Strauss, Johannes 130
"Sugar and Spice" 8
SunGun 2, 3, 5, 123, 126, 128
super/8, S/8 12, 33, 36, 37, 38, 44, 50, 63, 88, 102, 112, 116, 117, 118
Super 8 Sound, Inc. 38, 39, 117
SuperPanavision 108
super/16, S/16 16, 33, 44, 106, 107, 108, 109, 114
Superman 28, 48
supervised transfer 25, 43, 102
S/VHS 104, 118
Swan, Don 116
sync, synchronize 18, 26, 38, 40, 98, 99, 101, 102, 104
sync speed 23, 26, 85, 88
synopsis 85, 88, 92
synthesizer 10, 23, 130

take 22, 23, 35, 42, 52, 53, 55, 57, 68, 107
talent 20, 22, 23, 32, 53, 55, 68, 88, 90, 92, 93, 94, 95, 101, 120
tape 30, 38, 48
technical adviser 88
Technicolor Corporation 108, 109, 111
Techniscope 33, 34, 109
Telecine 118
television 38, 39, 43
Tempest 36

Temple of Doom 67
theatrical release 33, 34, 43, 106, 109
35mm 30, 33, 35, 36, 37, 43, 45, 59, 63, 68, 102, 103, 106, 107, 109, 110, 114, 115, 116, 117, 118, 120
3-M 38, 96
3-Perf, Three Perf 110, 111
time code see SMPTE time code
timing, timed work print 35, 102
title 36, 46, 47, 48, 50, 51, 102
"Tocatta and Fugue in D minor" 131
Tracy, Dave 23
transfer 26, 33, 35, 38, 39, 40, 43, 44, 48, 93, 98, 99, 102, 106, 109, 111, 117
traveling matte see matte
tungsten 37, 38
TV release 34
The Twilight Zone 90

unions 28

Vaughn, Gary 15
VCR 23, 99
VHS 25, 104, 105, 117, 119
video 26, 35, 74, 76, 98, 104, 109
video lab 71
video master 25, 43, 44, 102, 107
Video News Film, VNF 39, 59, 63, 68
video release 34, 36, 43, 44, 47, 90, 104, 107, 109, 111, 116
video store 27, 102, 116, 118
video transfer 35, 50, 117
VideoAssist 120
videotape 10, 23, 24, 25, 30, 31, 33, 34, 43, 48, 90, 96, 99, 101, 102, 104, 106, 111, 118, 125

Wall camera 115
Walters, Dick 17
Walters, Lorna 18
wardrobe 88, 90, 91, 93
West Side Story 131
wet gate see liquid gate
Wilson, Chris 25, 26
Wilson, Dave 23, 24, 26
work print 38, 39, 40, 43, 52, 67, 68, 93, 99, 107, 108, 114, 115, 116, 117, 118
Worker's Comp 42
World War II 71
writer, writing 15, 26, 31, 86, 87, 88, 91, 92, 93
Writers Guild 132
Wurker S/8 117

Xerox 20, 82, 87

Yale Laboratories, Inc. 38, 44
Yelton, Al 24

zero cut 107
Zippo (lighter) 76
zoom, zoom lens 50, 56, 57, 98, 106, 109, 120